The Making of AMERICA

From Wilderness to World Power

B. W. Beacroft, B.Sc. (Econ)., M.A.,
Deputy Headmaster (Administration)
Colne Valley High School, West Riding
and
M. A. Smale, B.A. (Oxon),
Assistant History Master,
Bury Grammar School

LONGMAN

LONGMAN GROUP LIMITED
London
Associated companies, branches and
representatives throughout the world.

© Longman Group Ltd 1972

First published 1972
Fourth impression 1975

ISBN 0 582 31236 1 Cased
ISBN 0 582 31239 6 Paper

Photoset in Malta by St Paul's Press Ltd
Printed in Great Britain by Lowe & Brydone (Printers) Ltd., Thetford, Norfolk

TO THE TEACHER

We hope this book will encourage the teaching of American history in secondary schools.
It is intended primarily for C.S.E. pupils and as a supplement to an 'O' level course.
The text is not a narrative outline history but consists of several basic themes and
related topics woven together to illustrate the making of the American nation. These
themes we think are both important in American development and interesting to read
about. Our aim is to provide more details than the conventional textbook, to arouse
the pupils' interest, to provoke thought and discussion and, on certain issues, to invite
personal commitment. Certain sections are necessarily difficult when examined in detail
and less able pupils will need considerable help through discussion and explanation.

CONTENTS

LIST OF MAPS

ACKNOWLEDGEMENTS

The authors wish to thank very sincerely Mr Richard Venner, Librarian, West Bridgford Public Library, for his unfailing courtesy and diligence in tracing and obtaining numerous specialist books on every aspect of American history referred to in this book. They also wish to express their grateful thanks to Mrs Denise Beacroft for her accuracy and zeal in typing and retyping the manuscript.

We are grateful to the following for permission to reproduce copyright material:
author's agents and Harper & Row Inc. for abridged extracts from *Why We Can't Wait* by Martin Luther King, copyright 1963, 1964 by Martin Luther King Jr.; Henry Regnery Company for extracts from *A Yankee Private's Civil War* by Robert Hale.

The author and publisher are grateful to the following for permission to reproduce photographs and drawings:

Page
vi From *The Fur Trade Vol. 1* Phillips, original drawing by Mary Baker
2 (*above*) Northern Natural Gas Company Collection, Joslyn Art Museum, Omaha Nebraska (*below*) Barnaby's picture library
3 (*above*) Aerofilms Limited
5 Rochester Museum and Science Centre
7 American Museum of Natural History
8 From *The Indian Tipi* R & G Aubin, University of Oklahoma Press 1957
10 Smithsonian Institution National Anthropological Archives, Bureau of American Ethnology Collection
13 From *Frederick Remington's Own West* Harold McCracken, Dial Press
15 The Bettmann Archive
18 U.S. Department of the Interior National Park Service photograph
24 James R. Dunlop Inc. Washington
33 Radio Times Hulton Picture Library
37 Caufield & Shook Inc. Louisville, Kentucky
41 United States Information Service
49 (*left*) United States Information Service (*centre & right*) Mary Evans Picture Library
51 The Bettmann Archive
55 United States Information Service
58 From *The Keelboat Age on Western Waters* University of Pittsburgh Press
59 From *Wagons Mules and Men* N. Eggenhofer, Hastings House 1961
62 The New York Historical Association
69 Mary Evans Picture Library
72 From *Wagons Mules and Men* N. Eggenhofer, Hastings House 1961
74 Walters Art Gallery
79 Utah State Historical Society
81 From *The California Trail* Eyre and Spottiswoode 1962
86 New York Public Library
98 Frederick Hill Meserve Collection, Courtesy American Heritage

Page
95 Library of Congress
96 (*above left*) From *Compact History Of The Civil War* by R. E. and T. N. Dupuy © 1961 by R. E. and T. N. Dupuy (*above, right and below*) From *Battles And Leaders Of The Civil War* 1956 A. S. Barnes and Co. Inc.
98 Illinois State Historical Library
99 From *Battles And Leaders Of The Civil War* 1956 A. S. Barnes and Co. Inc.
100 (*left*) From E. S. Miers *The American Civil War* © Western Publishing Co. Inc. and Ridge Press Inc. (*right*) From *Battles And Leaders Of The Civil War* 1956 A. S. Barnes and Co. Inc.
102 British Museum
107 From *Adventures Of America 1857–1900* Harper and Row
109 From *Adventures Of America 1857–1900* Harper and Row
110 (*above*) Culver Pictures (*below*) From *Frederick Remington's Own West* Harold McCracken, Dial Press
111 Radio Times Hulton Picture Library
112 Mercaldo Archives
113 The Library of Congress
115 British Museum
116 Smithsonian Institution National Anthropological Archives, Bureau of American Ethnology Collection
120 Mansell Collection
125 From *Adventures Of America 1857–1900* Harper and Row
126 From *Adventures Of America 1857–1900* Harper and Row
131 Mary Evans Picture Library
135 From *Adventures Of America 1857–1900* Harper and Row
137 From *Adventures of America 1857–1900* Harper and Row
138 Culver Pictures
140 From *Adventures Of America 1857–1900* Harper and Row
141 New York Historical Society
142 (*above*) The Library of Congress (*below*) Photograph by Jacob A. Riis. The Jacob A. Riis Collection Museum of the City of New York

Page
144 From *Adventures Of America 1857–1900* Harper and Row
145 Photograph by Jacob A. Riis. The Jacob A. Riis Collection Museum of the City of New York.
146 (*left*) From *Adventures Of America 1857–1900* Harper and Row (*right*) From *Adventures Of America 1857–1900* Harper and Row
152 The Library of Congress
153 Radio Times Hulton Picture Library
155 Culver Pictures
156 Culver Pictures
157 Culver Pictures
158 From A. Sinclair, *Prohibition* Faber and Faber Limited
159 United States Information Service
160 United States Information Serice
161 The Bettmann Archive
162 The Bettmann Archive
163 (*left*) United Press International (*right*) From A. Sinclair, *Prohibition* Faber and Faber Limited
165 United Press International
166 United Press International
176 United States Information Service
177 Camera Press
180 Associated Press
183 United States Information Service
185 Associated Press
186 (*left*) United Press International (*right*) Associated Press
187 (*left*) Associated Press (*right*) Associated Press
189 United Press International
190 Associated Press
195 Radio Times Hulton Picture Library
196 United Press International
197 Mary Evans Picture Library
198 (*above*) United Press International (*below*) Imperial War Museum
199 Culver Pictures
200 United Press International
203 United Press International
209 United States Information Service
210 United Press International
211 United States Information Service
212 Associated Press

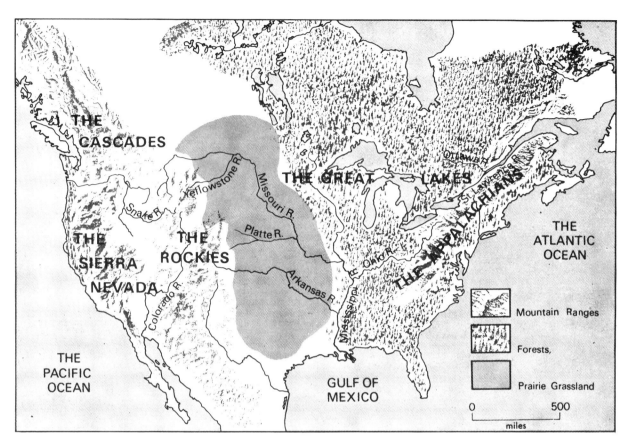

Map 1 The American
Wilderness

A Beaver

1 PRIMITIVE AMERICA

Five hundred years ago, before Europeans knew of its existence, North America was a vast wilderness of about three million square miles. It was a paradise for wild creatures and the home of primitive Indians. Our story begins here. Look carefully at Map 1 before you read on.

The Wilderness

The forests. From the Atlantic to the Mississippi, from the Great Lakes to the Gulf of Mexico, were enormous forests and extensive woods. In the far north white birches stood against dark spruces. Further south were great stands of elm. Fur-bearing animals were everywhere, their thick glossy coats later to be prized by the white man from the Old World. Here roamed black bears, moose, elk, deer, wolves and foxes. In summer the woods were filled with songs of birds and the sounds of crashing trees as beavers built their houses and swimming pools. In winter came a still whiteness. Thick ice covered the waterways. Animals slept and the birds flew south.

Further south still oak, sugar maple, walnut and hickory grew on sunny and dry hillsides. The slopes of dark ravines were clothed with hemlock. Sycamores and willows lined the streams; spruce and fir dotted the mountain ridges. Beneath the trees in wild profusion grew blueberries and strawberries, wild ginger and potatoes. The white-tailed deer and the woods-buffalo were as common as the fox, wolf, bear and beaver. Overhead flocks of geese, ducks and pigeons sometimes were so large that they darkened the sky. The rivers and coastal seas teemed with sturgeon, trout, salmon, cod, lobsters, crabs, and even walruses and whales.

The prairies and high plains. Beyond the Mississippi the forests gave way to a vast carpet of grass which stretched westwards a thousand miles to the foothills of the Rockies. The scenery was dreary and monotonous, only occasional strips of cottonwoods along the streams relieving the eye. It was a land of changing weather. Storms were common and often violent. Thunder crashed and roared round the low hills. Lightning cast its vivid glare over desolate ground. On other days in summer the skies were cloudless and the sun parched the grass below. In the dead of winter the northern and central regions became endless white meadows of deep snow and ice.

These lands were the home of antelopes, wolves, coyotes, badgers, prairie-dogs, rabbits and gophers. King of them all was the bison—usually called the buffalo. The males stood five to six feet high at the shoulder and measured about twelve feet from nose to tail. Always in large herds the buffalo roamed the plains searching for fresh grass, walking in single file along deeply rutted trails centuries old and hundred of miles long. One man wrote that he once saw a file of buffalo twenty-five miles long.

The mountains and deserts. The huge Mississippi valley was bordered east and west by great mountain ranges. To the east the Appalachians rose up through the enormous forests to 6000 feet. Movement through them from east to west was greatly obstructed by steep rock faces and river valleys strewn with boulders and tangled with trees and

1

thickets. The Western Mountains were a thousand miles wide. Mountain chains like the Rockies, the Sierra Nevada and the Cascades reached two or three miles high. Between them were deep valleys, ravines, canyons, basins and plateaus. Low down, beavers, deer, racoons and rabbits played in grassy meadows and wooded groves. Higher up, in the wide open valleys and plateaus, the scenery and wild life resembled those of the plains. Pines sprinkled the high mountain slopes, the home of the grizzly bear.

Away to the south lay wide areas of sand and rock wilderness. Only the hardiest of nature's plants and animals survived here, fighting grimly for life in a fierce and cruel environment, an existence reflected in their armoury of spikes and thorns, fangs and claws. This was the desert land of the cactus and mesquite, the rattlesnake and the lizard, the kangaroo rat and the horned toad.

These were regions of spectacular scenery. The Yellowstone Valley contained hissing geysers, hot springs, tall fountains of boiling water, pulsating mud volcanoes, and mountainsides torn open with cracks of bottomless depth. Nearby stood Amethyst Mountain which consisted of the fossilised remains of sixteen forests, one on top of another. In the Painted Desert fossils 160 million years old flashed deep reds and brilliant yellows and purples in the strong sunlight.

This wilderness confronted the white man when he entered the New World. He also came face to face with the Indian. The distribution of the main Indian tribes at this time is shown on Map 2.

3

The Red Indians

Map 2 The location of some important Indian tribes

The Indians were stone age people. They knew about fire and they used natural materials like stone, wood, bones and skins to make their tools, weapons, clothes and houses. Metal was unknown to them. The American Indians hunted, fought and travelled everywhere on foot or by canoe. The idea of the wheel never occurred to them. On land all loads were carried on the backs of the squaws (Indian women) and on travois pulled by dogs. The travois consisted of two long poles tied to the shoulders of a dog, the loose ends dragging on the ground; the load was placed across the poles. The use of squaws to transport goods was not laziness on the part of the men, who kept themselves ready in case of sudden attack or an unexpected chance to hunt.

The dog was the only animal the Indians domesticated. They were astonished by the horses, cattle, sheep, pigs and goats brought to America by the white man from Europe. Such animals did not exist in the wilderness. This lack of domesticated animals was the main reason why most Indians depended heavily on hunting and fishing. However, they also gathered wild foods and grew crops like maize, beans, squashes, pumpkins, sweet potatoes, tobacco and cotton. Indeed, the white man was equally astonished by the Indians' tremendous knowledge of the habits of wild animals and fish and the food value of plants. Probably 2000 species of these items were used in some way or other by the Indians in their daily lives. Crops like maize and tobacco were unknown in Europe before the white man discovered America.

However, the Indians were not alike in every respect. Even neighbouring tribes rarely had exactly the same language and way of life. Tribes far apart usually differed markedly in their appearance, speech and daily lives. The main reason for this was the wilderness. The forests, the prairies and the deserts each imposed a different pattern of life upon the Indian. Thus, the forest Indian was a different person from, say, the prairie Indian. To illustrate this point more clearly let us now describe the Iroquois and the Teton Sioux Indians in a little detail. These two peoples will appear in our story later on.

The Iroquois—a people of the forests. There were five Iroquois tribes—the Seneca, the Cayuga, the Onandaga, the Oneida and the Mohawk. They lived in the elm forests south of Lake Erie and Lake Ontario. Horticulture, hunting and fishing were their main activities.

The farming was done in forest clearings on soft and fertile soils. Maize, squashes and beans were the main crops. After the harvest they were cooked and preserved for winter use. For example, the corn was sifted through baskets into deep wooden mortars, ground by pestles, cooked in large pots over fires, and stored in large baskets. Wild herbs, powdered wood-ash and squashed ants were sometimes used to flavour the food. Sugar from maple trees and wild strawberries and blueberries supplemented this vegetable diet. Apart from the heavy work of clearing the forests and harvesting, all these activities were done by the women to whom the land belonged.

The men did the hunting and fishing. Skilled with bows and arrows, spears and slings, clever at disguising themselves as animals and imitating wild calls, and adept at making snares, traps and pits, they hunted deer, bears, rabbits, beavers, ducks and turkeys. Three of these weapons were also used in fishing, but another method was to dam the streams and catch the fish in nets made of vine branches. Usually the men hunted and fished in groups but in winter, when game was scarce, they often worked alone. Fresh meat and fish were usually boiled before they were eaten. Most of the meat was dried, smoked (to keep insects away) and preserved for later use. You can see that the Iroquois ate a wide variety of foods and had a well-balanced diet.

Animals and fish provided the Iroquois with materials for their clothes and some

This is part of a model of an Iroquois village in an American museum. How many separate activities do you see here?

4

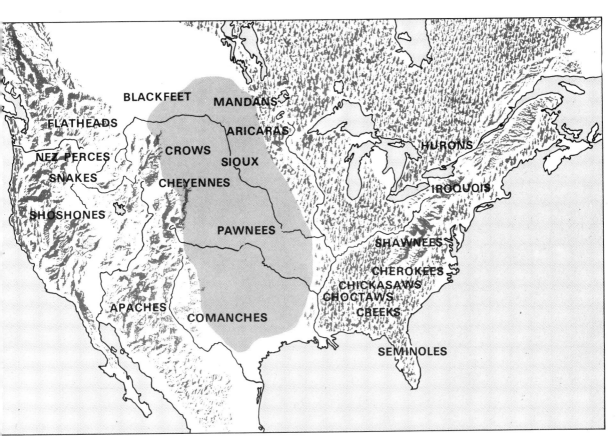

of their tools and weapons. Skins, particularly those of the deer and the doe, were scraped, dried and sewn into clothes. In summer a man wore a breechclout, a strip of buckskin passed between the legs and held up in front and behind by a belt round the waist, with a short kilt and moccasins: a woman wore a skirt and moccasins. In winter a man also wore a shirt and leggings and a woman a full dress. Small bones were used as needles and combs. The shoulder-blades of deer made satisfactory hoes. Bowstrings were made from the skins of turtles' necks or the sinews of deers' legs. Beaver teeth, which were long, sharp and strong, made good blades for hand-knives to slice meat, scrape skins, cut branches and scalp enemies.

The Iroquois made considerable use of wood. Their best bows were cut from hickory, but ash and white-oak were also used. Arrow shafts were made from viburnum wood and tipped with sharpened flints. Elm was commonly used to make canoes but the best wood for this purpose was birch, which gave a very light and manoeuvrable craft. Unfortunately, birch did not grow locally. The Iroquois were known to travel a long way north to cut birch or obtain it from other tribes either by trade or force. Elm was of prime importance in village-making and house-building. A village was usually encircled by a stockade made of elm logs. Inside were several large rectangular wooden huts with barrel-shaped roofs. These homes were called longhouses. They consisted of a framework of elm saplings covered by sheets of elm bark.

A dozen families or more lived in each longhouse. Each family occupied a room placed at right angles to a central corridor running from one end of the house to the other. A low platform round the sides of the room provided sleeping accommodation. It was covered with skins and furs. The family's belongings were stored on a shelf high up in the roof above. Each facing pair of rooms shared a fire lit in the corridor between them, the smoke rising through holes left in the roof. These homes were noisy and smoky but warm and weatherproof. The families within each longhouse all belonged to the same clan. Each clan was named after an animal or bird whose carving or 'totem' was outside above the doorway. The clans were headed by the women who owned the longhouses. On marriage the man went to live with his wife's clan. The older women in each clan were responsible for choosing the men to lead their clan. These men became the clan chiefs or 'sachems'. Their badge of office was a set of deer antlers. If they ruled unjustly or unwisely the women replaced them by other men. Clearly, the Iroquois women had an important position in their tribe.

At home the Iroquois were polite, kind and considerate towards each other. To outsiders they were fierce, cruel and aggressive. The Iroquois tribes feared each other and neighbouring tribes feared the Iroquois. The Iroquois certainly looked fierce; they painted their faces and shaved their heads, leaving only small scalp locks. From boyhood they were trained to think highly of fighting: to fear neither physical pain nor death. Bravery in battle won a warrior high social position in his tribe.

Both hunting and warfare were dangerous activities; men were killed and the tribes weakened. To overcome this the Iroquois took prisoners in battle. Captured warriors, if they impressed the Iroquois, were adopted into the tribe and treated as equal members of their new clan. The captives often proved their worth by 'running the gauntlet'. Each prisoner had to run between two rows of warriors armed with clubs who hit out as hard as they could as the victim passed them. Prisoners were also taken to be tortured slowly and offered as a sacrifice to Aireskoi, the spirit of war and hunting. Tortures were a great public spectacle. All the village was expected to watch as a mark of respect for the victims. Although the tortures were horrifyingly cruel, the Iroquois loved and admired those men who died fearlessly and cheerfully. Afterwards the bodies were eaten. The Iroquois believed that if they ate the flesh of a brave man it would make them more fearless.

So fierce was the fighting between the five Iroquois tribes that this probably explains why they formed themselves into a league which they called the 'Great Peace'. The five tribes agreed to stop fighting each other and unite to defend themselves against their common enemies. The league was governed by a council of fifty sachems drawn from the five tribes and elected by the women. This league was created before the white man entered America.

Religion was a very important aspect of the lives of the Iroquois. They believed firmly in gods and spirits, both good and evil. Ceremonies were held to encourage the good spirits and discourage the bad ones. Their New Year Festival, in early February, was to ensure the coming of spring and the victory of the Master of Life over the forces of evil. Some people, through dreams or 'visions', seemed able to contact the spirits easily and to know how they felt. These people were called shamans and they held important positions in Iroquois society. With the help of the good spirits shamans could cure sickness. The Iroquois believed that sickness was caused by False Faces— horrible heads without bodies that lived in the forests. Their evil spell could be broken by the shamans who formed the False Face Society. A sick person would be visited by a shaman wearing a grotesque mask and carrying a rattle. At the door of the sick person's longhouse the shaman would pause, pretend to enter several times, run his rattle along the door frame, and shout 'ho-ho-ho-ho-ho-ho'. He then entered, shook his rattle over the patient, dipped his hands into the ashes of the fire, and then rubbed them over the head and in the hair. The shaman's reward was a cornmeal pudding which he ate alone because he must not unmask in public.

A False Face Mask

The Iroquois believed there was a life after death. Their spirits left their bodies and went to live in beautiful villages beneath the earth. In this heaven there was no war or sickness and everyone had enough food and skins. They believed in ghosts as well. Ghosts were separate from spirits. After death the ghosts of the Iroquois remained nearby. They were said to take part in village life and follow the warriors on their expeditions.

The Teton Sioux—a people of the prairies. The Sioux called themselves the Dakota, a word meaning 'allies'. Other Indians called them 'Sioux' which meant enemy. Indeed, the Sioux have been called 'the Iroquois of the West'.

There were three divisions of the Sioux. East of the Mississippi lived the Santee and Yankton Sioux—woodland tribes who were farmers, hunters and fishermen. West of the great river, scattered across the north central prairies were the Tetons. The Teton Sioux were hunters. Gathering wild fruit and berries, fishing and trading were minor activities. They never grew crops.

These people hunted most of the animals of the prairies but the buffalo was their main target. Their very existence depended upon this animal which they called Pte. The following extract from a book about the Sioux shows this point clearly:

'Flesh for immediate cooking, dried meat and fat for pemmican* and other foods were only the obvious uses to which the bison was put. Heavy robes, made from the buffalo's thick hide, were the Indian's winter covering and his bed; in summer, the hides, tanned and with the hair removed, served him as a sheet or light blanket and made leggings, hunting shirts, moccasins and women's apparel. His tipis [conical tents] were of dressed cowhide.... The hide of tough old bull, stretched over a light frame of green willows, made the famous bullboat with which the Indian transported his family, goods and gear across the rivers; while the thick hide that guarded Pte's neck was shrunken into a circular shield that could turn the sharpest lance or arrow.

'Trunks and boxes to contain the Indian's smaller possessions were made from the raw hide of the buffalo, with the hair shaved off; sledge runners for their dog-drawn sleds were made from the rib-bones; hoes and axes were made from the shoulder blades; tools for dressing hides came from the ribs and cannon bones. The hoofs of the bison boiled made a glue for feathering their arrows and cementing their arrowheads; Pte's long black beard served as an ornament for their clothing, shields, or quivers. Bones for needles and sinew for thread and bowstrings also came from the buffalo's bulky body, while the long horns, peeled and polished, made ornaments, spoons and ladles. The green hide of the animal was sometimes used as a receptacle in which to boil meat, and the lining of the paunch served as an efficient water bucket. The skin of the buffalo's hind leg, cut off between the hock and the pastern, made a tough boot or moccasin; long brushes to keep off flies and other troublesome insects were made from the tail; and ... knife sheaths, quivers, bow cases, ... and scores of other miscellaneous articles, all *indispensable* to the prairie red man, came from the bison's massive framework.'

The main hunts were in spring and autumn. The whole tribe took part and worked as a team. A person who disobeyed orders and frightened a herd away might be put to death or have his possessions burnt. Buffalo were caught in several ways. One way was for the hunters to walk downwind of the herd and then stampede it over a cliff or into a closed valley. In the first case the animals plunged to their death: in the second they became trapped between a valley wall and a fence or net hastily erected by the Indians after the herd had run past them. Another way, if the herd was small, was for the hunters to surround it and then move in quickly with arrows and spears to kill the startled animals before they had time to gallop away.

*Pemmican was dried meat, pounded and mixed with crushed berries; melted fat and marrow was then poured over the mixture.

Sioux Tipis　　Because of their roving life the Tetons needed movable houses. They lived in tipis—a Sioux word meaning dwellings. The tipi was essentially a tripod of long poles covered with buffalo skins neatly sewn together and tailored to fit the frame. It was lined inside by brightly painted skins which acted as draught-excluders and wall-paper. Skins also covered the floor except where the fire was made. Undoubtedly, the tipi was one of the best movable houses ever invented. It was easy to erect and take down, very weather-proof, roomy, warm in winter and cool in summer. Each tipi housed one family.

In a Teton village no one was much wealthier than anyone else. Nobody owned any land. Can you think why? At death a man's belongings were shared out amongst the tribe. Rarely did a successful hunter refuse to provide food and skins for others if they were in need. His tipi was often crowded with guests. Generosity was a Teton virtue and children were taught it from an early age. The first time a boy killed an animal he gave it away. Later, he always shared his kill with others. Similar actions were expected of girls when they gathered fruit and berries.

Like most Indians the Tetons were very fond of their children. They never hit them. Good actions were praised and bad ones scorned. While the children were learning to hunt and fight or sew hides and gather plants they received names like 'long ears', 'big nose', 'flat head', 'hump on the rump', or 'without teeth'. Such names were thought to act as a spur to the children because once they had learned their tasks they received respectable names like 'Red Deer', 'Running Buffalo' and 'White Eagle'. Perhaps you can guess why names like these were chosen and why they seemed respectable?

Murder and theft within a Teton tribe were very rare. The women had equal voice with the men in tribal affairs. The Indian was taught to put the welfare of the tribe before himself. Yet when the white man came he said that all Indians were savages and inferior beings. Bearing in mind what you have just read do you think this opinion was sound? Were murder and theft rare among white men? Did they allow their women an equal voice in their everyday life?

The Teton believed in a Sky Father who watched over the world, protected the Indians and directed the animals. He thought that spirits were everywhere around him—in the thunder and lightning, the trees, the streams, the animals. If he pleased the spirits they would make him brave in hunting and war, generous to his friends, and faithful to his family and tribe. Only by being these things would he win the respect of his tribe which

9

might then choose him as a leader. The most important ceremony of the year was the Sun Dance. The highlight of this dance was when volunteers thrust skewers through their chests and attached them by long strings to the top of a large pole. Then they danced round the pole, praying and looking towards the sun all the time. The dance ended when the flesh was ripped away from the chest and the skewer and its strings fell to the floor. To the Teton this self-torture proved a man's bravery and he believed that the visions he had while dancing might make him a better hunter and warrior.

He also believed strongly in animal spirits. During youth he would sit alone on the prairie for days without food and water, praying for a dream in which an animal would tell him how to hunt properly. This animal then became his guardian spirit and the hunter kept a memento of it for the rest of his life. If it was a rabbit his memento might be a rabbit's foot or tail. If no animal appeared in his dreams the Teton would take gifts to a shaman and receive a guardian spirit and a memento from him. No Indian

The Sun Dance: a drawing by a Dakota Indian

was ever without one. After each buffalo hunt the Tetons always left the best hide of all on the prairie. It was a gift to Tatanka, the buffalo god, in gratitude for his help in catching the animals.

The purpose of this section is to show that because their natural environments were different the Indian tribes were not exactly alike. Can you now make a list of the ways in which the Iroquois way of life differed from that of the Teton Sioux?

Further Reading

Hulpach, Vladimir, *American Indian Tales and Legends*, Hamlyn, 1965.
Hunt, W. Ben, *Golden Book of Indian Crafts and Lore*, Publicity, 1954.
La Farge, O., *A Pictorial History of the American Indian*, Golden Press, 1960.
Platt, R., *Wilderness: the Discovery of a Continent of Wonder*, Dodd, Mead and Company, 1961.

2 THE COMING OF THE EUROPEANS

The year 1492 is of tremendous importance in American history. In that year Christopher Columbus landed at San Salvador near the Florida coast. He thought he had reached Asia by a westward sea passage from Europe. In fact he had discovered a 'new world', a wilderness, a land of opportunity for the wealth-seeking nations of Western Europe. Columbus's voyage began the invasion of America by Europeans which was to continue for well over four hundred years. In this time they have conquered the Indians and transformed the vast wilderness into the richest and most powerful country in the world.

The early discovery, exploration, settlement and development of America was done mainly by people from Spain, France and England. This chapter describes some of their work down to about 1750.

The Spaniards

The Conquistadors and Indian legends. Columbus made several more voyages to the West Indies after 1492. His stories about gold and pearls attracted the Spaniards to the area. Those who went called themselves the conquistadors—the conquerors of new lands who sought their fortunes from gold, jewels and slaves. At first they were very successful. They found and conquered the incredibly rich Indian civilisations of the Aztecs, Mayas and Incas whose lands stretched from Mexico to Peru. Not surprisingly, the Spaniards almost forgot about Asia. Very soon they turned to North America. They argued that if fabulous treasures existed in Mexico and Peru then why not in the north too?

Indian tales of weird and wonderful sights in the north lured on conquistadors. In Florida the Indians said there was a Fountain of Youth, a tribe of Indians with golden helmets, and a giant king who as a boy had been rubbed with grease and stretched to an abnormal size. Somewhere, too, there was a mountain crusted with diamonds. To the west lay the Seven Cities of Cibola, built of gold, silver and turquoise. There were rumours of strange tribes: one lived under water; another sat in the shade of their own enormous ears; in California was an Amazon queen with huge feet, and a race of bald-headed men. North America seemed to be a land of opportunity and wonder for fortune-seekers and the curious. In the 1530s Spanish conquistadors like Narvaez, de Soto and Coronado became eager to explore. Protected by metal armour, armed with guns and mounted on horses the conquistadors were more than a match for the stone age Indians who were greatly overawed by the thunder and the invisible killing power of the gun, and by the horses. No Indian had ever seen a horse before and at first he thought a man on a horse was all one strange and terrifying monster.

Yet they found neither glittering treasures nor strange people. Both Narvaez and de Soto died in the American wilderness. Nevertheless, these men are remembered because they were the first white people to penetrate the wilderness and leave records of what they saw. You can find out more about these people in some of the books listed at the end of this chapter.

The Rise of New Spain. Despite these setbacks the Spaniards remained in the American wilderness. Silver was found in New Mexico, fertile valleys like the Rio

The conquistadors and their soldiers were very few in number compared to the Indians but they had three enormous advantages: horses, metal armour and guns. Can you think why these were so important in battles with the stone-age Indians?

13

Grande supported ranches and farms, and the Indians were a challenge to the Spanish Catholic missionaries. However, the main reason why they remained was a defensive one. The Gulf of Mexico and the Caribbean Sea became favourite places for English, French and Dutch pirates to attack Spanish treasure ships taking home gold and silver from Mexico and Peru. Thus Spain encircled these seas with naval bases and garrisons in an effort to keep piracy in check.

After 1600 other European nations began to explore and colonise the American wilderness. As this international rivalry developed, Spain extended her own claims to the continent. The growth of English settlements along the Atlantic coast prompted her to encroach on Georgia. She built forts in Texas to curb the westward growth of French Louisiana. Competition from Russia and England on the Pacific coast resulted in the conquest of California. Map 3 shows the main rivals in America about 1750 and the directions of their exploration and settlement.

Presidios and missions. Within this Empire, however, were thousands of Indians. How was Spain to control these and to win them over to an acceptance of Spanish rule? The presidio or fort was one method. From the outset the king's policy was to give away mineral rights and blocks of farmland around the presidios to Spanish civilians and retiring soldiers. Each landowner was made guardian of a group of Indians. He was expected to protect and civilise them and make them Christians. In return, laws were passed forcing the Indians to work on the land and down the mines and to live nearby in small towns called pueblos. Unfortunately this well-meant idea was abused. The Indians became slaves. Some rebelled and many good-hearted Spaniards urged reform.

Map 3 The entry of the Europeans

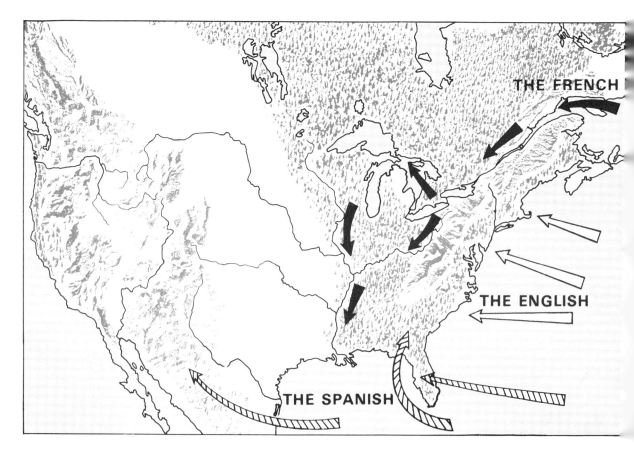

The job of converting and civilising the Indian was given to missionaries. These men, protected by soldiers garrisoned in nearby presidios, were told to go and live with a group of Indians, convert them, and then move on elsewhere. But they did more than this. They not only made Christians of many Indians, they also disciplined them to become peaceful and productive farm workers.

The missionaries introduced nearly every European crop and domesticated animal to the Indians of the Southwest who learned to rear cattle, sheep, goats, horses and mules and grow European fruits and vegetables like figs, oranges, peaches, apricots, pears, apples, cabbages, lettuces, onions, garlic and mint without any help from the Spaniards. The Spanish missions, therefore, were as important in the wilderness as the presidios. Not that they succeeded everywhere, but it is to their great credit that, in general, instead of destroying the Indian tribes they preserved them.

The French

Canada and the fur trade. The greatest French explorer of the sixteenth century was Jacques Cartier. In 1534 and 1543 he discovered and explored the waters and lands of the Gulf of St Lawrence. Like Columbus he was primarily interested in finding a sea passage to Asia and discovering Indian treasures of gold and silver. He found neither but he did report that the region teemed with fur animals and fish. No one took much notice except a few French fishermen who began to fish there and trade furs with the Indians. From such small beginnings grew the great fur trade of America.

The fur trade of Europe was an old one. Both rich and poor people wore hats, coats,

*uebec at the end of
e 17th century*

15

jackets, shoes, linings and trimmings made of fur. Furs were fashionable, warm and comfortable during the cold winters. By the end of the sixteenth century, however, the forests of Russia became depleted of animals and fur prices rose. Frenchmen and others began to look at the American wilderness with a new interest. It presented a golden opportunity for a brand new fur trade.

The first Frenchman to see this clearly was Samuel de Champlain. From 1603 he spent several years exploring both sides of the St Lawrence river, ranging north to Lake Nipissing and Georgian Bay and south to the lake named after him. In 1608 Champlain built a small settlement at the base of a huge rock standing at the head of navigation of the St Lawrence river. He named it Quebec after an Indian word, 'kebec', which meant a narrowing of waters. Later he built a fur post further up river where the Ottawa joins the St Lawrence. This was called Place Royale. It was to become the site of Montreal. Making friends with the Hurons and Algonquins, Champlain encouraged them to bring their furs to Quebec and Place Royale where they received in exchange trade goods like iron axes, knives, kettles, woollen blankets, vermillion paint, shining glass beads, mirrors and trinkets. Perhaps you can guess why these things pleased the Indians? In return for the furs these Indians expected Champlain to help them fight their mortal enemy—the Iroquois. The French guns undoubtedly astonished and frightened the Iroquois, some of whom were captured, tortured and eaten by the Hurons. Henceforth the Iroquois hated the French.

Slowly the area of the French fur trade expanded. As the forests in the east became depleted of beavers and other animals the French were forced to tap those further west. The St Lawrence and its tributaries, particularly the Ottawa, made natural routes into the heart of the wilderness. French explorers, fur traders and missionaries penetrated to the shores of the Great Lakes. Friendly contacts were made with other northern and western tribes who began to bring their furs to trading posts and missions which sprouted up along the rivers and lakes of the interior.

The coureurs de bois. In this extension of the fur trade to the north and west the coureurs de bois played an important role. These men were often retired soldiers, peasants or convicts who had come to America as 'habitants' or settlers. They rented land from the 'seigneurs' or landowners, cleared the forest and began farming the land. It was arduous work, often with poor returns. Many gave up, left their land, and took to the rivers, lakes and forests to earn their living by hunting and trading furs. They lived and dressed like Indians, travelled hundreds of miles on foot and by birchbark canoe, and remained in the wilderness for months or even years at a time. It is said that they were a gay, carefree and fearless lot. The woods rang with their songs. Yet many were wild, hot-tempered and frequently drunk on brandy. They encouraged the Indians to drink it, made them drunk and then cheated them of their furs. In the early days they were regarded as outlaws and pirates by the French government because they had received no official permission to trade in furs. Indeed, the coureurs de bois often smuggled their furs to France or sold them to the English at Hudson Bay or in New York colony.

La Salle on the Mississippi. The fur trade, the exploration of the wilderness, and the expansion of French territory in America went hand in hand. Indeed the French played a central part in the exploration of North America. In 1672, while the coureurs de bois and the missionaries were busy in the north and around the Great Lakes, Louis Joliet and Jacques Marquette paddled down the Mississippi to its junction with the River Arkansas. About the same time La Salle discovered and explored much of the Ohio River. Ten years later he retraced the journey of Joliet and Marquette, continuing on down the Mississippi until he reached the Gulf of Mexico.

La Salle, like Champlain, was an explorer, fur trader and empire builder all rolled into one. He was most impressed by the Mississippi valley:

'It is nearly all so beautiful and so fertile; so free from forests, and so full of meadows, brooks and rivers; so abounding in fish, game and venison, that one can find there in plenty, and with little trouble, all that is needful for the support of flourishing colonies. The soil will produce everything that is raised in France. Flocks and herds can be left out at pasture all winter; and there are even native wild cattle, which instead of hair, have a fine wool that may answer for making cloths and hats. Their hides are better than those of France. . . . Hemp and cotton grow here naturally, and may be manufactured with good results; so there can be no doubt that colonies planted here would become prosperous.'

La Salle realised that this area offered much more wealth than the north did. Canada had barren soils and winters of snow and ice. A man of vision, he dreamed of a great new colony, a whole new trading area for France, with furs and other goods moving from the north to south down the wide, icefree Mississippi to the Gulf of Mexico. But more than this, France already controlled the Great Lakes and the St Lawrence valley, the natural line of communications from east to west. If France took possession of the Mississippi valley, the very centre of the wilderness and the natural line of communication north to south, then she would control the whole continent. French forts here would hem in the English behind the Appalachians and drive a wedge between the Spanish colonies in Florida and the Southwest. Discuss this idea with your teacher. Draw a rough sketch map of the wilderness to explain La Salle's thinking and say if you think his idea sound.

Few people agreed with La Salle at this time. France was engaged in expensive wars in Europe and could not spare the soldiers, settlers, weapons and trade goods. French traders in the St Lawrence valley were opposed to a scheme which would funnel furs south rather than east. Can you think why? Some even encouraged the Iroquois to attack the forts built by La Salle and the Indians who were friendly towards him. Undaunted, La Salle and a few helpers tried to found the new colony of Louisiana by themselves. His plan was to carry building materials and trade goods by canoe and sailing ship from the St Lawrence across the Great Lakes to the Illinois and Mississippi rivers. There he would build forts, trade with the Indians, sell their furs in Montreal, and thus buy more equipment for new forts further south. Eventually La Salle hoped to penetrate to the mouth of the Mississippi where he would build a great port. Such a plan involved arduous journeys of hundreds, even thousands of miles, sometimes in the depth of winter. La Salle had an iron constitution and tremendous spirit. But he failed to build his empire. Perhaps you can think of some reasons why? In 1687 La Salle was murdered by some of his own men somewhere in the south.

La Salle's heroic failure was not entirely in vain. After 1700 the French created a small colony around the town of New Orleans near the mouth of the Mississippi. They called the colony Louisiana. Friendly trading relations were built up with the Indians to the east and west of the mighty river. Armed with French guns, knives and axes these tribes proved a menace to both the English and the Spaniards. Nevertheless, in 1750 Louisiana was not the thriving colony of La Salle's dreams. It was very weakly linked with the settlements in the north where most of the 90,000 French people lived.

The growth of New France. In the north the French seemed solidly entrenched. Indeed, under Louis XIV, determined efforts had been made to populate Canada. Retired officers had received grants of land and demobilised soldiers and peasants recruited in France were sent to Canada to work as tenant farmers. Regular shipments of girls were made to provide wives for the settlers. Single men were expected to marry within a fortnight of the arrival of a new batch of girls and couples who had large families of ten or more received money grants from the French government. Life in Canada was closely regulated. No one could return to France without permission. There were heavy punishments for speaking ill of royalty, swearing, and holding public meetings.

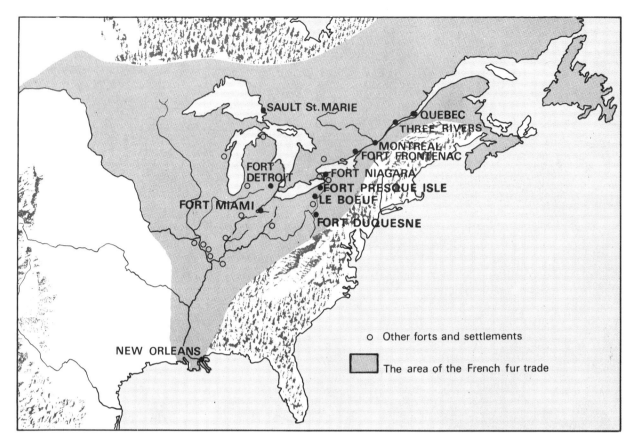

Map 4 *The French in North America about 1750*

Jamestown

18

Map 4 shows the approximate area of the French fur trade and the main French towns and forts in America about 1750. Notice the heavy cluster of settlements along the St Lawrence and the presence of the forts in the upper Ohio valley. These forts were not simply to control the Iroquois but to prevent the English fur traders and settlers from breaking through the Appalachians into the heart of the wilderness. In 1750 it looked as if France was to dominate the whole continent.

The English

Early English exploration. Columbus's discoveries also stimulated England to send explorers to North America. John and Sebastian Cabot, Martin Frobisher and Henry Hudson played an important part in searching for a northwest passage to Asia and mapping the shores of Canada. Like the French they found no passage, but the Hudson's Bay Company was set up to trade in furs.

But the Hudson Bay froze in winter. The land was too cold and infertile for farming. The English therefore looked further south. In 1585 an expedition organised by Raleigh claimed the whole of the east coast from Cape Cod to Florida, calling it Virginia.

Until well into the new century many believed that the bays of the Chesapeake and Delaware would lead to the Pacific or that some new source of gold or silver would be found inland. There were other reasons for colonisation too; a colony could supply naval stores, absorb some of the unemployed from England and provide a growing market for English products.

Captain John Smith and Virginia. Raleigh's settlement was wiped out—no one knows how. But in 1607 the Virginia Company established the first permanent colony at Jamestown; that it survived was largely the work of Captain John Smith.

The voyage took ten weeks longer than expected, so that spring had passed when the colonists arrived, and the ship's supplies were not enough to last until the next years's harvest. The company had instructed the colonists to explore and search for gold. Anticipating quick success, many would not share in building houses, and clearing land, though these were vital to survival in the winter. As soon as the ship had left, the President and Council, appointed by the Company, quarrelled over the organisation of the settlement and hoarded food for their private use.

The result of all these shortcomings was that famine and sickness broke out and an inadequately manned watch failed to stop Indian raids. Between May and September fifty men died. Many were saved only by friendly Indians who brought in corn. If the colony was to survive it had to be better organised. John Smith 'by his own example, good works and fair promises, set some to mow, others to bind thatch, some to build houses, others to thatch them, himself always bearing the greatest task for his own share; so that in short time he provided most of their lodgings'. Some despaired and only Smith's vigilance frustrated three plots to return to England. Trade with the Indians for food was essential. In spite of ignorance of their language and customs, Smith succeeded so well that the Powhatans started to bring in regular supplies. But this was after two of his companions had been murdered, himself captured and saved from execution only by the intervention of the chief's daughter, Pocahontas.

Smith's rivals were jealous. They offered the Indians more goods and higher prices than Smith did and tried to convince them that he had been cheating. Then in the middle of the winter, the settlement was accidentally burnt down, and the supply ship's captain wasted valuable time and supplies hunting for gold. Although Smith had been democratically elected as President, many still opposed him for their own profit. Some, for instance, secretly sold ship's supplies: 'Within six or seven weeks after the ship's return to Virginia, of two-hundred or three-hundred hatchets, chissels, mattacks and pickaxes, scarce twenty could be found.'

Clearly there were no quick profits to be made. In time, however, the ample good land would make the colony self-supporting and naval supplies from the forests could repay the Company's investments. Repeatedly Smith begged for 'carpenters, husbandmen, gardeners, fishermen, blacksmiths, masons and diggers-up of trees and roots' instead of fortune hunters.

In 1609 he was seriously injured by the explosion of his powder bag. He returned to England. As President he had restored good relations with the Indians, cut out laziness by threatening to transport idlers across the river to fend for themselves, built up a good reserve of supplies, including animals, and tried to establish respect for justice, fair dealing and hard work by his own leadership and example. Although the old troubles broke out again when he left, the colony was strong enough to survive.

Perhaps you will agree that Smith had more success than La Salle. Re-read the sections on the two men and then try to explain why.

Other English settlements. Not all English colonies started with a search for gold. For simplicity's sake one can list colonies under two headings; those founded to escape religious persecution and those started mainly for profit. There were exceptions to this. Find these exceptions by studying Table 1.

The Pilgrim Fathers probably had the most purely religious motives for emigrating, but they lived quietly and kept to themselves, and it was the commercially-minded Puritans, settled around Boston, who built up the colony of Massachusetts; although they did have strong religious motives, they expected to prosper, and were agents of a company which expected to make a profit. The colonists recruited by Lord Baltimore or the Carolina syndicate had various motives; some were escaping religious persecutors, many were poor, many just wanted an opportunity to better themselves in a new country where land was cheap.

The promoters of later colonies did not make the mistake of Virginia. Among the first arrivals in Pennsylvania were 'a Low Dutch cake-baker, an apothecary, a glassblower, a mason, a smith, a wheelwright, a cabinet-maker, a cooper, a cobbler, a tailor, a gardener, farmers, seamstresses. . . . ' These people were no fortune-hunters: they intended to make their lives in the colony.

Table 1.   The Development of English Settlement in North America

Massachusetts	1620	Pilgrim Fathers settled at Plymouth.
	1629	The King granted a charter to the Massachusetts Bay Co. and the first 400 settlers arrived, mainly Puritans who disliked the religious policy of Charles I.
Maine and New Hampshire		The settlers here did not have sufficient share in the government of the colony and broke away from Massachusetts to form their own.
Connecticut	1639	Small groups of settlers who drifted away from Massachusetts formed their own constitution and elected their own government.
Rhode Island	1644	Religious refugees from Massachusetts formed a new colony.
Maryland	1632	The King granted Lord Baltimore a charter to develop a strip of American coast. His aim was to make a profit by selling or renting land to colonists from Europe.

New York	1614	Had been settled by Dutch and Swedes as the New Netherlands.
	1664	Taken over and renamed by the English Duke of York when it was granted to him by Charles II on the basis of England's claim made in 1585 by Raleigh.
New Jersey	1664	Formed from grants by the Duke of York to two other noblemen who wished to speculate in land like Baltimore.
Pennsylvania	1681	A Royal Charter granted to the Quaker William Penn who wanted to found an ideal colony where all men could live in peace and with religious freedom. Developed very quickly by Scots-Irish and Germans who were less interested in Penn's ideals than in land for themselves.
Virginia	1608	Founded by the Virginia Co., who like the Spaniards believed that gold could be found inland.
North and South Carolina	1663	A syndicate of eight peers given a charter to develop them commercially. They hoped to produce semitropical foods and raw materials like sugar cane, tobacco and indigo.
Delaware	1704	The settlers obtained a separate assembly from that of Pennsylvania. Delaware did not become a separate state until after the war of Independence.
Georgia	1733– 1753	Settled as a military buffer between the English colonies and the French and Spanish ones.

By 1750 all these colonies had been taken over by the Crown to be governed as royal colonies, although the King accepted the various colonial governments which already existed.

The English colonies, then, were quite different from New France. They were founded for a variety of reasons and often on the initiative of enterprising individuals instead of by the government. Whereas France controlled its colonies closely, England did not attempt to do so. Within its colonies there were people of different religions and nationalities and a continuous movement to land outside government control.

It was these colonies which were to fight England for independence in 1775. By 1750 they were well established. What sort of lives had the emigrants made for themselves?

New England in 1750. First, look closely at Map 5. The four northernmost colonies are known as New England. Winters there are cold, the coasts rugged, the soil poor, and much of the land hilly with fast-flowing streams and thick forests. The settlers banded together in small villages to make the best of harsh conditions. The forests provided timber for shipbuilding, the rocky harbours offered security for fishing fleets and later for vessels trading all over the world, the streams drove flour and saw mills.

For the Puritan, prosperity was a sign of God's favour and he worked hard to ensure his success. Puritanism discouraged extravagance or showiness, so in spite of difficulties Massachusetts grew rich. Ships from Boston carried wheat, corn, peas, pork, beef, fish, oak, pine, resin and barrel staves to England and Europe. They took rum to Africa for slaves, which they sold in the southern colonies or the West Indies in exchange for sugar and molasses (a black treacle obtained as a byproduct of sugar making), with which to make more rum. They also profited from the fur trade with the Indians.

By 1645 20,000 immigrants had poured into Massachusetts—many of them Puritans. Although they disliked intolerance in England they proved intolerant themselves. They persecuted Quakers particularly harshly and only official members of the Church—a minority—were able to vote at the three-monthly courts which made laws and levied taxes. This intolerance led to the banishment of Roger Williams for 'spreading new and dangerous opinions against the authority of the magistrates'. Questioning the Puritan right to take Indian land was one 'dangerous opinion'. He founded Rhode Island. For similar reasons Thomas Hooker migrated and helped to found Connecticut. In both these, from the start, there was freedom of worship, free speech and a more democratic government.

But as the colonies became wealthier, even Massachusetts changed. All the settlers could attend town meetings and gradually they forced the Puritans to allow them more influence. The wealthy merchants relaxed some of their strictness, their wives and daughters rode in carriages and wore European clothes and jewelry.

Harsh conditions had bred a tough, independent outlook; living close together made meetings easy to arrange in order to voice grievances, and these gave practice in self-government; success in taming the wilderness brought confidence. For these reasons England did not find it easy to govern these colonies. For example, the Navigation Acts said that all colonial trade should pass through England where duties could be levied. But Massachusetts had persistently avoided the duties by trading directly with the Continent. As a result her Charter was withdrawn in 1684 and a Governor-General sent out to rule without a local assembly. In 1688 he was overthrown and William III

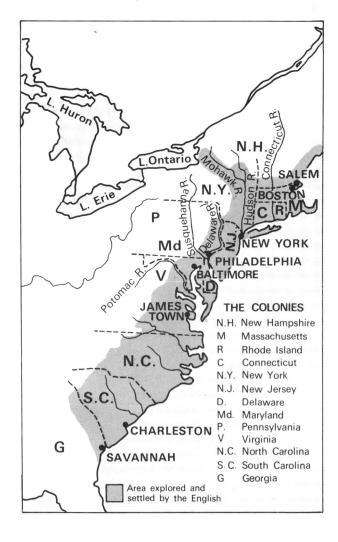

THE COLONIES

N.H. New Hampshire
M   Massachusetts
R   Rhode Island
C   Connecticut
N.Y. New York
N.J. New Jersey
D.   Delaware
Md.   Maryland
P.   Pennsylvania
V   Virginia
N.C. North Carolina
S.C. South Carolina
G   Georgia

Area explored and settled by the English

Map 5 British territory in America by 1750

allowed the Assemblies to meet again. But there was still constant bickering between the Assembly and the Royal Governor.

The Middle Colonies in 1750. The middle colonies—New York, New Jersey and Pennsylvania—were racially the most mixed, and many different languages were spoken in that area. New York had originally been settled by the Dutch, then by the Swedes, later by increasing numbers of English, Scots and Irish, and later still by French Huguenots. The aristocrats were the great merchants and landowners like Peter Schuyler and Caleb Heathcote. Often they were descendants of early settlers but with land, hard work and good luck any man could rise to the same position.

The country and climate were favourable enough to provide everyone with a living, but New York's wealth came from trade. A large part of the fur trade was conducted from Albany along the Mohawk and Hudson valleys, often at the expense of the French. Besides exporting the same sort of foodstuffs and raw materials as Boston, New York imported molasses, logwood (used to produce a black dye), indigo (a plant from which deep blue dye is extracted), mahogany, wine and grape brandy, elephant tusks, slaves, ebony, gold, rugs, tapestries, jewellery, gems, coins and European manufactures. What do you notice about the nature of these imports compared with the exports?

In the fertility of its soil and its reliance on trade, Pennsylvania was similar to New York. William Penn, a Quaker, intended it as an ideal state where men could live in love and friendship. He allowed religious toleration and partial self-government. Five thousand acres of land cost only £100 and small farms could be rented for a shilling per acre per annum. Penn advertised so successfully that English and Welsh Quakers, Germans, Dutchmen, and Scots and Irish Presbyterians poured in. By 1775 Philadelphia had become the largest English city after London.

By 1750 all these middle colonies were largely self-governing. New York had revolted with New England in 1688 and had been granted the right to an Assembly. As an attraction to colonists, settlers in New Jersey had been allowed one from the start, while in 1701 the Assembly of Pennsylvania had forced Penn to accept a constitution which made it virtually supreme. Here again though, it was only the pacifist Quakers in the east who held political power; the German and Dutch farmers inland only wished to be left alone, while the Scots and Irish on the frontier took little notice of the Quakers.

Like Boston, Philadelphia and New York traded directly with Europe in spite of the Navigation Acts. These three great commercial centres are an interesting contrast. In the north the dour, hard-headed Puritans becoming rich in spite of harsh, unfavourable circumstances, shunning pleasure and condemning any form of licence. In New York life was to be enjoyed and 25 per cent of all the buildings in the city were beer houses. Lastly, Philadelphia, the 'city of brotherly love', the richest of all, whose quiet, stubborn, wordly-wise Quakers were so respected and trusted that their paper currency was accepted at face value even in the other colonies. But much of the colonists' prosperity depended on English laxity in enforcing trade laws.

The South in 1750. The remaining colonies formed the South. Tobacco, the first product worth exporting on a large scale, required new land every three or four years. Wealthy Virginians had therefore brought huge estates bordering the rivers. They built their own jetties and exported their crop direct to England. There were no large towns. Their London agents would buy the European goods they needed. They relied almost exclusively on one crop and on Negro slavery to grow it. Smaller landowners could not compete and either became labourers or, more often, trekked west to break new land.

Used to wielding great power over their own vast estates, the planters had little patience with English interference. Francis Parkman has described them:

'Many of them were well-born with an immense pride of descent, increased by the habit of domination. Indolent and energetic by turns, rich in natural gifts and often poor in book-learning . . . high spirited, generous to a fault; keeping open house in their capacious mansions among vast tobacco fields and toiling Negroes . . . what they lacked in schooling was supplied by an education which books alone would have been impotent to give, an education which came from the possession and exercise of power and the sense of a position to maintain, joined to a bold spirit of independence. . . . They were few in number, they raced, gambled, drank and swore.'

Indeed, the planters despised both the dour religion and the careful book-keeping of the Puritans and the pacifism of the Quakers. The Puritans and Quakers believed the Southern aristocrats to be most unchristian.

The Carolinas were similar. But in the far south the planters grew rice and they did not despise trade like the Virginian aristocrats. Charleston was a wealthy city and a centre of fashion. But it was only a small élite which was rich. They made their money out of the labour of slaves on unhealthy, mosquito-ridden plantations from which they themselves retreated for half the year. Inland again, there were the poorer white farmers and frontiersmen, fiercely independent of both English and aristocratic control.

The Atlantic partnership. In 1750 the population of the thirteen English colonies was 1,200,000 and still growing. They all depended on British and European manufactured goods and some relied entirely on selling their products in Europe. In return Britain and Europe valued the colonies as sources of furs, naval supplies, foodstuffs and raw materials. The colonies were also dependent on Europe for people. English colonies had expanded faster than New France in part because land was made more easily available and there was less government interference, so that by 1750 a third of New England's colonists were people from northwest Europe. The colonies were a safety valve for the discontented, ambitious and persecuted and the immigrants provided the manpower colonial expansion demanded. This mutual dependence is known as the Atlantic partnership.

The western frontier. In 1750, however, the territory controlled by England in North America looked small in comparison to that of New France or New Spain. The English remained confined to the narrow coastal strip between the Atlantic and the Appalachians.

Throughout the period down to 1750 people in the thirteen colonies had been pushing west into the wilderness. There were two main reasons for this. As in New France, the fur trade in the English colonies lured traders and trappers ever deeper into the inland forests. The second reason was the existence of good, cheap farm land. As the population increased good farm lands near the coasts were occupied. Later immigrants who sought land were forced to move further and further inland to find it. Remember that most people came to America to find greater personal freedom and economic opportunity. To possess one's own land meant freedom from landowners and rent-collectors, and a chance to become better off.

There were good reasons why this westward movement was slow. The English settlers were mainly farmers and merchants, concerned with clearing land, making harbours and building towns and villages. This was a slow process. The rivers of the coast did not lead far inland and were not easily navigable. When the settlers did push inland, they quickly came to the impenetrable wall of the Appalachians. Powerful Indian tribes, the Iroquois and the Cherokees, blocked the routes north and south of the mountains. This was why pioneers moved southwest into the Shenandoah Valley instead of directly west.

The Boone family is typical of this movement. After emigrating from Devon in 1717 they settled in Pennsylvania, where Daniel Boone was born in 1734. His parents taught him to read and write but most of his education came from wandering the countryside, hunting, from the local Indians and from Henry Miller, a blacksmith friend who taught him all he knew about guns. In 1750 when his land became exhausted and he quarrelled with the local religious leaders, Daniel's father moved slowly to the Yadkin Valley in Carolina, in the foothills of the Appalachians. Before long, urged on by the French, Shawnee Indians attacked some of the farms, though not Boone's. Daniel took part as a wagon driver in Braddock's march on Fort Duquesne, and was lucky to escape with his life. On his return, he married and settled down as a farmer, hunter and trapper. Although furs were plentiful and profitable Boone never made very much money, as often he was caught by Indians and robbed of all he had caught, his rifle, his horses and his traps. But he came to know the wild country west of his home well.

This westward movement created tensions between the frontiersmen and the easterner. Life in the backwoods was hard, lonely and dangerous. Indians were a constant problem. Money to buy seeds and tools was short and debts piled up if crops or markets failed. Easterners grumbled about the Indian troubles and complained that the backswoodsmen were slow to pay off their debts. They tried hard through their control of the local Assemblies to settle these problems as best suited themselves.

If you have read this section on the English colonies carefully you will have noticed various tensions. There was tension between northerners and southerners, between eastern familes and western pioneers, between settlers and Indians, and between fur traders and the French. These tensions exploded into serious conflicts which were to reshape the future of America. To some of these conflicts we now turn.

Further Reading

Bakeless, Katherine and John, *Explorers of the New World*, Bell, 1959.
Grenville, J. A. S. and Fuller, G. J., *The Coming of the Europeans*, Longmans, 1962.
Peterson, Harold L., *The Book of the Gun*, Hamlyn, 1962.
Wright, Louis B., *Everyday Life in Colonial Times*, Batsford, 1965.
Longman 'Then and There' Series
   Gill, W. J. C., *Captain John Smith and Virginia*.
   Gill, W. J. C., *The Pilgrim Fathers.*
   Nichol, Norman, *Glasgow and the Tobacco Lords.*
Jonathan Cape 'Jackdaw' Series
   No 4, *Columbus and the Discovery of America.*
   No. 8, *The Mayflower and the Pilgrim Fathers.*

3 WARS AND REVOLUTION

The theme of this chapter is conflict. The entry of the Europeans into the wilderness and their contact with each other and the Indians created problems which were settled ultimately by force. Indian fought Indian, red man clashed with white, colonist rivalled colonist, and the English colonies finally rebelled against their mother country. This chapter gives some examples of these conflicts and considers the important and irrevocable results which followed from them.

The Indian Conflict

*The English and the Algonkins.** The early English settlers in the New World benefited from the knowledge and help of the Algonkin tribes they met. They learned from the Indians how to plant maize, make canoes, fish, hunt, smoke tobacco, fertilise their fields with seaweed and cook beans overnight in holes containing hot stones. Both Captain John Smith and the Pilgrim Fathers obtained corn from the Indians, and this greatly helped their settlements to survive the first months. Smith signed a peace treaty with the Powhatans and the Puritans made one with the Wampanoags.

But trouble was not long brewing. The English wanted land and as their numbers increased they pushed westwards. They chopped down the forests and killed or drove away the wild animals and birds. Resenting this destruction of their hunting grounds the Indians naturally tried to stop it. Some tribes were quickly crushed. In 1637, for example, pioneers pushing west in Massachusetts and Connecticut almost wiped out the Pequot Indians. In 1675 a Wampanoag chief called King Philip led several tribes against the New England settlements and began a two year war. This had terrible consequences for the whites. One-sixteenth of the adult male population of New England was killed. Twelve towns were completely destroyed, and half the New England towns suffered some damage. Nevertheless, the Indians lost. The settlers hit back strongly. On one occasion they attacked the fort at Kingston, the headquarters of the Narrangansetts, the strongest tribe. 600 wigwams were set on fire and the Indians shot as they tried to escape. About 600 Indians were killed and many more died in the cold winter that followed. A year later King Philip was cornered in a swamp and shot by an Indian on the side of the English. The chief's head was cut off and taken to Plymouth where it remained on display for twenty years. One of his hands was displayed in Boston. Such practices speak little for the English who said they were Christians.

These are only a few examples of the conflict between the English and the Indians. The books at the end of the chapter will give you other examples if you are interested.

The English and the Iroquois. Peaceful relations between the English and the Iroquois continued throughout the seventeenth and eighteenth centuries. These powerful Indians were too strong for the settlers to defeat and so they avoided the hunting grounds of the Iroquois. The English fur traders in New York colony encouraged the Iroquois to

*A general term for the east coast Indian tribes.

bring furs to them from the north and thereby injure the French fur trade. We will return to this point later.

The French peace with the Indians. The French fur trade depended greatly upon peaceful relations between the French settlements and the Indians. If you have read the section on the French in chapter 2 carefully you will understand why this was essential. Indeed, apart from the Iroquois, the French generally succeeded in winning and keeping the friendship of the tribes around the Great Lakes. Unlike the English, the French did not destroy the forests as they moved westwards. They were traders, not farmers.

In some ways the Indians benefited from the white man. He brought them metal and woollen goods like guns, axes, kettles and blankets which they could not have made for themselves. Such goods made farming and hunting easier and life more comfortable. In other ways they suffered. The European brought diseases like influenza and smallpox which the Indians had never known and to which they had no resistance. In return for furs he gave the Indians rum, whisky and brandy. Indeed, the fur trader (English as well as French) was often unscrupulous. He deliberately made the Indians drunk and cheated them of their furs. Drunkenness sometimes led to violence, robbery and murder. Not only were some Indians outlawed by the whites but by their own tribes as well.

Think carefully. Before the white man came the Indian way of life was adapted to survival in a hostile wilderness. Nevertheless, as we said in chapter 1, the Indians had a strict code of behaviour. The coming of the white man made hunting easier and life more comfortable. The Indian became increasingly dependent on the white man's trade goods. In his natural state too, the Indian had no strong alcohol and was unable to adapt to the violent effects of French brandy and English rum. The loss of his traditional hunting grounds, the effects of alcohol, and his dependence on white traders made hunting less important without providing any alternative outlet for the Indian's energy. At the same time these changes weakened his self-control and gave him real grievances. Not surprisingly, he became guilty of outrages which seemed barbaric to the whites.

The French fur trade and Indian warfare. From the time of Champlain the French and the Iroquois were enemies. At the same time as the French traders were building their fur posts along the St Lawrence the Dutch were building New Amsterdam (later to become New York) and the English creating Albany. Eager for a share in the fur trade the Dutch and English merchants encouraged the Iroquois to bring furs to them instead of to the French.

As the demand for furs grew the Iroquois depleted their own forests of beaver and then began to interfere with the trade of the Hurons and other northern tribes. This interference had serious consequences for the French and their Indian allies. The flow of furs to Montreal and Quebec was reduced because many were taken by the Iroquois to Albany or New Amsterdam instead. A glance at Map 6 will help you to see the situation.

Much bloodshed arose from the Indian competition for furs. In the 1630s and 1640s thousands of warriors died in battles between the Hurons and Iroquois. In 1637 a Frenchman was forced to watch the Hurons torture an Iroquois warrior. Afterwards he wrote that the prisoner was taken into a long cabin with eleven fires down the middle of it and platforms round the sides on which stood yelling Hurons holding firebrands. The captive was made to run round the fires while the Hurons burned his legs, making him shriek with pain. When he stopped to rest he was made to sit on hot ashes and burning coals. His ears were pierced with sticks and his fingers broken. Cold water was thrown over him when he fell unconscious. In the morning he was burned on a scaffold and finally killed with a knife. His head and body were eaten. The war, however, was won by the Iroquois who in 1649 completely overran the Hurons and wiped them out. In the next ten years the Erie, Neutral and Tobacco tribes were also annihilated by the Iroquois. For most of this time, too,

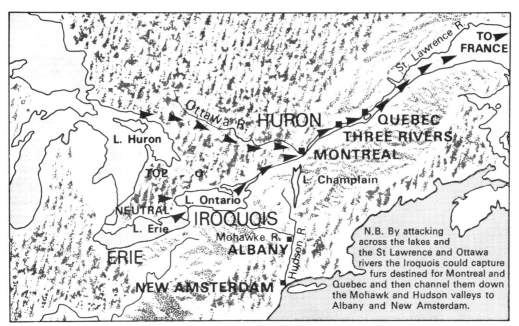

Map 6 The Iroquois
and the fur trade in
the North East

Labels within the map:

TO FRANCE

St. Lawrence R.

Ottawa R.

HURON

QUEBEC

THREE RIVERS

L. Huron

MONTREAL

L. Champlain

TOB

L. Ontario

NEUTRAL

IROQUOIS

L. Erie

Mohawk R.

ALBANY

ERIE

Hudson R.

NEW AMSTERDAM

N.B. By attacking
across the lakes and
the St Lawrence and Ottawa
rivers the Iroquois could capture
furs destined for Montreal and
Quebec and then channel them down
the Mohawk and Hudson valleys to
Albany and New Amsterdam.

the French fur posts were menaced by these fierce Indians. In 1665 an army sent from France managed to crush them and stop the Indian wars for a while. Nevertheless, the French and their Indian allies were never completely safe from Iroquois attack for another hundred years.

The Indian question is an interesting and important one. How do you think the Indians benefited from their contact with the white man? How do you think they suffered? What do you think were the main reasons for intertribal battles and the struggles between Indians and whites? Could these wars have been avoided? Do you think on balance Indians benefited or lost by their contact with the white man? Think about these questions, re-read this section, and then discuss them in class.

The Anglo-French Conflict

The reasons for growing hostility. In the eighteenth century the English and the French were the chief rivals for colonies throughout the world and for the fur trade in North America. In America their rivalry came to a head with the French and Indian War, 1754–63, which was part of the Seven Years War in Europe.

A long standing cause of this conflict in America was the fur trade. French resentment of the trade between the Iroquois and the English in New York and Albany had led in the late seventeenth century to an attempt to crush the Iroquois and to seize the Hudson-Mohawk region for New France. This only emphasised the importance of the fur trade and between 1715 and 1750 traders from New England, New York, Pennsylvania, Virginia, Carolina and Georgia began to journey west across the mountains to trade with the Indians. Pennsylvanian traders like George Croghan and Christopher Gist carried shrouds, blankets, calicoes, guns, knives, hatchets, kettles, belts, cheap jewellery and rum to tribes like the Delawares, the Shawnees and the Miamis. In return the Pennsylvanians received skins of deer, bears, racoons, foxes, muskrats, mink and beaver which in 1750 were valued at £40,000. By this time about 300 English fur traders were working in the Ohio valley. A Frenchman reported: 'Each (village) great or small, has one or more English traders...the English (are) well advanced on our lands, and, what is worse, under the protection of a crowd of savages.'

One of the most important of these villages was Pickawillany, whose chief was 'Old Britain'. Compared to the French, the English offered the Indians more goods for their furs. Another Frenchman said: 'It is true that they like our brandy better than English rum but they prefer English goods to ours and can buy for two beaver skins at Oswego a better silver bracelet than we sell at Niagara for ten.' Oswego was an English trading post in New York colony.

By 1750 there was another reason for the growing tension between the French and the English. Several English colonies claimed lands in the Ohio valley. Such claims were based on the seventeenth century charters issued to them by the English crown. By 1750 the line of English settlement had reached the Appalachians. It was clear that further settlement could only be made on the other side. Wealthy people in England and the colonies realised that large profits could be made by claiming virgin lands of the Ohio and selling them later to the highest bidders when the settlers arrived. The most aggressive colony in this respect was Virginia. In 1748 the Ohio Land Company was formed there which claimed 200,000 acres of land south of the forks of the Ohio. The possibilities of a permanent occupation of the valley by settlers from the English colonies was a grave threat to the French.

The French considered the Ohio their own territory and decided to drive out the English while they still could. In 1752 they led a band of Indians against Pickawillany. The inhabitants were massacred and 'Old Britain' was eaten. The following year they built Forts Presqu'isle and Le Boeuf.

The Indians too were fearful of English settlement in the forest of the Ohio. It was a serious threat to their own way of life. (Why?) In the ensuing war most tribes fought on the French side.

Virginia tried to take positive action against the French. In 1753 the Governor sent George Washington with a small escort of frontiersmen and Indians across the mountains to deliver a message to them:

'The lands upon the Ohio River in the western parts of the Colony of Virginia are so notoriously known to be the property of the Crown of Great Britain that it is a matter of equal concern and surprise to me to hear that a body of French troops are erecting fortresses and making settlements upon that river within His Majesty's dominion. . . . It becomes my duty to require your peaceful departure.'

The French refused to move.

Clearly, the position was serious. The upper Ohio was important to both sides and neither was willing to back down. Virginia's Governor decided to build a fort at the forks of the Ohio. This was only half-built when a thousand French soldiers appeared. Outnumbered ten to one the Virginians retreated. The French then built their own fort there. It was called Fort Duquesne. Map 7 shows the settlements and forts mentioned in this section.

The military situation in 1754. The English colonists greatly outnumbered the French. However, they were farmers and merchants, reluctant to pay the cost of a war or fight themselves, and divided into a number of separate squabbling colonies.

The Pennsylvanians had actively spread rumours that the Virginian Ohio Company intended to settle the land—which was true—in order to alienate the French and the Indians and embarrass their fellow colonists. Even after the war had started and Indians and French were massacring the frontier farmers, some Assemblies not only refused to cooperate with other colonies but even refused to grant their royal governors

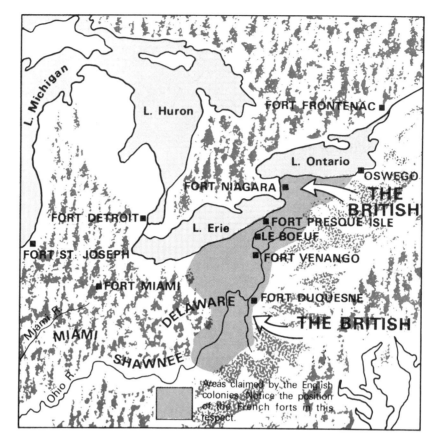

Map 7 Anglo-Frenc
rivalry in the Ohio
Valley about 1750

money for the war because they wished to use the emergency to extract greater independence for themselves.

The colonists could not count on the support of the Iroquois, for these Indians themselves now feared the settlement of the English in their forests. By contrast, many of the people of New France were soldiers and frontiersmen who obeyed the orders of the French king. The French also had many Indian allies.

By now, England realised the great value of the fur trade and the advantages of settlement beyond the Appalachians. The fur trade benefited its London merchants and the makers of beaver hats, fur clothes and leather shoes. New colonies beyond the mountains would enrich her own speculators and provide more food and raw materials for England herself. The government was not eager to pay the entire cost of the war: it expected the colonies to contribute money as well. In 1754 England sent two regiments and told the colonists to raise two more.

France held a strong position in America. Her forts were strung out in a great arc along the waterways from Louisberg to New Orleans. France controlled the great heartland of the continent which, as La Salle had said, offered opportunities for new colonies and trade. The Ohio and Mississippi valleys were worth holding. With good reason the French thought the colonists too disunited to oppose them. Six French regiments were sent to America.

To maintain this grip on America the French had to hold the St Lawrence, Hudson, Mohawk, Champlain and Mississippi rivers. The English, if they were to break through into the heart of America, had to capture some or all of these valleys. Can you say why? A crucial factor was likely to be seapower. Whoever controlled the sea could bring reinforcements and supplies to its own side and prevent its rival from doing so.

The French and Indian War, 1754–63. The English were unsuccessful in the early campaigns of the war. In 1755 General Braddock marched overland against Fort Duquesne. (Was this a good idea?) Largely through English ignorance of colonial methods of fighting, the attack failed. Braddock was killed and his second-in-command retreated to Philadelphia leaving the whole 350 miles of the Virginian and Pennsylvanian frontiers protected only by Washington, then twenty-three years old, and a mere 1000 colonials who thought military discipline next to slavery.

The French and the Indians used the opportunity to wipe out outlying settlements. In Pennsylvania frontiersmen protested: 'It is really very shocking for the husband to see his wife... her head cut off, and the children's blood drunk like water by these cruel and bloody savages.'

In 1757 Fort William Henry was surrendered. In spite of a safe conduct from Montcalm, the French commander, the Indians seized many of the English prisoners and took some of them off to Montreal. 'At two o'clock in the presence of the entire town, they killed one of them, put him in a kettle, and forced his unfortunate compatriots to eat him.' The French bought the rest for two kegs of brandy each.

As a result of this failure in war William Pitt came to power in England in 1757. He was determined to beat France by using English naval supremacy to seize her colonies. The struggle for the control of the American continent was now in deadly earnest.

In Canada he planned the four-pronged attack shown in Map 8. The most important thrusts were up the St Lawrence (Sir Geoffrey Amherst) and the Hudson (Sir James Abercrombie) routes. What do you think of this plan? Amherst had first to seize Louisberg. (Why?) He was successful but the French avoided surrender long enough to make the attack on Quebec impossible until the following year. Abercrombie reoccupied William Henry and marched on Fort Carillon. Although he had four times as many troops as Montcalm, his judgment failed and he lost the chance of an easy victory. The two minor attacks are more interesting.

Brigadier Forbes was to make another attempt on Duquesne. His march shows the difficulties of travelling overland in the wilderness. Francis Parkman describes them. Don't forget that the road had to be cut across three ranges of mountains:

'Autumnal rains, uncommonly heavy and persistent, had ruined the newly-cut road. On the mountains the torrents tore it up, and in the valleys the wheels of the wagons churned it into soft mud. The horses, overworked and underfed, were first breaking down ... they were forced to drag their own oats and corn as well as supplies for the army through 200 miles of wilderness.... This was no longer possible.... Above, below, around, all was trickling, oozing, pattering and gushing. In the miserable encampments the starved horses stood steaming in the rain, and the men crouched disgusted under their dripping tents.... The rain turned to snow, the descending flakes ... melting from sight in the trench of half-liquid clay that was called a road. The wheels of wagons sank into it to the hub, and to advance or retreat was alike impossible.'

But Forbes did get through, so ill he had to be carried on a litter. Before he could attack Duquesne, the French blew it up and retreated. But his care to pacify the Indians en route ended the slaughter on the frontier.

Colonel Bradstreet suggested and carried out the fourth attack, on Fort Frontenac, which was the chief supply depôt for all the western forts. Deprived of supplies they would have to surrender. Using a force of tough, armed boatmen he had recruited to supply Fort Oswego, his attack was a model of speed, efficiency and secrecy. It took him only twenty-four days to move 3000 men from the Great Carrying Place to Frontenac, destroy the fort and return. His success shows how effectively colonial troops could be used. He had an advantage over Forbes in being able to use natural

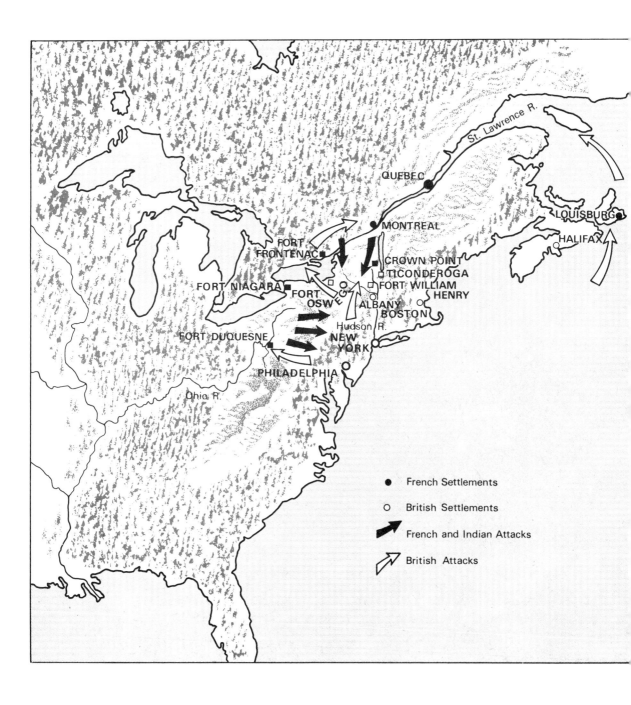

Map 8 The French and Indian War

waterways, but he used the toughness and knowledge of the frontiersmen to ensure the speed and secrecy which guaranteed surprise. In all he seized or destroyed seventy-six guns, 10,000 barrels of provisions and nearly one million livres of trade goods. His success led to the abandonment of Duquesne and later of the other western forts. A livre was a French coin valued at about 10 pence.

Pitt's plan was continued in 1759. William Johnson took Fort Niagara and Oswego was strengthened. Amherst replaced Abercrombie and the French retreated from Forts Carillon and St Frederick. The former was rebuilt by the English as Ticonderoga. The main action was James Wolfe's famous attack on Quebec.

Quebec in 1761

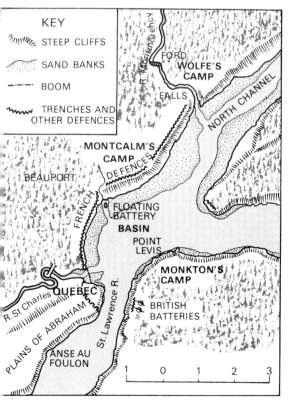

Map 9 Quebec, showing natural and man made defences at the time of Wolfe's attack

KEY

- STEEP CLIFFS
- SAND BANKS
- BOOM
- TRENCHES AND OTHER DEFENCES

R. Montmorency

FORD
WOLFE'S CAMP

FALLS

NORTH CHANNEL

MONTCALM'S CAMP

BEAUPORT

FRENCH DEFENCES

FLOATING BATTERY

BASIN

POINT LEVIS

MONKTON'S CAMP

BRITISH BATTERIES

R. St Charles QUEBEC

PLAINS OF ABRAHAM

St. Lawrence R.

ANSE AU FOULON

1 0 1 2 3

First look at map 9. You can make lists of the natural and man-made defences of the city. The picture shows some of the places named on the map. Montcalm had 12,000 men to defend this strong position; his best plan was to sit tight and let Wolfe exhaust his army trying to get to grips. As he relied on supplies from Montreal, he sent part of his army, under Bougainville, to patrol the upstream bank of the St Lawrence. Wolfe had 9000 men and twenty-two warships; his problem was to force Montcalm to fight before winter froze the river. Before reading on, look at the map and decide where and why you would attack.

He arrived on 27 June. It was thought too dangerous to make a frontal attack on Quebec. To land upstream might mean being caught between Bougainville and Montcalm. So he tried a simultaneous assault on Beaufort and the River Montmorency. He was defeated by a thunderstorm, which made the mud cliffs unclimbable. He next tried devastating the countryside to force Montcalm to give battle—but without success.

July and August passed without any progress and winter was uncomfortably close. At last he agreed to land at the Anse de Foulon on 12 September hoping to sever Montcalm's supply lines and force him to fight. He sent his landing force well upstream, to slip down after dark pretending to be a French supply flotilla. Luckily Bougainville had cancelled the flotilla but not told the cliff-top guards and the commander at the top of the Anse de Foulon had let many of his men go home to help with harvesting. Wolfe committed an advance party of only 150. If they failed, the whole army was ready to sail for home immediately to avoid the winter freeze-up.

A half hour before the dawn the first boats grated on the gravel beach, and due to magnificent naval teamwork, within a few hours 4500 men were drawn up on Abraham's Heights. Montcalm decided not to wait for Bougainville: 'We cannot avoid action; the enemy is entrenching. . . . If we give him time to establish himself, we shall never be able to attack him with the sort of troops we have.' The battle was won by superior English discipline. Wolfe died on the field and Montcalm shortly afterwards.

Wolfe has a reputation as a great general. Consider:
1. He hesitated for over two months, so that his final attack was a last chance and a big risk. What would his reputation be if he had failed?
2. That his landing was unopposed was largely good luck.
3. Once the army was ashore Wolfe's rigorous training and leadership gave him victory. Would it be fair to say that Wolfe had trained his men well and led them well on the field, but that he found it difficult to decide where to attack?

Although this proved to be the climax of the war, the English were only saved from having to surrender Quebec the following year by English ships being the first to arrive after the ice had broken. The armies from Oswego, Ticonderoga and Quebec then converged on Montreal and Governor Vaudreuil surrendered.

At the Treaty of Paris in 1763, Canada was handed over officially to England by France and her ally Spain surrendered Florida. To compensate Spain, France sold her Louisiana. (See Map 10.) France was eliminated as a colonial power in North America. Henceforth it was the English who developed the continent. The Treaty of Paris is significant because it marked the end of the Anglo-French struggle for supremacy in North America.

The Conflict Between England and her Colonies

The wars with the Indians and the French are easy to understand. The war between the colonies and England is more difficult. Let us consider the point of view of each side.

English attitudes and policies towards the thirteen colonies. Englishmen often had a condescending attitude towards colonists. Many frankly despised 'the scum or off-scouring of all nations . . . a mongrel breed of Irish, Scotch and Germans, leavened with convicts and outcasts'. The self-reliance and confidence of the colonists made them seem to the British 'haughty and insolent, impatient of rule'.

For most Englishmen 'the colonies were acquired with no other view than to be a convenience to us'. There was no intention that they should ever 'grow up' and become independent. Since they belonged to England, England had the right to give them laws, impose taxes and expect obedience. As the colonies became richer, they should expect to pay heavier taxes.

The colonies were a 'convenience' to England because they were a source of raw materials and food and a market for English goods. Colonial trade was regulated by the Navigation Acts. Certain goods, which England could not produce herself—rice, molasses, naval stores, furs, sugar, tobacco, dye-stuffs—had to be exported to England. These were called 'enumerated' goods. Duties were levied on these exports and many of the goods were resold at great profit by English merchants to continental countries. Similarly, all goods from Europe to the colonies had to pass through England where duty and handling charges raised the prices which the colonists paid. One-third of English shipping was involved in colonial trade and English merchants provided most of the capital to finance investment in America. In 1760 the colonies owed them £4 million.

The colonies did enjoy some benefits. For example, they had a monopoly of the market for tobacco in England and bounties were paid to colonial merchants on the naval stores they exported to the mother country.

This trading system profited the English more than the colonists. Yet the colonies

ap 10 The division
America after the
reaty of Paris 1763

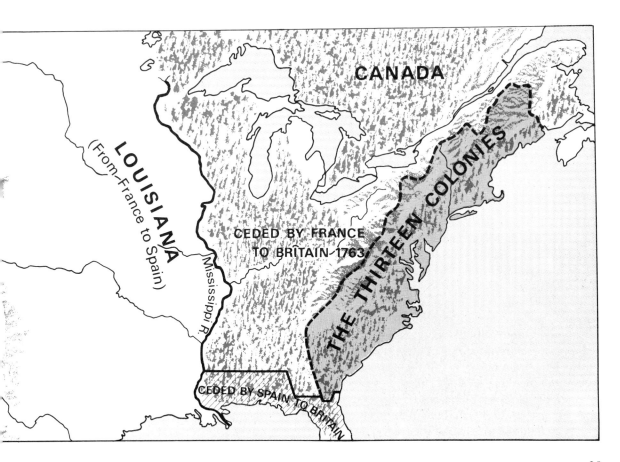

prospered because England was often lax in its operation of the system. For example, New England produced few enumerated goods but bought many English goods. To pay for these it needed £200,000 profit per annum from other trade, especially from molasses and rum. New England imported molasses from the French West Indies, made it into rum, and then exported it. In 1733 a Molasses Act had imposed a heavy import tax on foreign molasses which, if strictly enforced, would have seriously harmed New England trade. In reality molasses were regularly and easily smuggled into New England and so the rum trade thrived.

The real origins of the conflict between England and her colonies lie in the French and Indian War. First, this had been very expensive for England. The total war debt of the colonies was only £2,600,000. The interest alone on the English National Debt, largely incurred because of the war, was £5 million per year. Secondly, victory had given England a whole new territory to administer. Finally, the Indians remained a grave threat along the Appalachian frontier. In 1763, led by Pontiac, they had attacked frontier settlements in an attempt to drive the white man back to the east. Pontiac saw clearly the dangers to the Indians of the westward movement of the whites.

'This is but the beginning. . . . The invader has crossed the great sea in ships; he has not been stayed by broad rivers, and now he has penetrated the wilderness and overcome the ruggedness of the mountains. Neither will he stop there. He will force the Indian steadily before him across the Mississippi ever toward the West.'

Pontiac's Revolt failed but the Indian danger remained. And there was always the possibility that the French might use the Indians to help them win back their lost lands.

Thus in 1763 England needed money to pay off debts and to support an army along the frontier. At the same time she wished to minimise the risk of further Indian wars while profiting from the fur trade and sale of lands in the upper Ohio valley.

England therefore took steps to meet these needs. In 1763 a Proclamation Order prohibited settlement west of the crest of the Appalachians until proper treaties had been made with the Indians. (See Map 11.) The fur trade was regulated to prevent cheating. Fur prices were fixed, the sale of rum was forbidden, traders were licensed and official trading posts set up. In 1764 a Sugar Act was passed which reduced the tax on molasses imported into the colonies but tightened up the collection of it. The customs service was made bigger, the powers of the courts increased, and the Navy ordered to have a keener eye for smugglers. The Stamp Act in 1765 imposed a tax on all newspapers and legal documents like wills or bills of sale. In 1767 small import duties were put on paper, paints, glass and tea. These were known as the Townshend duties.

The colonial response. The colonists had always resented the way in which Englishmen talked of 'our colonies and our plantations in such terms and with such airs as if our property and persons were absolutely theirs, like the villeins and the cottages in the old feudal system'. After 1763 their resentment increased and the authority of the English government was either ignored or challenged very strongly by them. Those who had come from Europe, survived, and conquered the wilderness with little help from England, had strength, courage, initiative and determination. To them, the English ruling classes seemed insufferably snobbish, affected, lazy and often corrupt and incompetent.

To many colonists the ending of the war meant two things. They would be less dependent on England for protection and they would be free to settle and exploit the Ohio valley. The fur trader, the land speculator, the dissatisfied eastern farmer and the wealthier immigrants all looked west across the Appalachians. Yet no sooner had the west been opened up than an interfering government tried to close it again. But it turned out that England could not enforce her Proclamation Order. The boundary was simply a line drawn

AREA MADE PART OF BRITISH CANADA ACT OF 1774

HARRODSBURG • BOONESBORO

Ohio R.

Cumberland R.

Tennessee R.

WATAUGA

THE 13 COLONIES

Areas of land speculation and pioneer settlements

N.B. Just how far beyond the Proclamation Line the land speculators were going

— Proclamation Line

*ap 11 The Pro-
*amation Line, 1763
*d the Quebec Act
74

*statue of Daniel
oone put up in 1892

on a map. It was impossible to police it. The army was too small and the frontier too long. The Proclamation Line was ignored.

Daniel Boone's career illustrates this clearly. His farm in Carolina was not very profitable. Indians sometimes succeeded in stealing the furs he had hunted in the forests. As more people came to Carolina, as laws came to be enforced more effectively, as taxes became heavier and his creditors pressed more strongly, Boone spent more time exploring the Kentucky region west of the mountains. He early realised the profits to be made by selling western land but he lacked the money to buy it from the Indians. Local businessmen, however, were prepared to pay off his debts and finance him if he would prospect for the best land in Kentucky. After a two-year exploration he bought land for his backers from the Cherokees. In 1775 he set out with 500 men, cutting a path—the Wilderness road—for the wagons and families to follow. A settlement was built near the Kentucky River. Its name was Boonesborough and it was well beyond the Proclamation Line.

Meanwhile the Sugar Act had caused protests from the merchants of New England and in 1766 England reduced the duty on molasses. The Stamp Act, however, provoked a storm of protest throughout the colonies. Lawyers, merchants, printers, editors— educated people with political influence—quickly aroused public opinion against West-minster. Angry mobs burned stamps and the houses of the tax collectors. Riots occurred in New York and New England. Merchants refused to import English goods until the Stamp Act was repealed. Nine colonies sent representatives to a Stamp Act Congress in New York. A resolution was passed stating that the English Parliament had no powers to tax the colonies without their consent. The colonial rallying cry became 'NO TAXATION WITHOUT REPRESENTATION'.

37

This principle became the key issue. On the one hand, King George III and his English Parliament believed they had the right to tax the colonies and that it was only fair to do so. They did not admit a colony's right to representation at Westminster. On the other hand, England had never interfered too much in the government of the colonies. Indeed, there had grown up in the colonies a strong tradition of self-government, especially in New England which resented too much control by the royal governors. (If you have read this section carefully you will have noticed the leading role of New England in the protests against taxation and trade regulations.) In particular, the colonies had always insisted that they should control their own financial affairs.

The colonies made so much fuss about the Stamp Act that England repealed it in 1766, but retained the right to tax the colonies whenever it saw fit. But by then the colonists had begun to find all sorts of unfairness in the trade regulations. They were not allowed to export to each other many types of everyday goods, such as wool and hats. In 1767 iron was 'enumerated' to destroy the promising iron industry. One man complained:

'A colonist cannot make a button, horseshoe, nor a hobnail but some sooty ironmonger or respectable button maker of Britain shall bawl and squal that his honour's worship is ... maltreated, injured, cheated and robbed by the rascally American republicans.'

The colonists concluded that Britain wished to 'crush their native talents and to keep them in a constant state of inferiority', but that their protests might be effective.

The regulation of trade was quickly seen as a disguised form of taxation.

'Why is the trade of the colonies more circumscribed than the trade of Britain? ... Why [should not] trade, commerce ... and manufacturers ... be as free for an American as for a European? ... Under a pretence of regulating our trade, we may insensibly be robbed of our liberty.'

Acting on this belief New York refused to provide supplies for the English army, as it was supposed to do by the Quartering Act of 1765, or to pay new import duties. Its Assembly was suspended. When Massachusetts circularised the other colonies, even conservatives agreed to the principle of 'no taxation without representation'. In Boston customs officials who tried to collect duties were manhandled by a town mob. English troops moved in to protect the officials. In 1770 a mob snowballed and then attacked the troops. The soldiers fired killing three people and mortally wounding two. This incident became known in the colonies as the 'Boston Massacre'. In this same year England gave in to the trade embargo and the Townshend duties, except that on tea, were withdrawn.

Throughout, England did not act firmly enough. She sent insufficient troops to the colonies and failed to order those that were there to suppress disorder early enough. Consequently the colonists got away with one incident after another. Massachusetts Assembly was suspended for its circular letter but was allowed to sit again without retracting. In 1772 an English revenue cutter, the *Gaspee*, went aground and was burnt; but no colonists would admit to responsibility, and in the end nothing was done.

The Boston Tea Party. After 1770 the colonies largely evaded the tea tax by refusing to buy tea imported through England. Soon the East India Company had a surplus of seventeen million pounds of tea in its warehouses in England. Nine-tenths of all the tea drunk in the thirteen colonies was smuggled in by colonial merchants. In 1773, to help the Company, England passed the Tea Act which gave it a monopoly of the colonial tea trade and allowed it to take tea direct to the colonies without stopping in England. The purpose of the Act was to force the price of tea down and knock the bottom out of the smugglers' market.

The Tea Act aroused new anger in the colonies. Colonists opposed the idea of monopoly.

Those merchants who made profits from smuggled tea quickly made their protest heard. Throughout the colonies the agents of the East India Company were pressed to resign and tea brought in by the Company was either sent to England or placed in warehouses. In Boston, however, the Company's agents refused to resign and made plans to import the tea. This action greatly annoyed Samuel Adams, a Massachusetts 'patriot'. He organised a group of men dressed as Indians, who boarded the Company's ships and destroyed the tea by throwing it into the harbour. This event is known as the Boston Tea Party.

It was now England's turn to be angry. The colonies were punished. Boston's port was closed until the tea was paid for. Massachusetts could no longer govern itself. Elections were forbidden there: the members of the colony's Assembly were now appointed by the King. Town meetings were prohibited without the prior consent of the royal governor. More British troops were moved in.

Liberty—the rallying cry of the colonists. All the colonies now rallied in support of Massachusetts. The watchword was liberty. It was a word and an idea which appealed not only to colonial merchants but to people throughout the colonies—to frontiersmen, fur traders, land speculators, farmers, lawyers, editors, immigrants, taxpayers. What did liberty mean to all these people?

To understand this you must remember the nature of the New World, the type of people who went there, and their reasons for doing so. America was a wilderness. To live there the white man either had to live like the Indian, to return to a stone age existence, or he had to convert the wilderness into a civilised community. To convert the wilderness meant determination, patience, perseverance, hard physical work. It meant risking disease, Indian attack, failure and death. The people who went there— English, Scots, Irish, Germans, Swedes—all knew this. America offered them a better life than Europe. It offered them religious and economic liberties—freedom from oppressive governments and taxes, religions, landlords and masters. To fashion their new life in America they wanted freedom to trade, to manufacture, to farm when and where they saw fit. The Navigation laws, taxes, restrictions on westward movement, all interfered with these freedoms. The colonists believed they had a right to these. They united together against too much government, too much authority. Thus the American War of Independence was really about liberty.

Radicals and conservatives. These ideas about liberty were most strongly held by the 'patriots' or radicals. Support for the radicals came from all sections of colonists but particularly from the frontiersmen, the western farmer and the lower classes in the town. These had little political influence and resented not only British authority but also that of the colonial ruling classes—the wealthier merchants in Massachusetts, the Quakers in Pennsylvania, the planters in Virginia. Radical leaders like Samuel Adams deliberately exploited this resentment to strengthen their hand against the conservatives. Their motives were not entirely patriotic. Patrick Henry of Virginia openly admitted that he appealed to the radical frontiersmen because he wanted power and reputation. Samuel Adams used the mobs in Massachusetts to intimidate the conservatives. The radicals wanted independence. The conservatives were more cautious: they wanted self-government but not complete separation from Britain. The conservatives did have the same grievances as the radicals about taxation and the restrictions on trade and westward expansion.

Three things helped to unite the conservatives and the radicals. First was the Quebec Act of June, 1774. (See Map 11.) By this, the Upper Ohio valley was absorbed into Canada which benefited the French fur traders of Quebec at the expense of their rivals in the thirteen colonies. Settlers from these colonies were also restricted there. So it seemed to the thirteen colonies that their gains from the French and Indian War had been lost. Even worse, England tolerated Catholics, whom the Puritans of Massachusetts hated, and allowed the Canadians no self-government. Many colonists imagined the British government wished to rule all its colonies in this way. The Quebec Act united the colonies in calling a Continental Congress at Philadelphia.

Meanwhile, the British troops in Boston, led by General Gage, had tried to seize a radical arms-dump at Concord in 1775. On the way the troops dispersed some armed minute-men* at Lexington. The first shot of the American War of Independence had been fired. The troops only partly destroyed the arms dump and were harassed by colonists all the way back to Boston.

The conservatives believed it was the British government that was corrupt and they had remained loyal to the King. Up to this point they had never considered complete separation from Britain. Their loyalty to the King was destroyed by an English radical's pamphlet, *Commonsense*, which showed that it was the King himself who was responsible for English policy towards the colonies. When the King tried to hire German mercenaries (paid foreign soldiers) to kill his own colonial subjects the conservatives were finally won over by the radicals. On 4 July 1776 the Declaration of Independence written by Thomas Jefferson, was accepted. Here is the best-known part:

'We hold these truths to be self-evident, that all men are created equal, that they are endowed by their creator with certain inalienable rights, and that among these are life, liberty and the pursuit of happiness. That to secure these rights, governments are instituted among men, deriving their just powers from the consent of the governed. That whatever any form of government becomes destructive to these ends, it is the right of the people to alter or abolish it, and to institute new government. . . .'

The War of Independence, 1775–83. You can follow the progress of the war on the following maps and table. There were no dramatic large-scale battles and the campaigns were not planned as clearly as in the Seven Years War. So it is not intended to go into detail. Here is a chance for you to do some work by yourself. Use the books listed at the end of the chapter and any that you have at school to write your own account of the American War of Independence. For example, try to include details about particular battles and generals, the different methods of fighting by colonists, Indians and English soldiers, and the weapons used. When you have finished try to suggest the main reasons why the colonists won the war. A careful reading of the table will help you.

Table 2.   The Main Stages of the American War of Independence

PART ONE: IN THE NORTH

By the middle of 1776, English authority had been completely overthrown. The English soldiers, shut in Boston since their defeats at *Lexington, Concord* and at *Bunker Hill*, had been forced to evacuate when the Americans brought up the guns they had captured at *Ticonderoga* in 1775. An American attack on Canada had failed.

The English had to pacify a whole country. Inevitably this meant spreading their army out. American strategy, therefore, was to force England to keep her army together by creating a continental army herself, and to use every opportunity to harass the English forces with militia, especially when they were separated from sea-borne supplies. It did not matter in the least if England captured major cities.

*Radical supporters who were ready to take up arms at a moment's notice.

IN CONGRESS, JULY 4, 1776.

The unanimous Declaration of the thirteen united States of America.

The Declaration of
Independence

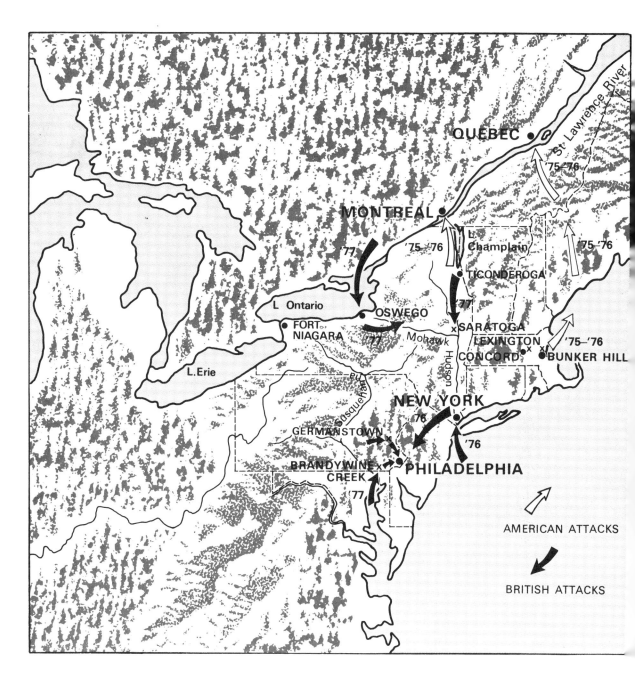

1776   The English successfully captured *New York* as their main base, but Washington— *Map 12 War in the*
         the American general—stopped their march on *Philadelphia* and the colonists   *North*
         delayed an English invasion from Canada.

1777   Lack of concerted strategy led to disaster. One English army, led by General
         Burgoyne, started along the Champlain/Hudson valley but suffered irreplaceable
         losses to colonial militia. Support from the Mohawk Valley failed to arrive and a
         second English army chose to divert Washington by attacking Philadelphia. It was
         successful at *Brandy wine Creek* and *Germanstown* but gained no military advant-
         age. Meanwhile it could not come to the aid of Burgoyne's army which after ruin-
         ous losses at Bemis Heights and Freeman's Farm had to surrender at *Saratoga*.

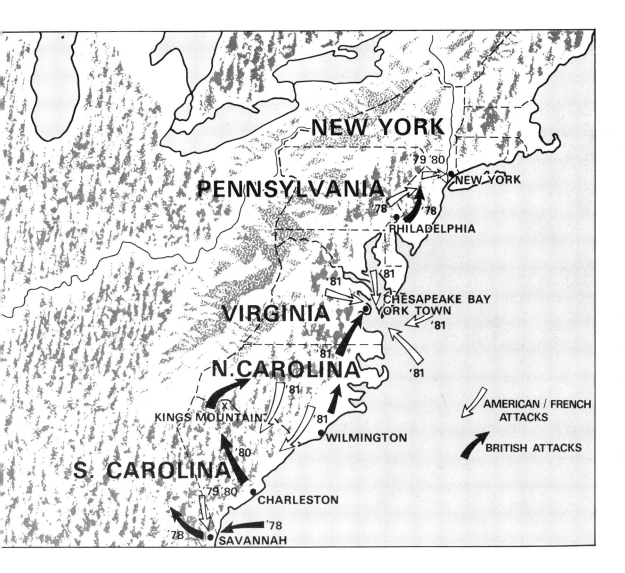

NEW YORK

PENNSYLVANIA

'79 '80

NEW YORK

'78

'78

PHILADELPHIA

'81

'81

CHESAPEAKE BAY

VIRGINIA

YORK TOWN

'81

'81

N.CAROLINA

'81

'81

AMERICAN / FRENCH ATTACKS

KINGS MOUNTAIN

'81

WILMINGTON

BRITISH ATTACKS

'80

S. CAROLINA

'79 '80

CHARLESTON

'78

'78

SAVANNAH

France, convinced that the colonists would win, now recognised American independence, and in 1778 joined in the war against England.

PART TWO: IN THE SOUTH

England decided to hold New York, while attacking the south, where she expected more support from loyal colonists.

1778   Philadelphia was evacuated but Georgia was captured easily.

1779–   Washington found it difficult to organise practical co-operation with the
1780   French navy and colonial attacks on *New York* and *Savannah* both failed. Co-operation with the French army was easier and 5000 French soldiers joined him.
        The English attacked and took *Charleston* in South Carolina. They then invaded North Carolina but were stopped at *King's Mountain*.

1781   Washington sent an army south and although it was beaten, it forced the English to retire and reorganise and used the opportunity to sweep South Carolina and Georgia free of English troops, except for Charleston and Savannah.

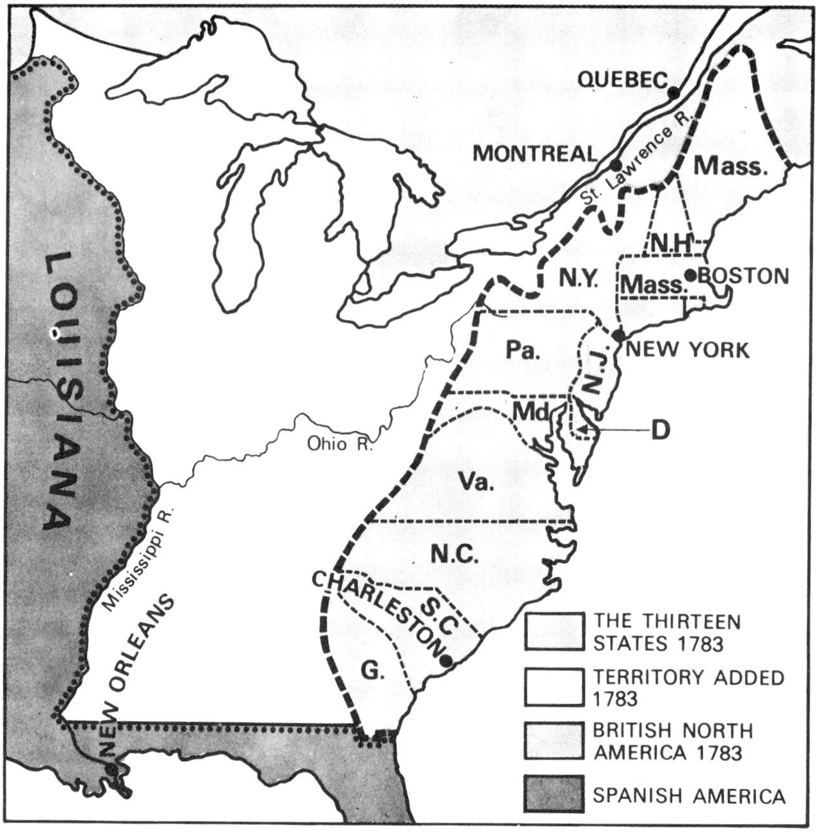

Map 14 America after the Treaty of Paris 1783

Note that it did the English little good to retain control of a few cities when the rest of the colonies were perfectly free. Whenever the major English force moved to a new location, its previous one was vulnerable.

> The English could not bring the Americans to battle so they retired to *Yorktown*. This was an excellent position provided that England controlled the sea.
>
> Unfortunately the Americans and French at last managed to coordinate a major offensive. A large French fleet sealed off Chesapeake Bay and landed 3000 troops. Washington moved south with 7000 more to join the Virginian army to cut off the English army by land.
>
> The position was hopeless and the English surrendered on 17 October.

England still held important cities, but it was clear that this would not win the war. The loss of control of the sea was temporary but fatal. The English government had always believed that the rebellion was the work of a small minority, but by this time it was convinced that few Americans were prepared to fight to restore English rule. The war was expensive. Peace was made and Independence recognised in 1783.

Further Reading

Bakeless, John, *Daniel Boone*, Stackpole, 1965.
Connell, Brian, *The Plains of Abraham*, Hodder & Stoughton, 1959.
Tourtellot, Arthur B., *William Diamond's Drum*, Hutchinson, 1960.
Wellman, Paul I., *Indian Wars and Warriors East*, Houghton Mifflin, 1959.
Longman 'Then and There' Series;
   The Struggle for Canada.   The American Revolution.
Jonathan Cape 'Jackdaw' Series;
   The American Revolution.   Wolfe at Quebec.

4 THE NEW NATION

The Americans had consciously turned their backs on Europe. In its place they had declared their ideal of a new democratic nation carved out of the wilderness. But in 1783 they were still thirteen separate quarrelling states, troubled by both economic and political problems.

The Problems of Independence

Economic problems. The war only briefly interrupted trade across the Atlantic. England and Europe still needed naval supplies, furs, dyes, fish, tobacco and grain and 90 per cent of Americans still worked on the land to feed themselves and provide products for export. America still relied on England and Europe for manufactured goods, immigrants, and money for investment.

But American merchants now found themselves cut off from trade with all the British colonies, and in the case of the West Indies this affected their trade with the southern states as well. (Why?) When they looked for new markets they had to compete with England, the world's greatest commercial power at that time. For some years after 1783 many northern ships were laid up and northern sailors unemployed. In the Napoleonic wars England blockaded most of Europe and this cut off Americans from important markets and even led to a second war between America and Britain between 1812 and 1815.

One solution was to cut down imports of manufactured goods. But England had allowed industry to develop only on a small scale. Craftsmen were few in the eastern cities as many of them migrated to the West. England guarded the secrets of her cotton and iron industries carefully, prohibiting the export of machines and migration of skilled workers, searching ships and punishing smugglers heavily. Without this knowledge, Americans could not hope to compete against the flood of cheap English goods. So merchants were unwilling to invest in industry and indeed few Americans wished to work in factories when they could have land of their own.

Although the merchants of the northeastern cities were only a small proportion of the population, they were wealthy and important. Clearly they would support a policy designed to strengthen trade.

Radicals v. conservatives. During the war 'Radical' parties gained control of most states. They were more strongly opposed to England and wanted more democratic government than the conservatives. The 'Patriots' of Massachusetts were Radicals. Their support came from the smaller farmers inland. They alarmed the wealthy by widening the franchise and abolishing primogeniture.* (Look at the footnote and then say why these measures alarmed the wealthy.) They were so suspicious of any form of government, that in some areas they failed even to maintain law and order. As farmers they were less affected by the economic difficulties in the towns, and did little to help the unemployed find work or the merchants to pay their debts.

*Primogeniture means the right to pass on all one's property to one's eldest son. This practice enabled families to build up their wealth.

Jealousy between the states. Radicals particularly feared any central government for all the states, which might be as hard to control as the English government had been. Most Americans sympathised with this view, and even before the war was over each state had started printing its own money, and setting up its own legal system and customs regulations. New York taxed vegetables ferried across from New Jersey. In revenge New Jersey demanded rent for the Sandy Hook lighthouse at the entrance to New York harbour but on Jersey soil. More serious rivalry arose over developing the West. Pennsylvania and Connecticut almost fought for possession of the Wyoming Valley. Such quarrels were dangerous when the individual states were too weak to force England to give up her western garrisons and when Spain might close the Mississippi to American trade. (How and why might Spain do this?)

Responsible Americans realised that no European nation would take the United States seriously while they were so divided and that to develop the West and revive trade cooperation was needed. So in 1787 a Convention was held in Philadelphia, attended by all the states except Rhode Island. Its problem, as Franklin put it, was 'to make thirteen clocks strike as one'.

Table 3.   The Federal Government of the United States of America

LEGISLATURE

Congress

1. *The Senate*
   Two members from each state regardless of its size and population, elected for six years.

2. *The House of Representatives*
   The number of members for each state dependent on its population—elected for two years.

EXECUTIVE

President

Elected for four years (Vice-President also elected).

Appoints Secretaries to all important departments of the Federal government and to many other offices as well.

DUTIES

1. Enacts laws.
2. Votes taxation.
3. Decides on war and peace.
4. Accepts or rejects Presidential Policies.

1. Formulates all major policies.
2. Chooses ministers.
3. Responsible for day-to-day running of the government.
4. Enforces laws.

This government is allowed to: Conduct foreign policy.
Regulate trade.
Raise taxes to pay its expenses.
Enforce its decisions by using the Supreme Court.

Questions: 1. Why should not the Supreme Court be elected like the rest of the government?
2. Why were the States represented differently in the Senate and the House of Representative.

The Founding of the New Nation

The American Constitution. The men who met in Philadelphia are known as the Founding Fathers. They were all wealthy, highly educated, able. They wanted to protect their own property from the chaos of too little government by the Radicals, but also to guarantee the individual's right to 'life, liberty and the pursuit of happiness', for which they felt the war had been fought. They wanted the states to cooperate with each other, but did not wish to take away their independence. Lastly they wanted them to be prosperous and powerful in the world. They believed they could only achieve these aims by setting up a central government to settle disagreements, control rivalry and negotiate with other nations. They tried to combine democracy with order and efficiency. You might discuss in class how far this is possible in a school. Table 3 is a summary of what the Founding Fathers decided; it is also the basis of the present United States Constitution. Look at it carefully before reading on.

Fearing a Federal government might become too powerful they took elaborate precautions to prevent it doing so. First, the Constitution was supreme; not even Congress

JDICIARY

upreme Court

dependent of state or direct popular ontrol. Justices nominated by the esident and confirmed by the Senate.

Interpretation of laws.
It has acquired the duty of deciding if laws passed by Congress are in accordance with the Constitution.

could go against what it said and it could only be changed after a complicated process involving all the States. Second, Federal powers of government were not concentrated into one person or one body. America did not want any sort of absolutist government. Federal powers were divided threefold: the Presidency, Congress and the Supreme Court. Each acted as a check and a balance to the other. To pass legislation the President needed the support of Congress. Laws passed by Congress had to be in keeping with the Constitution. Their constitutionality was decided by the Supreme Court. Third, the Constitution stated what the Federal government could do. The State governments kept all other powers for themselves, even to deciding who could vote in Federal elections. Still suspicious, the Virginians insisted on drawing up a list of the rights they felt were most important; such rights as freedom of speech, freedom of worship and trial by jury. Discuss why these were valuable and think what the rest might be. Ten of these were grouped together as the Bill of Rights and added to the Constitution in 1791.

These ten 'amendments' as they were called, helped to convince the doubtful states that they could safely accept the Constitution. Another important factor was that George Washington, the President of the Convention, supported the scheme. In 1789 he was fifty-seven years old. Tall, grave and taciturn, he was slow to make decisions and had been reluctant to return to public life after the bitter years of effort in holding the colonies together in the war. He was the only man universally admired for honesty and fair-mindedness. Although the states feared that the Federal government might be controlled by a small group for its own benefit, they also felt that Washington was the one man who could be trusted to put the interests of the nation first. He had had experience of politics in the Virginia Assembly and of administration during the war and in spite of all the difficulties he had persuaded the states to cooperate effectively. He was elected unanimously as first President of the United States in 1789 when it was still uncertain whether all the states would join.

The significance of the Constitution and the birth of America. The making of the Constitution and the birth of the American nation are immensely significant events not only in the history of the U.S.A. but also in the history of the world.

Remember that the War of Independence was a revolution by thirteen separate and different colonies temporarily united against the absolutism of the British monarchy. That is, they felt the king was too powerful. He restricted the liberty of his subjects. The colonists wanted freedom—freedom to move west, freedom to trade, freedom to manufacture, freedom to express their opinions about their own affairs, freedom from taxes. In a nutshell: freedom from TOO MUCH GOVERNMENT. Liberty was the watchword in 1776—liberty for the individual from too much authority of any kind, liberty for the colony from the oppressive central government in London.

Remember this and you will understand more clearly the meaning of the Constitution and the reason for the Federal form of government. Having won their freedom colonists and colonies wanted to preserve it. The Constitution was a written guarantee of their future liberty. The Federal government was not all-powerful. The absolute government of London was not replaced by an absolute authority in Washington. The thirteen states surrendered as few of their powers of self-government as possible. The Bill of Rights clearly marked out and protected the liberties of the individual.

The new American nation had no absolute monarchies, no ruling aristocracies, and no rigid social classes. It was not a settled country but a baby republic in a huge continental wilderness. It was not the Old World but the New. Its Constitution and forms of government were the product of the will of the people acting together and based on the idea of liberty. In 1789 began a great experiment: an attempt to carve a democratic nation out of a hostile wilderness. Democratic not in the sense of one man one vote—although this was soon to come—but in the sense that all men had certain basic rights, irrespective of their social class or their wealth. Founding Fathers

*George Washington –
First President of the
U.S.A.*

Alexander Hamilton

Thomas Jefferson

like Thomas Jefferson believed that given such rights men would live together peacefully as a nation, accept the rule of law and conduct their affairs with reason and common sense. In Europe the monarchs of undemocratic nations like Britain, France and Spain shuddered and hoped the American democratic experiment would fail. If it worked then their own subjects might demand similar liberties from them.

None of this means that the new Constitution laid down hard and fast rules about how the new government was to function in practice. Opinions of statesmen remained divided on just how strong or weak the Federal government should be.

Two views of the United States: Hamilton and Jefferson. Alexander Hamilton was Washington's Secretary for the Treasury. He belonged to the wealthy merchant class of New York. He believed democracy was inefficient and looked forward to the growth of a powerful nation based on trade, industry and finance. He wanted a strong, Federal government to enable him to encourage trade. He wished to impose import duties on manufactured goods to allow American industry to grow; to check the westward movement by charging high prices for land, thus forcing labour into industry; to use the money gained to build roads and canals which would make trade within the colonies easier and the distribution of industrial goods cheaper. He wanted a National Bank to keep the value of money stable and interest rates high to encourage investment.

To the planters of the South and the western farmers this looked just like what many of them had feared—a conspiracy of a few wealthy merchants to make a strong Federal government for their own profit. Thomas Jefferson, the Secretary of State* and a Virginian planter brought up on the frontier, expressed their fears best.

He saw the desire for land and personal freedom as the whole reason for the wars against France and England and the massive migration from an overcrowded Europe. He hated the idea of industry, huge cities, slums and factories which he had seen in England, and dreamed of a land of farmers, each independent and free to live as he wished. Import duties would make the manufactured goods farmers needed more expensive; high interest rates would make it more difficult to borrow money; most important, immigrants needed to be able to buy land cheaply. In fact Jefferson had no wish for the United States to be powerful in Hamilton's way at all and wanted as little Federal interference in the rights of states and individuals as possible.

These views illustrate two themes in American history, which you have already seen in action and which will recur again and again.

*The American name for the Secretary of Foreign Affairs.

49

1. The conflict between Atlantic partnership and western expansion.
2. The conflict between those who believed in a strong Federal government and those who supported the rights of states and individuals.

You have already seen that states differed in what they thought was important. This was partly because they earned their livings in different ways. Merchants differed from farmers. In the following sections you will see how these differences, especially between South and North, increased. If the Federal government supported one group, should the other give in or should it leave the Union? This was the problem that caused the Civil War in 1860.

The Expansion of the Northeastern States, 1815–50

The Golden Age of commerce, 1815–50. Although the northeastern states did face difficulties after 1783 and had to trade to survive, they had important assets. Behind them were years of experience in trade, in shipbuilding and in sailing. As early as the 1780s they had begun trading on a worldwide scale and their ships were often away for years. Boston sailors, for example, might take manufactured goods to Oregon to exchange for furs. These would be sold in Canton for tea, silks and china, which in turn would be sold in Europe or the northern colonies, often in exchange for more manufactured goods. After the War of Independence this world trade was expanded as quickly as possible and Americans also became carriers of other nations' trade, for which of course they were paid in goods or in gold and silver. Still other Americans ignored English regulations and smuggled goods in and out of the British West Indies.

But the bulk of American trade still crossed the Atlantic. Apart from the products we mentioned earlier, Americans exported cotton, tobacco, rice, potash, leather, timber, fish, rum, flour, lard and meat, most of them in return for manufactured goods. Between 1821 and 1861 England took 50 per cent of all American exports and provided 49 per cent of her imports. In other words the basis of American trade was still the same as in colonial times—an Atlantic partnership in which food and raw materials were exchanged for manufactures.

In fact the partnership grew stronger as a result of the expansion in the trade in one product—cotton. And this expansion also saved the northern states and created a Golden Age of commerce.

Wild cotton was common in the southern states and there was a rapidly growing market for it in the Lancashire textile industry. But it was so difficult to separate the cotton from the seed that a slave could pick only one pound of cotton in a whole day. In 1793 Eli Whitney invented a simple device, the cotton gin—a drum with wire prongs which drew the cotton through slits too narrow for the seeds to follow. A slave could now pick fifty pounds per day. This invention revolutionised the southern states. Cotton plantations spread quickly across the South and into the Mississippi valley. By 1821 raw cotton accounted for 40 per cent of the value of all American exports and by 1851, 60 per cent.

New Orleans became the chief outlet for the cotton trade. Look at a map and say why. From there the cotton went either direct to Europe or often to New York or Philadelphia. In either case most of the trade was carried in American ships from the northern states and it was northern merchants who bought from the planters and supplied them with manufactures. It was the trade which enabled them to overcome the economic problems of independence and created a Golden Age of commerce, and which bound the United States closer to Europe and especially to England.

The growth of industry, 1783–1860. Industry was much slower to develop. Even in 1860 it was largely carried out by skilled craftsmen in local workshops and smithies and *New York Harbour*

contributed only 12 per cent of the American national income. It was only in the sixties in response to the railway boom that the coal industry expanded strongly and iron foundries moved out of the forests onto the coalfields, so that they could use coke instead of charcoal for smelting.

One industry, textiles, did thrive; and again you can see the importance of the Atlantic partnership, this time in providing the technical knowledge and the labour and skill of British immigrants. It grew up early partly because Samuel Slater, an ambitious young Englishman, had arrived in America in 1789. He had served an apprenticeship in the Belper cotton mill of Jedediah Strutt and Richard Arkwright, and had risen to share in the management. After several years' hesitation he had decided to emigrate and passed the Liverpool customs disguised as a farmer, carrying in his head full details of Arkwright's machinery. (Why did he pretend to be a farmer?)

On his arrival, penniless, at Rhode Island he was fortunate to meet Moses Brown, a rich businessman, who had been trying to perfect a water-driven spinning machine. He agreed to give Slater 50 per cent of the profits if he would build a mill like Arkwright's. The first mill was in production by 1791 and others followed, in Massachusetts as well as Rhode Island. Samuel Slater was soon a wealthy man.

Few were as successful as Samuel Slater, but many British immigrants, looking for higher pay and more responsibility and opportunity, brought their skills and knowledge to America. The Pennsylvanian iron industry was modernised by Welshmen, and Yorkshiremen helped to build up the woollen industry.

You have already seen some of the reasons for this slow growth of most of America's industry, on pp. 38 and 45. There were two main ones, lack of capital and the cost of transport. Rich men preferred to invest in trade and land where profits seemed more certain, so there was little money for starting new industries. Overland transport was expensive. Even after a National Road had been built it cost thirteen dollars to send one barrel of flour from Philadelphia to Pittsburgh, so it was cheaper to make goods locally and local markets could not support large-scale factory production. Alexander Hamilton had realised both these difficulties but he did not realise that as Americans moved west they would create a huge new market, and that once transport problems had been solved, this would be a great stimulant to both trade and industry. It was the railways of course which solved the transport problems. In the meantime, the states remained dependent on manufactures from Europe.

The Southern States, 1815–60

The growing of cotton brought a new era of prosperity and expansion to the South. Much of the newly-broken land was devoted to cotton. But the expansion had two other consequences which were of the utmost importance.

Slavery. First it revived slavery. In 1776 this had been in decline because for many tasks paid labour proved more efficient, especially as soil became exhausted and more careful, scientific cultivation was needed. But cotton cultivation was simple, slow, monotonous work involving a great deal of manpower in humid conditions. White men wanted land of their own and were unwilling to work on the plantations. Planters therefore bought Negroes. Between 1783 and 1861 the number of slaves in the southern states rose from seven hundred thousand to four million. Cotton became so overwhelmingly important that the whole way of life of the South was coloured by the growth of great plantations depending on slave labour. Even the poor whites who owned no slaves and had to work in the fields themselves came to look on the Negro as inferior, in some way less than human. How this attitude came about you will find explained in chapter 5.

Debt. The second consequence was that southerners became increasingly indebted to Europeans and northern merchants. You will remember that earlier plantation owners had sold their crops to agents who had conducted all the business transactions their clients required, including the buying of manufactured goods and luxuries. This system was continued after cotton became important, and it meant that much of the profit went into the pockets of the merchants who bought, transported and sold the cotton. Scattered over a vast area it was difficult for planters to combine together to control prices in their own interests.

Cotton growers had heavy expenses. They had to clear the land, build houses and roads and buy equipment. The slave trade had been abolished in 1808 and although slaves were certainly smuggled in, they were not so plentiful and prices rose steeply. To pay these costs planters had to borrow money, often promising to pay it back out of the profits of the next cotton crop. Sometimes the crop failed and they had to borrow even more heavily to keep going, or sell out. Often, as we shall see, they gambled, dressed and entertained extravagantly. As the northern merchants grew richer they lent money more heavily to the southerners. You can understand why planters objected to Hamilton's desire to keep interest rates high, and charge duties on imported manufactured goods. They came to feel that northern merchants and bankers were growing rich at their expense.

In blaming their misfortunes on the greed and dishonesty of the northerners, the planters were not entirely just. Brought up on great estates and to a feeling of aristocratic superiority, many of them despised trade and industry. With Jefferson they believed in America as a land of independent farmers so they were hardly fair in complaining of northerners monopolising the cotton trade to their own advantage. Someone had to market the cotton. More serious was that little or no industry grew up in the South. Again like Jefferson they disliked the noise and dirt of industrial development. Skilled British immigrants could find no work and did not settle there.

The southern states became then completely dependent on farming, and especially on one main crop. They were at the mercy of the merchants who bought the cotton and supplied them with manufactured goods. They became increasingly resentful of their dependence and indebtedness to these same merchants.

In this chapter we have shown very briefly the way in which the new nation was founded and developed. Different parts of the United States were interested in different policies. Hamilton's policy of improving communications, putting a heavy duty on imported manufactures and providing cheap labour by preventing settlement in the West, would go far towards solving the industrialists' problems. High interest rates, and the value of money kept high by a National Bank would encourage investment in industry and please merchants who lent money. It is not surprising that the wealthy northeastern states, which were the most commercially-minded, supported him.

If industry was slow to develop in the North, it hardly developed at all in the South. Here planters, who often had to borrow money, wanted low interest rates, and cheap land and manufactures. They found natural allies in the western settlers. Quarrels over these different views were long and bitter and each group elected representatives to the Federal government who would support its own view. At first the northeastern states with the largest population were successful, but as the frontier was pushed back, the farmers of the West and the planters became stronger. The next chapter deals with this expansion and change.

Further Reading

Longman 'Then and There' Series
   Clarke, Clorinda, *The Young American Republic.*

5 WEST TO THE MISSISSIPPI

In 1783 the Mississippi marked the western boundary of the new American nation. With the way west open Americans and immigrants were ready to pour across the mountains into the new land. But moving west had its difficulties.

The Indian Problem

Indian treaties. During the War of Independence most of the forest Indians west of the Appalachians had fought against the thirteen colonies. When the war ended they were undefeated but on the losing side. Under the Treaty of Paris their hunting grounds now became part of the new America. To the Indians, however, this meant nothing. As always they remained an obstacle to the westward movement of the settlers.

The Founding Fathers realised the seriousness of the Indian problem. Like the English government between 1763 and 1776 they knew they could not stop settlers crossing the Appalachians. Can you think why? The frontier would become a battleground as settlers clashed with Indians.

To try to prevent this bloody warfare the Federal government made the Indians surrender their claims to the forests. In return for these lands the tribes received blankets, food, tools, jewellery and annuities (annual payments of money or goods). They must end their roving life and settle down as farmers on lands reserved for them either in the forests or the western plains. Most tribes were too small and weak to refuse these conditions and they submitted peacefully. Some bigger and more powerful tribes did not submit so easily.

Tecumseh. Perhaps the greatest of the Indian war chiefs who tried to resist the American advance after 1783 was Tecumseh, a Shawnee. Tecumseh believed strongly that the forest belonged to the Indians. Realising that the white man was a grave threat to the Indian way of life he insisted that the Americans should leave a large area of forest between the Ohio and the Great Lakes for the Indians and that they must not take any land from a tribe unless *all* its members agreed. This was a real problem. The Americans argued that a chief had the right to sign away the lands of his tribe. Tecumseh said that a chief had no authority to do this. A chief was chosen for his wisdom and advice: his word was not law. Members of his tribe could disagree with him. Tecumseh was right but to do it his way created serious difficulties for the American government. Can you see why? The situation led to war.

Tecumseh knew he would have to fight. He tried to unite the forest tribes into an Indian confederation and to obtain the support of the British in Canada. He failed. In 1811 his Indian warriors were defeated by a volunteer American army at Tippecanoe and two years later Tecumseh himself was killed at the Battle of the Thames during the Anglo-American War. The Shawnees were sent to Indian Territory on land west of the Mississippi. This land was bought by America from France in 1803. It was considered unsuitable for farming by the white man and so Indians were sent there from the east. Between 1820 and 1840, for example, the American government sent about 100,000 unwanted Indians there.

The fate of the Cherokees. Some Indians tried to prevent the American advance by peaceful means. Take the example of the Cherokees who lived between Georgia and the Mississippi. These Indians had learned much from the white man and in 300 years had changed themselves from a stone age tribe to a civilised community. By the early nineteenth century they farmed on a large scale, dressed like white people, lived in houses and went to church and school. They had a written language and published a newspaper printed in both English and Cherokee. By 1826 they had even drafted a constitution and elected a principal chief.

Unfortunately, the Cherokees obstructed Georgia's expansion and the land-hungry speculators and settlers had a powerful ally in Andrew Jackson, the American President. Congress was persuaded to pass a series of acts to dispossess the Cherokees. Georgia's boundaries were extended to include the Cherokee lands and the land was divided into sections for auction. The Cherokees protested but new laws were passed to forbid these Indians giving evidence in court against white men, making contact with white people, or assembling publicly for any purpose. The Indians therefore appealed to the Supreme Court, which upheld their protests. But even this did not help. The President refused to support the Supreme Court's decision.

In 1835 a Treaty of Removal was signed between America and the Cherokees. Only 500 of the 17,000 Cherokees and none of their elected leaders were present at the signing of this treaty. By this the Cherokees were to go to Indian Territory where seven million acres of land were reserved for them. Often they moved west with few possessions and

Battle of Tippecanoe

they suffered terribly while on board ship and on the march. Diseases and starvation were common. The worst year was 1838 when an American army of 7000 troops rounded up many thousands of Cherokees and forced them west during a very hot summer and a very cold winter. In the winter alone a quarter of the 16,000 migrants died en route. When the Cherokees arrived in the West they found unimproved and infertile lands, dishonest traders, and hostile plains Indians who resented giving up part of their hunting grounds to them. Remember, too, that the Cherokees were forest Indians. Their way of life was not geared to the prairie wilderness.

Discuss the Indian problem in class. Do you think the problem was a difficult one or not? Do you think the Indians were treated fairly by the Americans? Can you think of any other ways the Americans could have tackled the problem?

The Westward Movement

Land laws. Meanwhile the Federal government passed a series of land laws designed to control and direct the flood of settlers pushing west.

The entire forest as far as the Mississippi was divided into two Territories shown on Map 15. These were then subdivided into smaller ones. For example, the Northwest Territory included the Territories of Ohio, Indiana, Illinois, Michigan and Wisconsin. As each Territory was formed it was placed under a governor elected by Congress. When its total population reached 5000 it could elect its own legislature. A Territory became a State of the Union when its population reached 60,000. Each Territory was divided into townships six miles square and then into thirty-six smaller sections of one square

Map 15 New territories in the West

mile. As each township was surveyed and its sections marked the land was auctioned. Sometimes, whole townships were bought by land speculators aiming to sell later at higher prices to settlers coming from the east. Much of the land, however, was sold in sections or parts of a section to poor people whose demands were recognised by the Federal government which sold the land to them on increasingly favourable terms.

THE TERMS ON WHICH THE LAND WAS SOLD

Year	Minimum amount allowed for purchase	Price per acre dollars	Time allowed for payment
1800	a half section	2	4 years
1804	a quarter section	2	4 years
1820	a half-quarter section	$1\frac{1}{4}$	nil
1832	a quarter-quarter section	$1\frac{1}{4}$	nil

One reason for these laws was the Indian problem. The American government tried to remove the Indians from an area, survey it and then open it to the settlers. In this way settlers would not meet hostile Indians and bloodshed would be avoided. These laws also reflect the conflict between Hamilton and Jefferson. Hamilton wanted to keep the westward movement closely in check. Why? He felt that land sold on stiff terms would hold back the settler. You can see that at first these laws reflected Hamilton's attitude. Slowly, however, the Jeffersonians got their way, as the table shows.

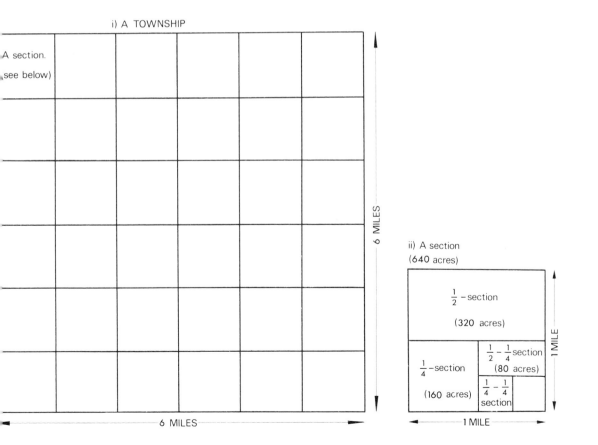

i) A TOWNSHIP

A section. (see below)

6 MILES

6 MILES

ii) A section (640 acres)

$\frac{1}{2}$ – section

(320 acres)

$\frac{1}{4}$ – section

(160 acres)

$\frac{1}{2} - \frac{1}{4}$ section

(80 acres)

$\frac{1}{4} - \frac{1}{4}$ section

1 MILE

1 MILE

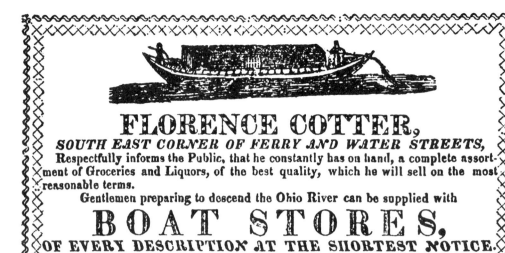

All this is not to argue that these laws were a completely effective control of the westward movement. Many settlers pushed ahead of the government surveyors. They marked out their own plots and paid no money for the land. When the surveyors and auctioneers arrived these squatters proved difficult and obstinate. Indeed, in 1841 the Federal government recognised the problem by passing a new act which exempted these settled lands from auction provided the settler was willing to pay the minimum price per acre. However, he could only buy up to 160 acres and even then only if this did not make his total land holding greater than 300 acres.

The westward impulse. The West was indeed a magnet. Into the northwest poured Americans from New England, New York and Pennsylvania, English, Scots, Germans, Swedes and Norwegians. The New Englanders outnumbered every other group, but each state and nation became well represented in the region. The southwest attracted rich and poor southerners, particularly from the Carolinas and eastern Georgia.

Why was the West so attractive? This is a most important question. To those moving west the wilderness was a land of promise, a land of opportunity. The abundance of free or cheap land and the virgin soils offered a chance to start life anew, a chance to be free from landlords and employers, rules and regulations, a chance to be one's own master and to live one's life according to one's own ideas and feelings. To New Englanders tired of scratching a living from thin hilly soils, to poor southerners bought out by the rich plantation owners, to European peasants oppressed by landowners and taxes, the west promised fulfilment of their dreams. They saved hard, sold out and went west.

Look at the following table which shows the growth of population in the West and the dates when each territory became a state. Remember, this occurred when the population reached 60,000. Draw an outline map of the area and plot on it, in order, the states named in this table. (Copy the state boundaries from an atlas.) If you do this you will get a good idea of the main directions and timing of the western movement between 1783 and 1860. Shade the states of the northwest a different colour from those of the southwest.

The way West. Down to 1818 there were three routes across the Appalachians. In the south was the Wilderness Road which connected Virginia to Kentucky via the Cumberland

Gap. Further north, Braddock's Road along the Potomac valley and Forbes' Road along the Susquehanna connected the middle states to Ohio and its river. These roads were not surfaced, but rough tracks about the width of one wagon and full of tree stumps, ruts and holes. People walked or rode with their families and possessions on horses, pack animals, small farm carts and wagons. Their average speed was about two miles an hour.

Once across the mountains many migrants headed for the Ohio river. Here they transferred their families and belongings to flatboats which they either made themselves or bought from local boatyards. Flatboats were rafts anything from 20 to 100 feet long and 10 to 20 feet wide. The largest ones sometimes had small barns for the cattle and cabins for the family. The smallest were simply floating platforms with no shelter of any kind. Once the flatboat was ready the migrants pushed off and floated downstream from Pittsburg or some other town to their destination. It was not always easy. Rapids could upset the raft and people, wagons, seeds, tools and animals might be lost in the river. Most people, however, made it. Once at their destination the rafts were either sold or broken up and the timber used to build a home.

In 1818 the National Road was opened between Cumberland and Wheeling. By 1837 it had been built through Ohio and by 1850 it spanned Indiana. This road was built by the Federal government. It was 30 feet wide in the mountains and twice as wide elsewhere. The roadway was made of stones and cambered with drains on both sides. This was a great improvement on the earlier roads; it became a busy line of communication between East and West lined with inns, hotels and wagon stops. It was soon used by farmers, freighting companies and migrants with their carts, wagons and Conestogas. The Conestogas were large vehicles suited to heavy loads on good roads over flat or rolling country. Pulled by at least six horses it easily carried 6000 pounds of freight. Its body or 'box' was undercurved to prevent the loads moving backwards and forwards on a hilly road. The box overhung the wheels so that a large load could be combined with a short wheel base (which made for easier pulling) and a reasonably short turning circle (which helped movement round tight corners). Many migrants used the Conestoga or a modified version of it after 1818.

Just before the opening of the National Road the first steamboat was used on the Ohio

River. By the 1820s steamboats were plying all the navigable rivers of America and the Great Lakes. Settlers moving down the Ohio now abandoned the flatboats and bought a deck passage downstream. This meant sleeping on the open deck, cooking one's own food and helping to feed wood into the boat's boilers. It was little different from roughing it on a flatboat but it was cheaper, quicker and safer.

In 1825 the Erie Canal was opened between Albany and Buffalo. It was hardly more than a large ditch but it provided many settlers with a new route westwards. They travelled by road to the canal, by barge to Buffalo, by steamboat across Lake Erie to Detroit and then by road across Illinois and Wisconsin. Map 16 shows these various routes.

Table 4.   Population Growth on the Movement Westward

State	Year of statehood	Population in thousands		
		1790	1820	1860
Kentucky	1792	74	564	1156
Tennessee	1796	36	423	1110
Ohio	1803		581	2340
Louisiana	1812		153	708
Indiana	1816		147	1350
Mississippi	1817		75	791
Illinois	1818		55	1712
Alabama	1819		128	964
Missouri	1821		67	1182
Arkansas	1836		14	435
Michigan	1837		9	749
Iowa	1846			675
Wisconsin	1848			776
Minnesota	1858			172

Life in the Northwest

The pioneer farmer. Many types of people migrated to the northwest. First came the fur-traders and hunters, men like Daniel Boone, who blazed the early trails west through the forests. Behind them came the cattle graziers, the first cowboys, who fed their herds on the patches of rich grass in the forest openings. Also close behind came the pioneer settlers armed with rifle, axe and plough. Part hunter, part farmer they roughed out the first fields and sowed the first seeds. An impatient and restless breed, many of them did not stop long in one place. Abandoning their clearings or selling out to a neighbour they moved on, following the hunter. Moving slowly west too came lumbermen and miners of coal and iron. Finally came more permanent settlers like farmers, tradesmen, crafts-men and professional people who converted the rough clearings into profitable farms, widened the forest trackways into roads, began a thriving trade in forest and farm pro-ducts, and created the first villages and towns.

Obviously there was no one way of life. Most representative, however, was the life of a farmer which we now describe.

Once arrived at his half- or quarter-section the pioneer's first job was to build a home which was a very simple and crude log-cabin. This took two or three days depending on the number of strong sons or neighbours he had. Then, if it was not too late in the year, he made a small clearing and planted his corn and vegetables among the tree stumps. He killed the other trees by cutting girdles around their trunks, but it took several years to chop them down and pull out their stumps—long and tiring work. His plough was often nothing more than a forked stick and at best only a straight wooden tool tipped with iron dragged along by at least four oxen. In the first year the land produced little. The pioneer was forced to hunt and to depend on his few cows. Often the family existed on starvation rations. Most pioneers were ordinary people with little money. Their savings were swallowed up in travelling west and buying their land. Indeed most had borrowed money to do all this. This burden of debt is a most important point. Keep it in your mind. In the first year they had little or no money to buy food or clothes even if a town was nearby. You can guess what they made their clothes and bedding from.

Before the following spring the clearings were extended. Almost everywhere in the North the pioneer then planted by hand his corn, wheat, flax, beans, peas, potatoes, onions, turnips, beets, cabbages, pumpkins, cucumbers and melons. In favoured areas like Ohio tobacco and hemp were grown too. His cows, pigs, sheep and poultry bred their

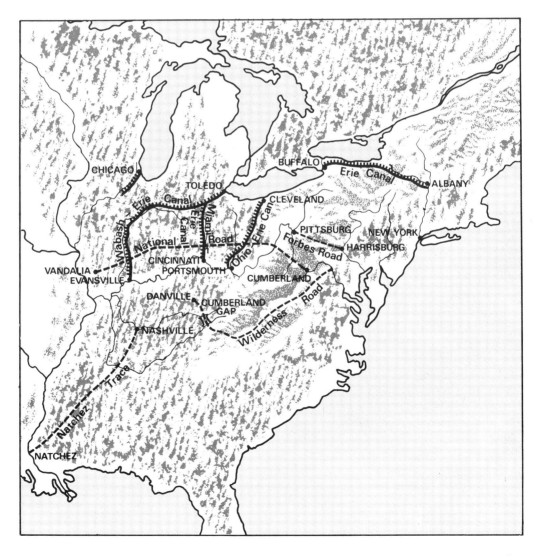

Map 16 Ways west across the Appalachians

young and his growing herds and flocks roamed the surrounding woods or were penned in small enclosures. By now the farmer could expect a slightly better existence. In summer his diet was a very varied one. In winter, however, he existed on corn-whisky, corn-meal, salted pork and pickled or dry fruits and vegetables.

Slowly, year by year, the pioneer improved and extended his land. Trees were felled and stumps removed. As the crops and animals multiplied he went to the nearest rivers and villages to sell his surpluses. His income began to rise and gradually he paid off his debts, bought better seeds, animals and tools, improved the dress of his family and built a bigger house. Sometimes the original log-cabin was extended. More often an entirely new building replaced it called the log-house.

Of course, not everybody succeeded. Many did not persevere and sold out. Others were victims of natural disasters like weather, poor soils and disease, or economic ones like low prices, high costs and ruinous debts. Some suffered from surprise Indian raids.

Nevertheless most farmers made progress. It was their dream come true. By their willingness to brave the dangers and the risks of the wilderness, by hard physical work, patience and perseverance they were successful. They had made something enduring and they had become their own masters. No more were they English tenant farmers, Scottish crofters, German peasants or New England hill country farmers but free Americans living their own lives as they wanted to.

The westerner. These feelings of independence, achievement and optimism were shared by many other people who had come west. True, they were not farmers but in building up their banks, warehouses, workshops, hotels, saloons and stores they also had taken risks, borne debts, been patient and persevering and worked hard to succeed. Like the farmers they too had made something permanent from the wilderness. The West grew because of all their efforts.

Indeed, the westerners had much in common with each other. They traded together, knew each other's business problems, fought side by side against Indians, attended the same churches, went to each other's christenings, marriages and burials and shared the same sports and pastimes. Men and boys enjoyed footraces, wrestling, jumping, swimming, hunting, shooting, log-lifting and horse-racing. These activities were combined with whisky-drinking, gambling, and tobacco-chewing and spitting. To be good at these things was to be 'manly' and many were bad-tempered and unhappy if they lost. Victory encouraged bragging and showing-off. Dancing was always popular and was accompanied by practical joking, drinking and kissing games (which helped courting and marriage).

Thus, in their work and play these people tended to ignore their different nationalities and religions. New Englanders, Germans, Scots and so on all mixed freely together and adopted each other's words and sayings, clothes, foods and ideas. Taming the wilderness drew them together. Since they all shared similar experiences they came to think of themselves as one body of people—westerners—equal with each other and as good as anybody in the east or in Europe. To the westerner who made good the new nation of America was fulfilling the words of the Declaration of Independence—'life, liberty and the pursuit of happiness'.

The westerners were united in their political aims and methods. From the outset the West was a very democratic place. Whenever they met, at work or at play, they spoke about politics. The village and town had their regular political meetings where every man had the right to speak and vote. Unlike the East, there was no ruling class here. The northwest had no groups of rich merchants or planters who monopolised political life. The politicians in the West were farmers, storekeepers, lawyers, bankers—anybody who could win the support of his neighbours and friends. These were the sort of men who governed the towns and states and represented the West in the Federal government in Washington.

The main political aims of the westerners were quite simple. Above all they wanted a continual supply of cheap land, cheap manufactured goods and cheap money, i.e. money borrowable at low interest rates. In other words the westerners stood opposed to the ideas of Alexander Hamilton. They wanted the Federal government to sell the western lands at very low prices, they opposed tariffs on imported manufactures and they hated the idea of a monopolistic central bank. The westerners feared that the wealthy businessmen in the East would use such a bank to restrict the supply of paper money and thus raise rates of interest. This would benefit creditors like wealthy easterners but penalise borrowers like western farmers and tradesmen. What westerners wanted was a large number of banks each issuing its own money and lending it at low rates of interest.

Now that you have read and thought about these points perhaps you can see that life in the West centred on the small farmers and that the westerners as a body felt themselves to be free and equal citizens. Their way of life, aims and ideals were those dreamed of by Thomas Jefferson who wanted America to be a land of small farmers owning and working their own land happily together. By the 1820s this agrarian democracy actually existed in the Northwest. Jefferson's dream had become a reality.

Andrew Jackson—champion of the common man. Jefferson died in 1826 but a new champion of the small farmer had arrived. This was Andrew Jackson, born in the backwoods, one who knew the hardships of pioneer life, a saddle-maker's assistant, a teacher, a lawyer, a military hero and finally a politician. In his later life he became a rich landowner and slaveowner but his appeal to the westerner remained. Unlike the eastern and southern gentlemen politicians with their careful talk and behaviour, Jackson spoke simply and plainly and worked in his office with his coat off and braces showing. The farmers felt he was one of them and called him 'Old Hickory'.

Jackson believed that government should be organised to benefit 'the great body of the people of the United States . . . the planter, the farmer, the mechanic and the labourer'. These very people voted him President of America in 1828 and again in 1832. His first reception at the White House was attended by both rich and poor. At the party his supporters trampled their muddy boots over the carpets and furniture, smashed glass and china, and drank punch galore. Jackson escaped from the festivities by climbing out of a window. Nothing had been seen like this in Washington before. The 'respectable' people of the city were shocked.

During his Presidency Jackson made ninety-four Indian treaties, sent many tribes across the Mississippi and took their land for the western settler. The Cherokees were one of the tribes dealt with by Old Hickory and we have already discussed the treatment they received. But Jackson was popular with the westerners. He also reduced the tariffs on imported manufactures and closed the second Bank of the United States.

'Old Hickory' kept Jefferson's ideas alive. These ideas now went under the name of Jacksonian democracy. The Republican Party of Jefferson became the Democratic Party of Jackson. We shall refer again to Jacksonian democracy later in this chapter and in chapter 10.

Life in the South

The southern economy. Like the northwest the South was mainly agricultural. Both areas were interested in cheap land and manufactures and low interest rates and they shared the trade of the Mississippi. After about 1820 cotton became the main crop of the South. There were other important cash crops: tobacco in Virginia and Maryland; rice along the coasts of Georgia and South Carolina, and sugar-cane in the rich soil around New Orleans. But the organisation of plantations to grow these crops was not very different from that of cotton and they all produced a similar wealthy land-owning, slave-owning class.

Andrew Jackson

But this class was a minority. In 1860 there were about 9 million whites in the South and 4 million Negroes. Of these whites only 46,274 owned more than twenty slaves each. Allowing for families this means about 6 per cent of the white population. Only 3000 whites owned more than one hundred slaves each and only eleven owners more than five hundred. Most white farmers owned none at all, and there was considerable variation from one part to another. 72 per cent were without slaves in North Carolina, only 40 per cent were without on the rich soil of the Alabama Black Belt. Most farms were too small.

These were the farms of the yeomen of the South, the majority of the population. The whole family worked on the farm. They were independent and very like the farmers of the Northwest except that in a crisis they would usually follow the lead of the planters. This is the sort of family Davy Crockett came from. Below them came the 'white trash', who lived in the simplest possible way and were often lazy and unreliable. Nowadays it is thought that many of them suffered from malaria, hookworm or deficiency diseases which made them apathetic and unable to work.

Despite their small number the aristocratic planters were the natural leaders of the South. They dominated the agriculture, the social life and the government of their region. They often marketed the crops of the poorer farmers and imported manufactured goods for them. The prosperous planters had the time, the money and the education to take part in politics. Their plantations were usually nearer the towns and to good river communication. The government of a large estate accustomed the planter to using authority and making decisions. But by 1860 the strongest bond uniting the southern whites was the threat to abolish slavery which had been growing in the North. There was the fear of a slave revolt, there was fear of competition, but most important was that though the poorer whites had little they could feel superior to a slave. Abolition would make slaves their equals, and perhaps some slaves might even do better.

Therefore, if we are to understand the life and thought of the South we must look to the large cotton plantations and the slave-owning aristocracy.

The management of a cotton plantation. A cotton plantation was an expensive affair. The planter had to buy and clear land, build houses for himself and his slaves, cut roads and erect landing places on the river. He had to buy equipment. The most expensive pieces of equipment were the slaves themselves. Cotton required much cultivation and hard physical labour all the year round, much of it in weather considered too hot for white workers. Negro slaves were much sought after. The slave trade had been forbidden in 1808 and although smuggling went on, slaves were in short supply. In 1795 a prime field hand fetched 350 dollars. By 1806 1800 dollars was a normal price. Planters encouraged their slaves to marry and have children to ensure a supply for the future but this of course meant that they had to feed many more mouths. The slaves too had to be clothed and kept in good health all the year round, every year, however good or bad his crop was. When John Burnside bought five plantations in 1857 he had to pay 500,000 dollars for the 937 slaves alone.

The planter, like all farmers, suffered from natural hazards. A late frost could kill the young plants and planting had to be started again. He dreaded insect pests like cutworm, the boll weevil and the army worm. Hurricanes sometimes wrought great havoc on crops, and diseases like cholera could kill many slaves at a time.

Of course, the success or failure of a plantation was not just a matter of luck. Much depended on the amount of work an owner could get out of his slaves. Many contemporaries noticed that they did one-third to one-half of the work of a northern farmer. They had no incentive since they would gain nothing by working harder. For the same reason they were often careless with tools and animals. We shall see how owners varied in their treatment later. His success also depended on his skill and the care he took of his land. Early settlers, knowing they could always move on to new land did little to stop erosion. There is one case recorded where in twenty years a gully had grown to a ravine 180 feet wide and 55 feet deep and 300 yards long. On the other hand even poor land could be made profitable by elaborate systems of drainage ditches, continuous crop rotations and heavy manuring.

The crop varied enormously from one soil to another but on average a farmer might expect an acre to yield one to one and a half bales of cotton, i.e. 500–750 pounds, but the price he would get for this fluctuated from year to year. This table will give some idea of the size of the fluctuations:

Year	cents per lb
1800	23
1812	7–8
1818	33
1819	8
1835	15`
1844	4

On these fluctuations depended the prosperity or bankruptcy of thousands of planters, and in the season the price of cotton was almost the only topic of conversation.

With so many difficulties and dangers you may be surprised that plantations spread so rapidly. The fact that they did is the best evidence that they were on the whole profitable, although part of the movement was due to the desire to be the first to break, and get profits from, good land, which was often quickly exhausted. Profits could be very high. Stephen Duncan had eight plantations which produced a total of 4000 bales per annum. At an average price of ten cents per lb this meant 200,000 dollars per annum. Even allowing for expenses, he was a very wealthy man, and his success was unusual. It is very difficult to decide how profitable ordinary plantations were. The profitability of well-run plantations varied markedly. A plantation on poor land might expect 4 per cent return per year on investment: one on good land 12 per cent.

It was certainly easier to grow cotton on a large plantation than on a small farm. Planters gradually bought out the small farmers who often were the first to settle and clear the land. They usually gained most of the best soil and consolidated it into much larger units. This happened all over the southwest between 1800 and 1860. The small farmers moved further west.

But cotton demands 200 growing days free from frost—this excluded Virginia and Kentucky. It also needed twenty-three inches of rain per annum so the western limit was Texas. So fast was the expansion that both these limits had been reached by 1860.

The treatment of slaves. Slaves were an expensive investment so that they were not likely to be generally so badly treated as to make them less useful. On the other hand slaves had no great incentive to work hard and owners would want to get as much out of them as possible.

There were two main ways of organising the work of slaves. In the 'task' system a set amount of work was laid down for each day. Once the slave had finished it he could spend the rest of the day as he wished. The 'gang' system was harder, a group of slaves working under a 'driver' (armed perhaps with a whip) might spend the whole day in the field.

The punishment for failure to work was usually flogging. Bennet Barrow was a young, strong owner whose slaves had a healthy respect for his right arm; he got excellent results. But he also rewarded good services with extra clothes or holidays or gifts such as whisky. Overseers seem to have relied on the whip more than their owners and slaves may well have suffered when owners did not keep strict control over their property. Many owners carried out punishments themselves or laid down strict rules for overseers to follow.

Those slaves who ran away rarely escaped. Bennet Barrow appears in a more brutal light in this entry in his diary: 'The Negro-hunters came this morning. Were not long before we struck the trail of Ginny Jerry, ran and trailed about a mile, treed him, made the dogs pull him out of the tree. Bit him very badly, think he will stay home for a while.'

It is very difficult to generalise about the treatment of slaves. At one extreme were the planters and their wives who looked after their slaves very carefully, feeding and clothing them properly, not overworking them, nursing them when they were sick and caring for them when they grew too old to work. For example, a planter named John McDonough showed how much slaves could achieve if they were encouraged. They were allowed to work overtime to earn money for their fare to Liberia in Africa. This took fifteen years. He acted as banker and when they had enough, he granted them their freedom. He appointed a Negro overseer and punishments were imposed by a jury of the slaves themselves. He encouraged them to read and write and learn skilled trades; many became mechanics or clerks and two went to college. In response his slaves were more loyal, more hardworking and more reliable.

At the other extreme were estates where the planters were absent and left affairs in the hands of white overseers. Here food, clothing and medical care were the bare minimum, the slaves overworked, the cottages and hospitals dirty, ill-ventilated and in a bad state of repair. Here, too, Negro families might be broken up, the father or mother being separated from their children when planters bought and sold slaves. On other plantations conditions were neither as good nor as bad as these extremes.

The most unhealthy sign that slavery was not acceptable to all Negroes was the widespread fear among the whites of a slave revolt. There were in fact only three important revolts, two of which were betrayed. But Nat Turner's revolt in 1831 resulted in sixty white deaths and alarmed the whole South. Most of the subsequent fear was based on rumour but one can understand the feelings of a planter whose family could be outnumbered many times over by his slaves and who might be remote from the nearest town or even from his neighbours. After 1831 the state laws were ferociously strict. Here are some examples. Slaves could not—leave their plantations without written permission
　　　　　　—meet in groups of more than five without a white man
　　　　　　—learn to read or write
　　　　　　—own property
　　　　　　—give evidence against a white man.

Marriages between slaves were not legally binding and a master was not guilty if a slave died in the course, or as a result of, reasonable punishment.

The planters set up a system of night patrols. Any Negro caught out after curfew was whipped on the spot. Law courts were usually made up of landowners and since much mistreatment would only be witnessed by the slaves themselves it would often be impossible to punish cruelty. In practice the law was seldom enforced strictly.

The planters' way of life. The planter was the gentleman of America—or so he often liked to think. He modelled his clothes, his house and his manners on the fashions of England and France. Sometimes he claimed descent from the English aristocracy. He built large, often luxurious houses, entertained lavishly and imported clothes and furniture from Europe where his children were often sent to be educated.

Opportunities for getting together were eagerly seized. Many of the gentry of the coastal areas would meet at Virginia Springs in the mountains in the late summer, when the tidal lands became unhealthy. Charleston Race Week attracted planters from all over the South. They tried out their own horses, for many were skilled breeders and gambled heavily on the races. The whole town took a holiday.

Many planters were high spirited, impetuous and proud. Born to riding, hunting and shooting, they gambled, drank and swore, lived in luxury and were often deep in debt. Others were among the most highly educated, civilised and able men of their time. Such a one was Robert E. Lee, the southern general. Still others were hard-working, practical men who had risen to wealth and power by their own efforts. They were united in opposition to commercial interests and in support of slavery. They looked down 'on the trading communities of the northern states . . . with that habitual sense of superiority, which men born to command, and above all others slave-holders, always cherish'. Although their incomes were large they were uncertain but their way of life was expensive. As we have seen they often had to borrow money—and usually from the same merchant. 'Perceiving himself therefore the debtor and quasi-slave of the man he despises, his pride, his interests and his passions, all combine to rouse his indignation.' In 1860–61 New York estimated the planters' total debt to northern merchants was 200 million dollars.

Earlier some southerners had thought slavery was wrong. Washington had actually freed his slaves. The expansion of cotton growing and the Nat Turner revolt in 1831 hardened opinion. The attitude to slavery varied with how many slaves there were in a given area. In 1831–32 the Virginian Assembly debated the abolition of slavery; 31 per cent of the representatives of the western counties where only 10 per cent of the whites were slave owners favoured liberation, but for the eastern areas where over 50 per cent owned slaves, 95 per cent of the representatives opposed liberation. You can see this division reflected in the Civil War. The Deep South was solidly in favour of slavery.

Further Reading

Clark, Thomas D., *Frontier America*, Scribner's, 1959.
Eggenhofer, Nick, *Waggons, Mules and Men*, Hastings, 1961.
Twain, Mark, *Life on the Mississippi*, Chatto & Windus, 1961.
Wellman, Paul I., *Indian Wars and Warriors East*, Houghton Mifflin, 2 vols., 1959.
Longman 'Then and There' Series
   Geoffrey Taylor, *The American South before the Civil War.*
   Bernard Martin, *John Newton and the Slave Trade.*
Jonathan Cape 'Jackdaw' Series
   No. 12, *The Slave Trade and its Abolition*
For reference only—contemporary documents
Billington, Ray Allen, *The Westward Movement in the United States*, Van Nostrand, 1959.
Van Noppen, I. W., *The South: a Documentary History*, Van Nostrand, 1958.

6 MANIFEST DESTINY

In 1783 the U.S.A. was only one of several nations in North America. Encircled by European colonies the young nation felt insecure and still hemmed in. John Quincy Adams said: 'The world should be familiarised with the idea of considering our proper dominion to be the continent of North America.' This American desire to control the whole continent has been called 'manifest destiny'. Americans believed such control was the natural and right thing for them to pursue. Ever since the founding of Jamestown the common man had regarded the American wilderness as the land of promise. This was why the Europeans came to America and colonists trekked westwards. Indeed, the basic cause of the wars against France and Britain was their resistance to the colonists' attempts to move westwards.

The Louisiana Purchase 1803

Danger in the West. In 1783, however, Spain still blocked the way across the Mississippi. Look carefully at Map 14 on page 44 and explain why. Yet the danger from Spain was exaggerated. Spain had neither men nor money to prevent the Americans moving west. The Mississippi was not fortified or patrolled by Spanish soldiers. But before America could profit from this weakness Spain sold to France the Mississippi delta, including New Orleans, and her claim to the vast area west of the river. America was alarmed. France, led by Napoleon Bonaparte, had definite plans for a new French colony in North America. Indeed, in 1802 20,000 French troops landed in the West Indies and the new French governor of Louisiana temporarily cancelled the privileges of American traders in New Orleans. If Napoleon succeeded in his plans France once more might come to dominate the heart of the continent. America was rescued by the turn of events. In 1803 Napoleon's relations with England worsened and war seemed likely. Napoleon needed money to fight the war. Possibly he feared America might help England. In 1803 he sold Louisiana to America for 15 million dollars.

The significance of the purchase. This purchase was of enormous significance to America. It gained the whole of the Mississippi Valley: she possessed the very heart of the continent. The U.S.A. now was much safer from attacks from the south and west. The way west was open to her pioneers. No wonder Thomas Jefferson boasted he had bought enough land to satisfy Americans for a thousand years. In time this western half of the Valley would support farms, mines, oil-wells and industries which would contribute greatly to America's prosperity.

The Lewis and Clark Expedition

Louisiana and the Northwest Passage. Jefferson had long been interested in Louisiana for another reason. He believed that the headwaters of the Missouri and Columbia rivers lay close together: that they were separated by the Rocky Mountains which were neither wide nor high. Here was the water passage to Asia which had eluded explorers since the time of Columbus. If Americans discovered this passage then the U.S.A. could extend its boundaries as far as the Pacific. The very profitable fur trade between the Pacific

coast and China might then fall into American hands. (Notice, once again the fur trade was encouraging new explorations.)

As early as 1783 Jefferson had tried to form an expedition to seek this passage. In 1803 such an expedition was finally ready. At first its mission was kept secret since Jefferson had not expected to buy Louisiana. Suddenly, Louisiana became American territory. It was transferred from France to America in March 1804. Ten weeks later Meriwether Lewis and William Clark began their momentous expedition.

Lewis and Clark. A recent writer has said:

'The expedition's most valuable resource was its leadership. It has been said of Meriwether Lewis and William Clark that the only two things they ever disagreed on were the taste of dog meat and the need for salt—both of which Clark could gladly do without. Both were experienced army officers, expert rivermen and hunters, adept at all the frontier skills, and each man was the natural complement of the other. Lewis, the better educated of the two, had the mind of a born scientist; Clark, largely self-taught, had an engineer's resourcefulness and a feeling for geography that approached genius. For the next two and a half years they would work together as harmoniously as two human beings ever managed to do.'

Actually, Lewis had been chosen as the leader but he insisted that Clark should have equal rank.

Their expedition to the Pacific. Originally the expedition numbered twenty-nine men. It was very well equipped.

'The keelboat carried two heavy swivel guns fore and aft, and was fitted amid-ships with stout wooden lockers whose lids could be raised to form breastworks against Indian attacks. Below decks were fifteen of the new Harper's Ferry rifles the first regulation U.S. firearm, shorter and more powerful than anything used previously; twenty-four pipe tomahawks, handy in peace and war; twenty-four large knives; and Lewis's patented airgun, a recent invention that worked by compressed air, and which was used mainly to impress the Indians. Among the Indian trade goods were 4600 assorted needles, 2800 fish hooks, 130 rolls of tobacco, 132 knives, 72 pieces of striped silk ribbon, 48 Calico ruffled shirts, and 73 bunches of beads in assorted colours. There were also thirty gallons of spirit, mainly whisky, in six wooden kegs.'

Map 17 shows the route taken by the expedition. The round trip was nearly 4000 miles and took nearly two and a half years. Nature posed serious problems. In many places on the Missouri the men walked shoulder-deep in the cold river, pulling the boat against the swift and treacherous currents. It took thirty-one days to carry the boats and supplies eighteen miles by land around the Great Falls of the river. Ten weeks were taken to cross the Rockies. The trail was often thousands of feet high and the party was shrouded in mist and cloud. Horses were killed to provide meat and snow melted for drinks.

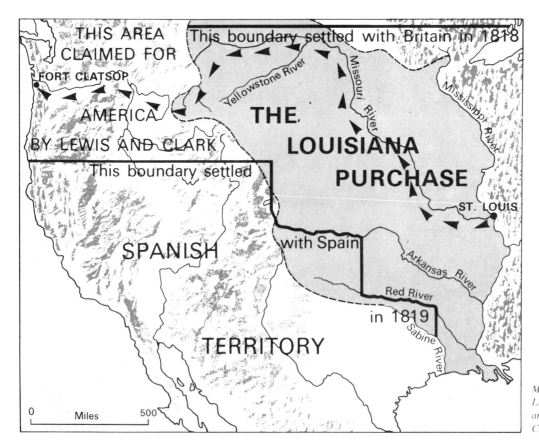

Map 17 The Louisiana purchase and the Lewis and Clark expedition

Descending the Columbia the party climbed down waterfalls and was whisked along by rapids. Temperatures varied from 90°F (32°C) in the summer to sub-zero in winter. There were violent hailstorms on the prairies which cut and bruised the skin. The mountains and the Columbia Valley were wet, cold and windy.

Indians gave problems too. The Teton Sioux caused most trouble. They refused to let the party pass unless more trade goods were given as presents. On one occasion Clark was surrounded, threatened, and handled roughly by the Sioux warriors. He was not intimidated. Next morning all guns were trained on the Indians while the boat left its moorings and started upstream.

Some Indians gave valuable assistance. From the Mandans Lewis and Clark learned much about the Rockies and the difficulties of crossing them. The expedition would need horses. These could be obtained from the Shoshones. It took the party four months to find these Indians who not only supplied horses but provided two chiefs to guide the party down the Columbia to the coast. They helped the Americans to run the rapids and they saved lives when one boat capsized. Their presence also gave the party safe conduct past the Indians of the Columbia valley.

The expedition reached the Pacific on 14 November 1805. It remained here through the miserable winter rains and set off back in the spring of 1806.

What was the significance of the expedition of Lewis and Clark? It was the first American expedition to cross overland from the Mississippi to the Pacific Coast. The Missouri and the Columbia, their headwaters, and the mountains between these two great rivers were mapped for the first time. The two leaders claimed all the lands they had explored beyond Louisiana for America. Most important of all Lewis and Clark discovered that the Northwest Passage did not exist. They shattered Jefferson's belief that there was an easy passage from the Missouri to the Columbia. In 1806 Americans learned how high and extensive the Rockies really were—a great barrier preventing any easy passage from east to west. This was a great disappointment. On the other hand the expedition reported these lands to be rich in furs and it was not long before Louisiana and the Rocky Mountains became a new centre of the American fur trade.

The Acquisition of Texas

The Santa Fé trade. We have mentioned the growing weakness of Spain. By 1819 she had lost Florida to America and two years later the Mexicans revolted against her and successfully declared their independence. Suddenly and dramatically Spain was driven from the continent after more than 300 years of occupation.

In 1821 the new Mexican government invited Americans to trade at the Texas town of Santa Fé. This invitation was speedily accepted and trade between America and Texas grew very quickly. From 1822 large wagon trains of conestogas (six-horse, broad-wheeled covered wagons) laden with red blankets, knives, mirrors and beads left the River Missouri and lumbered 800 miles across dry prairie and desert to Santa Fé. They returned with silver coins, gold, furs, buffalo robes, horses and mules. Wagons did not require daily packing and unpacking and they gave much better protection than pack-mules to both goods and men from bad weather and Indians. These trains were pulled by oxen and mules which were far more able than horses to withstand the daily hauling of heavy loads for weeks on end.

Each man carried 50 lb of flour and bacon, 20 lb of sugar, 10 lb of coffee, salt and beans. His implements were a frying pan, iron kettle, coffee pot and butcher knife. Once in buffalo country men from the trains hunted for fresh meat. It was much better than salted bacon. He was careful to fill his five gallon water cask before the train crossed the Cimarron desert.

Travelling with the trains were a motley crowd of people. There were traders wearing

their long coats, trappers in their greasy buckskins, bullwhackers and muleskinners dressed in blue jeans and woollen shirts and jumpers, and Mexicans under their great sombreros, ponchos and serapes (Serapes were shawls, often gaily coloured, worn by the men.) They bristled with weapons—rifles, scatter guns, pistols, repeaters and knives. Some trains even towed small cannon. There was safety in numbers. The Apache and the Comanche Indians were fierce fighters.

The Santa Fé trade was an important stimulus to a renewed westward movement by the Americans. Not only traders and trappers went to Texas but so too did a growing number of settlers. They were attracted by the empty fertile lands of the Texas valleys spoken of by the traders and trappers. It was not the first time settlers trusted such reports and followed in their footsteps. Think of some earlier examples.

American settlers in Texas. At first the American settlers were encouraged by the Mexican government. Not only did it wish to promote trade but to develop its lands too. The Mexican government sold land very cheaply—12½ cents per acre—and gave the settlers six years to pay. Land salesmen each received 25,000 acres free for every 100 families they brought to Texas. Many Americans were keen to act as salesmen. (How did this compare with the American government's system of land disposal described on page 57?) Farm tools were allowed into Mexico free of taxes. The settlers paid no taxes for six years and half taxes for the next six. No wonder the number of Americans in Texas rose sharply: 10,000 in 1827, 20,000 in 1830, and 35,000 in 1835. Most of them came from Kentucky and Tennessee, some from New England and a few from Germany and Ireland.

Mexico quickly regretted her policy of encouragement. Very soon the Americans outnumbered the Mexicans in Texas. They complained about rising taxes, quarrelled over land, and regarded the Mexicans as an inferior race. The Mexican government opposed

Santa Fé
il. Wagons
sing the
arron River

p 18 The Santa-
rail and the
as revolution

the idea of slavery introduced from Kentucky and Tennessee. In 1830 it tried to stop new settlers passing into Texas. But vacant fertile lands were a magnet to the Americans. The border was too long and the Mexican army too small to patrol it effectively. This dissatisfaction with Mexican rule led some agitators to demand that Texas should become part of the U.S.A. The leader of these agitators was Sam Houston.

The Texas Revolution. It is possible that Andrew Jackson, keen to absorb the southwest into the U.S.A., privately encouraged his close friend Sam Houston to start a revolution in Texas. Such a revolution did occur. No American army was involved. Jackson did not want a war with Mexico. Nevertheless, American frontiersmen like Davy Crockett and Jim Bowie went to Texas to fight against the Mexican army led by Santa Anna. They were all killed at the battle of the Alamo but not in vain. Houston later defeated Santa Anna at San Jacinto and in 1836 proclaimed the independence of Texas (See Map 18). He now asked the U.S.A. to annex Texas. Unexpectedly, America held back. Texas was a slave state. Many northerners, opposed to slavery, did not want another slave state in the Union. We will discuss the question of slavery in the next chapter. Texas was annexed by America in 1844.

Mountainmen and the Western Fur Trade

The Rocky Mountain Fur Company. Meanwhile, encouraged by the reports of Lewis and Clark about the great wealth of furs in the West, American traders and trappers tried to create a fur trade along the upper Missouri. Two companies were involved: the Missouri Fur Trade Company and the Rocky Mountain Fur Company. Unfortunately, British traders from the Hudson Bay and the St Lawrence had taken over the old French trade there and had won the friendship of the Mandan and the Blackfeet Indians. The Lewis and Clark expedition had clashed with the Blackfeet who became the enemies of the Americans. Opposed by both British and Blackfeet the Americans failed to establish a worthwhile trade along the upper Missouri.

Faced with this competition the Rocky Mountain Fur Company decided to abandon the Missouri trade. In 1822 it sent a party of trappers, under Jed Smith, by horseback west across the plains to the mountains. Smith spent a year trapping furs there and exploring the headwaters of the Yellowstone, the Colorado and the Columbia. His report was very favourable. The gamble had paid off. The Company had pioneered a new fur trade in the great Western Mountains which was to thrive for over twenty years.

The trappers. It was not simply a new area. The Company adopted new methods. It abandoned the traditional practice of forts and trading posts where Indians came to exchange their furs for the white man's guns, axes, kettles, brandy, blankets, and mirrors. Instead, the trappers were sent out into the wilderness to catch beavers and other animals themselves. A writer at the time described each trapper's equipment which

'consists usually of two or three horses or mules—one for saddle, the others for packs— and six traps, which are carried in a bag of leather called a trap-sack. Ammunition, a few pounds of tobacco, dressed deer skins for mocassins, etc, are carried in a wallet of dressed buffalo skin, called a "possible" sack. His "possibles" and "trap-sack" are generally carried on the saddle-mule when hunting, the others being packed with the furs. . . .

'Over his left shoulder and under his right arm hang his powder-horn and bullet-pouch, in which he carries his balls, flint and steel and odds and ends of all kinds. Round the

Joseph Walker and his Squaw

waist is a belt in which is stuck a large butcher-knife in a sheath of buffalo-hide, made fast to the belt by a chain or guard of steel; which also supports a little buckskin case containing a whetstone. A tomahawk is also often added: and, of course, a long heavy rifle is part and parcel of his equipment.'

Once in the mountains the trappers split up and scattered in ones, twos or threes throughout the wilderness. Their keen eyes searched the ground for 'sign' of the beaver. Where the 'sign' was fresh the trapper

'sets his traps in the run of the animal, hiding it under water, and attaching it by a stout chain to a picket driven in the bank, or to a bush or tree. A "float-stick" is made fast to the trap by a cord a few feet long, which, if the animal carries away the trap, floats on the water and points out its position. The trap is baited with the "medicine", an oily substance obtained from a gland in the . . . beaver. . . . A stick is dipped into this and planted over the trap; and the beaver, attracted by the smell, and wishing a close inspection, very foolishly puts his leg into the trap, and is a "gone beaver".'

The trapper remained alone or in tiny groups for six to nine months. All this time he stored or cached his furs in holes in the ground. When he had finished his season's hunting he visited his caches, loaded up his furs, and headed for the rendezvous.

The mountain rendezvous. The rendezvous occurred in the summer in a mountain valley chosen by the fur company the year previously. The Rocky Mountain Fur Company held its first rendezvous at Henry's Fork on Green River in 1825. This meeting of trappers became a great annual event in the Rocky Mountains between 1825 and 1840. At the rendezvous the furs from the trappers (and Indians) were collected by the company's representatives who then carted them off to St Louis or other towns on the Missouri. In return, the trappers received whisky, tobacco, coffee and fresh equipment for their next season's hunting. You can imagine what sort of occasions these rendezvous were. Here is one description:

'The rendezvous is one continued scene of drunkenness, gambling, brawling and fighting, as long as the money and credit of the trappers last. Seated, Indian fashion, round the fires, with a blanket spread before them, groups are seen with their "decks" of cards, playing at "euker", "poker", and "seven-up", the regular mountain games. The stakes are "beaver" which here is current coin; and when the fur is gone, their horses, mules, rifles, shirts, hunting packs and breeches are staked. Daring gamblers make the rounds of the camp, challenging each other to play for the trapper's highest stake—his horse, his squaw (if he has one), and, as once happened, his scalp. There goes "hos and beaver!" is the mountain expression when any great loss is sustained; and, sooner or later, "hos and beaver" invariably find their way into the insatiable pockets of the traders.

'These annual gatherings are often the scene of bloody duels, for over their cups and cards no men are more quarrelsome than your mountaineers. Rifles, at twenty paces, settle all differences and, as may be imagined, the fall of one or other of the combatants is certain, or, as sometimes happens, both fall to the word of "fire".'

The trappers become mountainmen. The trappers of the west became known as mountain-men. Some, like Jim Bridger, Tom Fitzpatrick and Kit Carson, became famous in their own lifetime and now occupy an important place in American history and legend. Most of them drifted west from the towns and farms east of the Missouri. They felt the call of the wild and loved the hard, vigorous and dangerous life of the mountain trapper. Cold winters, blizzards, floods, buffalo stampedes, avalanches, grizzlies and hostile Indians they took in their stride. Above all, the wilderness offered them freedom from the restrictions and routines of everyday life back east. Once they had breathed the fresh, cool mountain air and seen the beauty of the landscape few returned home.

The mountainmen lived like the Indians around them. Indeed, they adapted themselves to the mountains as well as any Indian. A man who knew them well wrote:

'Such men could live for months without food except what the country afforded. Nothing escaped the vision of these men—the propping of a stick, the breaking of a twig, the turning of the growing grass, all brought knowledge to them, and they could tell who or what had made it. A single horse or an Indian could not cross the trail but that they discovered it, and could tell how long since they passed. Their method of hunting game was perfect, and we were never out of meat. Herbs, roots, berries, barks of trees and everything that was edible, they knew. They could minister to the sick—dress wounds— in fact, in all my experience I never saw Bridger, or any other voyagers of the plains and mountains meet any obstacle they could not overcome.'

They were an odd assortment of men. Jim Bridger was 'six feet tall, spare, straight as an arrow, and agile. . . . He was hospitable and generous and was always trusted and respected. He possessed in a high degree the confidence of the Indians'. Jed Smith remained religious all his life. He read his Bible regularly, never swore or smoked, and rarely drank. One of his ears was badly formed. It had been torn off by a grizzly and sewn back on by a friend. Bill Williams was a Methodist minister before he became a mountainman. 'About six feet one inch, gaunt, red-haired, with a hard, weather-beaten face marked deeply with smallpox, he was noted for his high-pitched voice and dirty, greasy appearance'. Hugh Glass had been a shipmaster and later a pirate. Becoming discontented, he mutinied, jumped overboard in the middle of the night, and swam ashore.

In their travels the mountainmen had no respect for political boundaries. They were not afraid to venture into lands claimed by other countries. Indeed, a few of them were very conscious of the 'manifest destiny' of Americans and they urged the U.S.A. government to absorb the far west before other countries did. It was not long before the American government took their advice.

Wagon Trains West

The attractions of the far West. The mountainmen were impressed by the Pacific coastlands. At their rendezvous they talked of the rich soils, the warm wet winters and hot dry summers, the large forests, the rivers, bays and sea, and the abundant wild life. They spoke of the opportunities for farming as well as the fur trade. Such favourable verdicts were passed down the Missouri by the fur traders and their agents. Soon the news spread east, into Missouri and Illinois and then beyond. By about 1840 missionaries, adventure writers like James Fennimore Cooper and explorers like Charles Fremont who had been west all echoed the opinions of the mountainmen. Once more excitement gripped the pioneer farmers in the East. They looked around them and saw the lands of the Ohio and Mississippi filling with people. Virgin land was becoming scarce. The whole region was in the grip of a trade depression. Prospects seemed better in the far West. Their forefathers had moved west across the Appalachians. They would now continue the westward movement and cross the prairies and the Rockies. So began a new era of westward migration by pioneer farmers.

The problems of travel. To make up one's mind to move to California or Oregon was one thing. To transport one's family and belongings there was quite another matter. One way was to travel east to New York or Baltimore and then sail there via the Gulf of Mexico or Cape Horn. Another way was to travel west overland using either the Santa Fé Trail or some other route. Most people chose the overland route. Even this decision raised thorny problems. What was the best overland route? Who could lead them? How far was it and how long would it take? How friendly or hostile were the Indians? How

Map 19 The Californian and Oregon trails

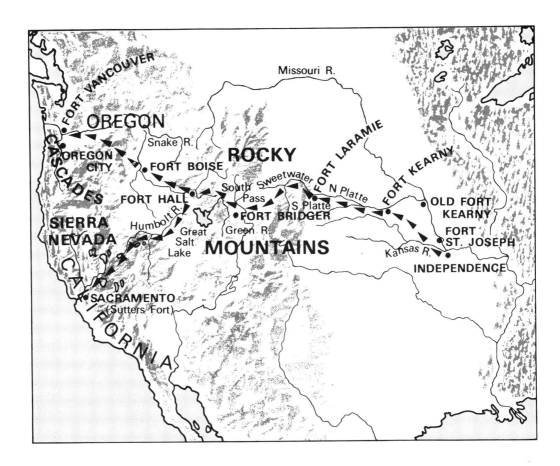

much food and what sort of equipment was needed? How were wives and children to be carried? What sort of animals were best for such a journey? These were only some of the problems. Can you think of some more?

The first families to travel overland to Oregon went in 1839 and the first to California a year later. In the next five or six years 5000 people reached Oregon and 1000 reached California. These pioneers suffered many hardships in their crossings. They ran short of food and water. Indians stole horses and cattle and sometimes killed those who strayed away from the main party. The mountains proved an enormous obstacle to wagons. Indeed, in the first years no wagons actually arrived on the Pacific coast. In 1841, 1843 and 1844 for example, the Californian immigrants found themselves stuck in the mountains with winter approaching. They abandoned their wagons and much of their equipment, put their families on horseback, and rode through to safety.

Trails, wagons and animals. Valuable experience was gained from those early migrations which was used by those who crossed later. By 1845 trails to both California and Oregon had been found which were suitable for covered wagons. The trails most commonly used are shown in Map 19. People realised that covered wagons were the best means of transport. A covered wagon was a home on wheels, a luggage van, an ambulance, a hospital, a fortress, and a weather shield all rolled into one. Conestogas, however, were not really suitable. The mountains had many steep gradients and narrow sharp bends. Smaller wagons with shorter wheel bases proved better than conestogas. Why? Oxen and mules became the favourite draught animals. Fierce arguments often developed about the relative merits of these two animals. One side said oxen were more docile than mules, stronger and less attractive to Indian thieves. Mules were said to be faster, able to eat

77

off even the poorest vegetation and far less prone to sore feet. The deciding factor for most migrants was cost. Oxen were a third of the cost of mules and therefore they were the most common draught animals on the California and Oregon trails.

At first the migrants believed that they required to take little food since game was plentiful en route. However, hunting sometimes took too long and drew men away from the wagons leaving them more defenceless if Indians attacked. It soon became customary to take enough food to last for five or six months: flour (up to 100 lb); yeast; crackers; corn meal; salted bacon; salt; sugar; coffee; dried fruit; special delicacies like tea, maple sugar, vinegar and pickles; and a few canned foods like beef, sardines, fruit and cheese. The diet was supplemented by game when and where it could be caught easily. Cattle were driven along too to provide spare teams and fresh meat and milk. Besides food the migrants also took spare clothes, blankets and tents, arms and ammunition, spare parts for the wagon and other useful articles. One migrant wrote a useful list:

'Knife, whetstone, axe, hammer, spade, saw, gimlet, hatchet, scissors, needles, palm and pricker [for sewing canvas], last, awls, nails, tacks, needles, pins, thread, wax twine, shoe leather and pegs, staples, ropes, whipthongs, cottoncloth, beeswax and tallow, soap, candles, opodeldoc [a linament], herbs, medicines, spyglass, lantern, patent-leather drinking cup, washbowl and campstool.'

Clearly one had to watch the total weight of the provisions and equipment. The wagons carried between three-quarters and one ton. For this reason spare parts for the wagon, for example, were kept to an absolute minimum.

The organisation of the wagon trains. How were these wagon trains formed and organised? Emigrants arrived in Independence from the East about April. Sometimes there were enough families from the same area to form a wagon train west. In these cases the train stopped at Independence to buy supplies, make last minute repairs and wait for the early May grass. Usually, however, emigrants and their families reached the Missouri alone or in groups too small to cross the wilderness safely. Small trains were obvious targets for Indian war parties. Therefore at Independence—or other towns along this stretch of the Missouri—the emigrant families joined together into larger groups. Whether a train was big enough depended not only upon the number of families and wagons but also upon the number of able-bodied men, their shooting skill, and the number of guns and rounds of ammunition they had. Even so, few trains left the Missouri with less than about twenty wagons. Many, of course, were much bigger than this.

The danger of Indians and lawless whites and the need to maintain some formation in travelling made for a military organisation of each wagon train. Each train had a captain, several lieutenants and a quartermaster to ration out the food. The captain usually was elected before the train left the Missouri. His job was a hard one. Many men were not good captains and new leaders were often elected before the trains reached California. When you have finished reading this section on wagon trains think carefully about the sort of man needed to captain a wagon train of settlers. Remember that wagon trains were usually formed hastily by people who were strangers to each other and bear in mind too the nature of the trail to California. Table 5 summarises the main parts of the trail. (You can pretend all your class are emigrants. Hold a meeting and elect a leader.)

Each day the wagon started in single file, or two or three abreast if space permitted. In fact, the trail was often very wide indeed and wagons tended to spread out and get out of line—which was dangerous in Indian country. On the other hand it was difficult to keep the train together. Some animals were stronger and fitter than others and pulled ahead. Some wagons were overloaded and broke down easily. The boys found it hard to herd the cattle along together at the same pace as the wagons. At midday there was usually a halt for several hours while the animals fed and rested. In the evening the wagons were

drawn into a circle or rectangle. The animals were led away to graze. Guards were posted to protect them and the emigrants from wild animals and Indians. Inside the ring of wagons tents were pitched, fires lit, meals cooked, meetings held, games organised, banjos and fiddles played and songs sung. And this life went on for five or six months until California was reached and the emigrants went their respective ways.

The way to California. Table 5 summarises the main stages of the most usual route to California. The trains could not start until early May. Why? They had to be across the Sierras by October when snow began to block the passes. Clearly conditions varied enormously from stage to stage. Some stages were easy and the emigrants enjoyed the travelling, the scenery and each other's company. The mountain and desert stages tested the endurance and spirit of people and animals. Look carefully at the table and study the conditions during these hard stages. What do you imagine were the feelings and thoughts of the men and women at these times?

Between 1845 and 1860 about 175,000 people travelled overland to California from the Mississippi. Many thousands more went overland to Oregon in these years. Clearly, this covered wagon migration was substantial and significant. Indeed, its significance is difficult to exaggerate. The covered wagon and the California and Oregon trails were the symbols of the most impressive conquest of the wilderness that Americans ever knew. Between 1607 and 1840 Americans had pushed their way slowly inland as far as the Mississippi-Missouri, i.e. about 1500 miles in 200 years. For years settlers had marked time at the rivers, regarding the land westwards as impassable. Now after 1845 thousands of families journeyed another 2000 miles through the wilderness in only five or six months. Indeed, those families went as far west as it was possible for any American to go on land. Americans now lived along the east and west coasts. They spanned the continent. The Americans were fulfilling their 'manifest destiny'.

Oregon and California. In 1845 neither Oregon nor California were on American soil. Britain and America both claimed Oregon but their dispute was not settled. British fur traders at Fort Vancouver had been active along the Columbia valley for many years. When the American pioneers arrived they settled in the Willamette valley, and asked their government to protect them. The United States government refused at first. It was clear, however, that the presence in Oregon of both British and American people required a settlement to the dispute.

Table 5. Main Stages along the California Trail

Stage	Miles	Days	Terrain and Weather
1. Independence to Kansas River	100	6	Grassy plains—rainy days.
2. Kansas River to Platte River	220	14	Rolling plains—grass and wild flowers.
3. Along Platte River to its South Fork	135	10	Grassland, with hills, bluffs, streams with occasional trees. Weather drier. Buffalo more plentiful.
4. South Fork to Fort Laramie	180	12	Trail rising very gradually. Grass brown. Hot days, cool nights. Mainly dry with occasional hailstorm. Some remarkable rock formations.
5. Fort Laramie to the North Fork of the River Platte	130	10	Trail up and down through the Black Hills.
6. North Fork to Independence Rock	50	3	Trail along canyon. Dry.
7. Independence Rock to South Pass	100	8	A well-watered, grassy and easy trail. At South Pass—trail at 8000 feet. Very cold at night.
8. South Pass to Little Sandy Creek	20	1	Downhill trail.
9. Little Sandy Creek to Bear River	100	7	Hardest going so far—desert, mountains.
10. Bear ~~River to Fort Hall~~	125	10	Good going.
11. Fort Hall to Raft River	40	2–3	Trail along south bank of Snake River.
12. Raft River to Goose Creek	65	5–6	Easy going, harder at end.
13. Goose Creek to Humboldt River	95	5	Still easy going. Rough, dry areas but grass and water available. Hot in day.
14. ~~Humboldt River to Hum- boldt~~ Sink	365	21	Trail crosses and recrosses River Humboldt. Grass and water plentiful. Marsh swamps, salt flats at the Sink.
15. Humboldt Sink to Truckee River	55	3–4	Mainly desert—some hard going, Most difficult so far.
16. Truckee River to Bear ~~Pass~~	70	7	Steady uphill pull—hard going at end. Through pleasant pine forests
17. Bear Pass to Bear Valley	30	5	Hardest going so far—across the Pass. The heart of the Sierra Nevada Mountains.
18. Bear Valley to Sutter's Fort	85	7–8	Hard downhill trail across forested slopes and ridges, through canyons to the low flat Sacramento Valley.

Main Problems Encountered

Learning to handle wagons and animals.
Second thoughts about going to California—homesickness.

Swollen streams.

Now in Sioux territory.
Wagons in tight circles at nights with strict guard.

Still in Sioux country. Trade with Indians needed care, a strong will and weapons to hand.
River Platte deep—wagons had to be ferried.

Alkaline water—poisoned animals. Sioux.

Shortage of grass and water.
Weaker oxen fail.

Bannock Indians—not very friendly.

Shoshone Indians—thieves.

Paiute Indians—more warlike than Shoshones.
A long monotonous haul.

No water, no grass—have to be carried from Sink. 55 miles taken in one pull—no camping. Animals weakened. Paiutes—steal or kill cattle.

Haulage of wagons uphill. Damage to wagons on rough downhill side. Lowering wagons by rope into Bear Valley.

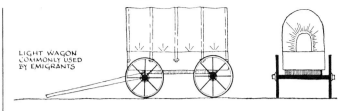

LIGHT WAGON COMMONLY USED BY EMIGRANTS

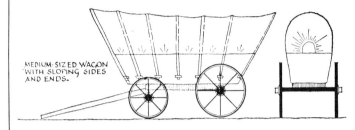

MEDIUM-SIZED WAGON WITH SLOPING SIDES AND ENDS.

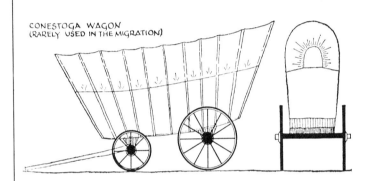

CONESTOGA WAGON (RARELY USED IN THE MIGRATION)

Types of wagons on the California Trail

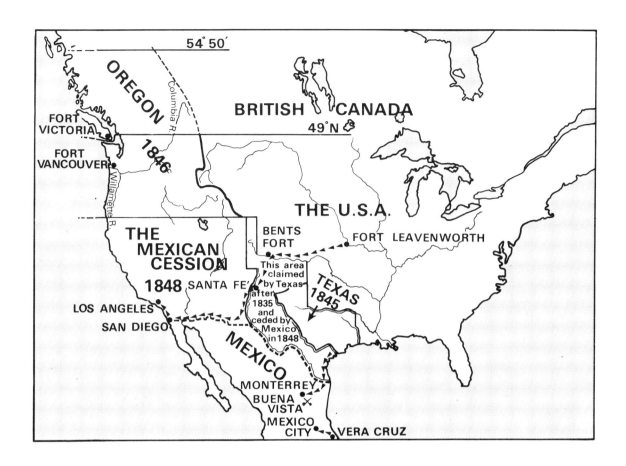

Map 20 Oregon and
the Mexican cession
1848

The situation in California was different. California had long been settled by white men. Once part of the Spanish Empire, it now belonged to Mexico which permitted the Californians to make their own laws and run their own governments. These governments, however, had little power. California was really controlled by a few wealthy Mexican and American landowners and businessmen. The Americans willingly conspired with Andrew Jackson and later presidents to place California in the hands of the U.S.A. Meanwhile they welcomed the settlers from the California Trail. As the number of Americans in California grew quarrels with the Mexicans increased. It was the Texas situation all over again. Tension developed between Mexico and the U.S.A.

America gains the far West. By the mid-1840s the activities of her traders, trappers and settlers had brought America to the brink of war. Mexico claimed both Texas and California and Britain claimed Oregon. The Americans in those areas expected their country to protect them by annexation. The U.S.A. was in an unenviable position. To satisfy its far westerners would mean war. At this point events suddenly moved quickly. Map 20 will help you to follow the rest of this section.

In 1842 Britain recognised the independence of Texas. Trade grew between the two countries. In 1844 Britain proposed a treaty between herself, France, Mexico and Texas, with each country pledged to protect each other from outsiders. This proposal never materialised but it angered and alarmed the U.S.A. James Polk, campaigning to be the next President, urged America to annex Texas and take Oregon. The Americans voted him their next President. John Tyler, the existing President, realised the mood of the Americans and with the approval of Congress annexed Texas.

When Polk became President a war with Mexico was near. This forced him to be cautious about Oregon. He could not risk a war with Britain as well. Thus, Britain was told that America would agree to a boundary along latitude 49° North and drop her claim to all lands north of that line. No American settlers lived there and so there were no lives to protect. Britain rejected this offer. The Hudson Bay Fur Company's headquarters at Fort Vancouver was well south of 49° North. Polk now became more aggressive and reverted to America's original claims to all lands as far north as 54° 40′. Tension mounted but the crisis was relieved when the Hudson Bay Company moved its headquarters from Fort Vancouver to Fort Victoria. The Company feared that the Americans in the Willamette valley might attack Fort Vancouver and destroy its goods valued at £100,000. Fort Victoria was out of harm's way and it was very accessible for trade. The fur trade of the Rocky Mountains was in decline anyway and a fort on the Columbia was less necessary. The two countries now agreed to divide Oregon along latitude 49° North with Vancouver Island remaining in British hands. This was in 1846.

Meanwhile a war with Mexico had begun. For America it proved short and sweet. Mexico stood little chance. It had never had a stable government. Internal revolutions were frequent. In the very year the war began many leading Mexicans in California were talking of revolution and annexation to the U.S.A. The country remained poor and it had few resources to fight a war. America put three armies in the field. The first swept through the country from the Texas-Mexico border to Monterey in Mexico. There it defeated a weak Mexican army under Santa Anna. At the same time, and unknown to the U.S.A., the explorer John Fremont and American settlers and sailors had executed their own revolution and declared California independent. The second American army entered Mexico along the Santa Fé Trail and subdued New Mexico. Entering California it met Kit Carson galloping east with the news that Fremont was in control. Far to the south the third American army landed at Vera Cruz and captured Mexico City in 1847. Mexico was forced to surrender and at the Treaty of Guadalupe Hidalgo in 1848 she ceded to America all her land north of the Rio Grande and Gila rivers in return for only 15 million dollars.

American expansion was at its greatest between 1783 and 1848. This was a period of tremendous success. America quadrupled its size and won such fabulous resources that she became the world's largest industrial and agricultural nation by 1900. Perhaps you can summarise this expansion by one map. Draw outlines of the U.S.A. and show the areas gained in 1783, 1803, 1819, 1845, 1846, and 1848. Label each area. The various maps in this chapter will help you.

Further Reading

Bakeless, Catherine and John, *Explorers of the New World*, G. Bell, 1960.
Billington, Ray Allen, *The Westward Movement in the United States*, Van Nostrand, 1959.
Blacker, Irwin R., *The Old West in Fact*, Ivan Obolensky, 1962.
Eggenhofer, Nick, *Wagons, Mules and Men*, Hastings, 1961.
Hamilton, W. T., *My 60 Years on the Plains: Trapping, Trading and Indian Fighting*, Univ. of Oklahoma, 1960.
Hawgood, John A., *The American West*, Eyre & Spottiswoode, 1967.
Leonard, Zenas, *Adventures of Zenas Leonard, Fur Trader*, Univ. of Oklahoma, 1959.
Parkman, Francis, *The Oregon Trail*, Oxford, U. P., 1954.
Stewart, George R., *The California Trail*, Eyre & Spottiswoode, 1964.
Tomkins, Calvin, *The Lewis and Clark Trail*, Harper & Row, 1965.
Longman 'Then and There' series
    Currie, Barbara, *Pioneers in the American West, 1780–1840*.

7 CIVIL WAR: VICTORY AND FAILURE

While the Union was expanding at its fastest, growing tensions between the South and the other states were threatening to split it apart. This chapter shows how the Civil War came about. The desire to leave the Union—secession—was the cause of war, but the struggle over secession arose from the different attitudes towards slavery. The North and West won the war; the Union remained intact. But the beliefs and prejudices of the South were not so easily defeated. Although free, the Negroes remained inferior to the whites. The attempt to 'reconstruct' Southern society failed.

The Approach of War

Sectionalism. In chapter 4 you saw that the Constitution could be understood in different ways. Chapters 5 and 6 showed how different regions of the United States each had needs and interests of their own. At any one time the region with the most influence in Congress and with the president tried to use Federal power to impose its own measures on the other states. For example, the Northeast had tried to impose Hamiltonian ideas, the West had supported Jacksonian democracy. The minority states claimed the central government was tyrannical and supported the right of any individual state to secede— i.e. to leave the Union—if it could not get its own way. The Constitution did not say whether this should be allowed or not.

This division of the Union into regions with different interests was called sectionalism. A section could protect itself providing it had a minimum of exactly half the membership of the Senate. You remember that each state elected two senators.

In 1819 when Missouri, a slave state, applied to join the Union, there were eleven free and eleven slave states. Missouri was part of the Louisiana Purchase, which the South assumed was all open to slavery. If this was so the North faced the prospect of a permanent minority in Congress as new slave states were admitted. The solution was the Missouri Compromise of 1820. Maine was admitted to balance Missouri and there was to be no slavery north of the Mason-Dixon line, the Ohio River and latitude 36°30′N (See Map 21).

From 1828 to 1833 there was an even more serious battle between South and North, over customs duties. John Calhoun declared that a state could nullify a Federal law if it wished. Many southerners spoke openly of leaving the Union, but again a compromise was found. Andrew Jackson in 1837 claimed: 'The Tariff was only a pretext, and Disunion and Southern Confederacy the real object. The next pretext will be the Negro or Slavery question.' The next part of this chapter shows how this prophecy came true.

The Abolitionists. In chapter 5 you saw how dependent the planters were on slavery and how their opinions hardened after 1830. One of the reasons for this change was the growth in the North and West of a movement to abolish slavery.

Most Americans had no wish for Negro social and political equality. Even by 1860 only New England had given the Negro equal voting rights. Most northern states had restricted Negro rights. The early abolitionists were freed Negroes and a few who thought slavery morally wrong. Their main activity was helping fugitive slaves to escape by the 'underground railroad'* to Canada. Slaves were valuable property and successful escapes set a bad example, so southerners got Congress to pass a new Fugitive Slaves Act in 1850. All citizens had to help to recapture slaves; all Negroes were assumed to be slaves unless they could prove they were free; magistrates were paid twice as much for convicting a Negro accused of escaping, as for declaring him free. Freed slaves were sometimes tricked into handing over their papers, which were then destroyed. There was no redress for the Negro and many were returned to slavery unjustly by this method.

Those who favoured abolition in the South were considered traitors and driven out. Some of them settled in the North and became leaders of the abolitionists. Because they were afraid and believed they had so much to lose the southern planters tried to suppress even discussion of slavery.

Their practical reasons we have already seen. Faced with the abolitionists' attack they tried to show that slavery was a positive benefit to slaves, to masters and to the economy. They pointed out that they were not responsible for introducing slavery, but that it was now an integral part of their existence, and that the Negroes had gained: '... Show us on the continent of Africa, or elsewhere, three million of blacks in as good a condition—physically and morally—as our slaves.' They claimed slavery was

Map 21 The Missouri compromise

*The routes by which Negroes were secretly smuggled out of slavery.

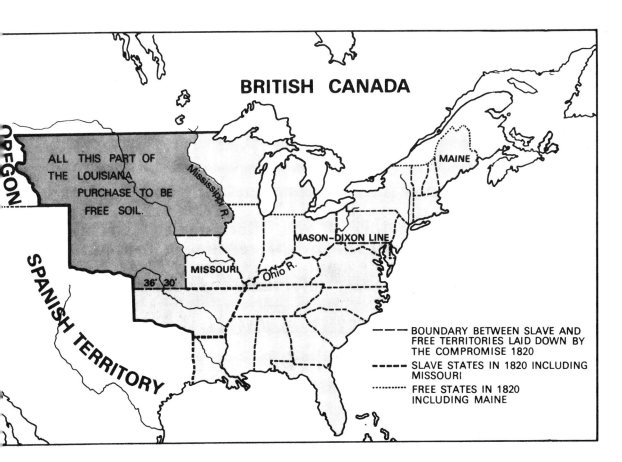

BOUNDARY BETWEEN SLAVE AND FREE TERRITORIES LAID DOWN BY THE COMPROMISE 1820

SLAVE STATES IN 1820 INCLUDING MISSOURI

FREE STATES IN 1820 INCLUDING MAINE

CAUTION!!

COLORED PEOPLE

OF BOSTON, ONE & ALL,

You are hereby respectfully **CAUTIONED** and advised, to avoid conversing with the

Watchmen and Police Officers of Boston,

For since the recent **ORDER OF THE MAYOR & ALDERMEN**, they are empowered to act as

KIDNAPPERS
AND
Slave Catchers,

And they have already been actually employed in **KIDNAPPING, CATCHING, AND KEEPING SLAVES.** Therefore, if you value your **LIBERTY,** and the *Welfare of the Fugitives* among you, *Shun* them in every possible manner, as so many *HOUNDS* on the track of the most unfortunate of your race.

Keep a Sharp Look Out for KIDNAPPERS, and have TOP EYE open.

APRIL 24, 1851.

economically necessary because white men could not work in the heat and other forms of agriculture were too expensive. Freedom would be a hardship to the slaves because 'the free black . . . assumes all the cares and responsibilities of self-support'. They quoted from the Bible and from classical Greece and Rome to show slavery was not morally wrong. Judge Harper summed their attitude up neatly: 'Our proudest and most deeply cherished feelings . . . our most essential interests, our humanity and consideration for the slaves themselves, . . . forbid that this should be done by our own act.'

In reply the abolitionists argued that poorer whites did work in the South and that paid labour could be profitable. More powerfully they said that Negroes were human beings and that Christianity demanded that they should have the elementary rights of human beings. Many of the abolitionists were priests who emphasised that slavery was a sin. It was also contrary to the Declaration of Independence. (Can you explain why?) To this, the South replied that under the Constitution the Federal government had to protect private property and slaves were private property. In ferocious pamphlets the abolitionists exaggerated the cruelty and injustice of slavery. Slaveowners were described as totally corrupt and dishonest, evil in their motives and deceitful in their methods, and planning to gain power over the whole Union. This personal abuse was particularly painful to proud southerners.

Perhaps even more effective was the claim that slavery led to tyranny, to censorship and to inequality of justice. Expelled southerners could speak from personal experience and most had seen the Fugitive Slave Act in operation. Some states, although they did not favour Negroes, passed personal liberty laws guaranteeing all men the basic rights of freedom of speech and equality before the law. Many Americans thought it against the Constitution that these rights should be denied in new states and saw slave-owners' demands as a threat to freedom throughout the Union. So civil rights supporters joined the abolitionists.

To slave-owners—not surprisingly—it seemed that the North was determined to destroy them.

Westward expansion. The South believed that it had to expand to survive. If it did not it would be outvoted in Congress and eventually slavery would be abolished. Also, new land was needed to replace exhausted estates. Those who realised that the practical limits of cotton growing had been reached wanted to use slaves in mining in Texas, which would absorb slaves from the East and enable plantations to diversify as well as providing a base for industry.

We have already seen the rivalry which led to the Missouri Compromise of 1820. By 1848 there were fifteen free and fifteen slave states. The admission of Texas, where slavery already existed, had been discussed for several years when in 1850 California asked to join but declared against slavery. Eventually California compromised by allowing slavery in the rest of the territory taken from Mexico and by the passing of the Fugitive Slave Act.

But this was unsatisfactory for the balance of senators was now thirty-two to thirty against the South and the Fugitive Slave Law proved unworkable. The North saw its fears of Southern expansion and restriction of liberty justified.

The Republican Party. The great controversy led to the formation of a new party. You remember that Jacksonian democrats had united the northern and western farmers with the planters against the merchants, financiers and industrialists who thought western expansion was a distraction from the development of trade. Some of the merchants were now realising that the West was a very profitable market as it was opened up by roads and railways. In the West the democratic small farmers were competing with the planters

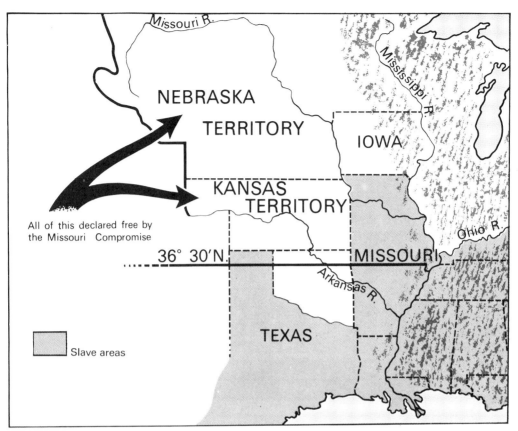

Map 22 The Kans
Nebraska crisis

NEBRASKA
TERRITORY

IOWA

KANSAS
TERRITORY

All of this declared free by
the Missouri Compromise

36° 30′ N.

MISSOURI

TEXAS

Slave areas

for land and over the type of state government which should be set up. On the other hand some of the wealthiest merchants, from whom the planters had borrowed, now favoured the Southern point of view. Some New York Democrats broke away from the party and coined a new slogan: 'FREE TRADE, FREE LABOUR, FREE SOIL, FREE SPEECH, and FREE MEN'.

This appealed widely to western farmers, to northern industrial workers (why?), to abolitionists and to Civil Rights men. To them the alliance of wealthier merchants with planters, of 'money power' with 'slave power', seemed a sinister alliance against democracy.

The next crisis was over the admission of Kansas and Nebraska. This is illustrated in Map 22. Senator Douglas proposed each should choose for itself whether to be slave or free. Since both were north of the Missouri Compromise Line the South accepted quickly and moved settlers in, who, using blatantly dishonest methods, set up a legislature and passed laws to protect slavery. The abolitionists replied by marching in with Beecher's Bibles (i.e. rifles) and forming their own rival government. Federal troops were required to suppress the violence. In 1854 the Kansas—Nebraska Act allowed states to choose by popular vote whether to be slave or free. This meant that all the area made free by the Missouri Compromise was now open to slavery. In Congress debates became so heated that Senator Sumner of Massachusetts was attacked afterwards with a walking stick. He never fully recovered but Massachusetts refused to fill his seat. The southerners re-elected his assailant. This incident shows how passionately both sides clung to their beliefs.

The new party christened itself Republican and in the presidential elections of 1856 polled one million votes. In the following year the Supreme Court added to the growing tension by its decision in the Dred Scott case. It decided that Scott, a Negro, was a slave, and therefore not a citizen and not entitled to sue in court for his freedom; that visits to free states did not make him free; and that the Missouri Compromise was unconstitutional because it limited the protection of private property. The Kansas—Nebraska Act, and this decision, enabled the southerners to get Kansas and Oregon admitted to the Union as states where slavery was legal, and Nebraska Territory recognised as slave territory. They implied that not even a popular vote, in favour of a personal liberty law for instance, let alone Congress, could interfere with a slave-owner's property.

The South was jubilant, the North enraged. Two years later John Brown, a fanatical abolitionist tried to free slaves by force at Harper's Ferry. His effort was hopeless and he was rightly hanged but the South took this as a foretaste of what would happen if the Republicans got into power. They were not reassured by the Republican programme of 1860. Although it condemned John Brown, it approved the Declaration of Independence. Although it promised no interference with existing slave states, it opposed slavery in new territories and was against secession. Effectively this meant that the South would be in a permanent Congressional minority. As they suspected the Republicans also intended to repeal the Fugitive Slave Act and reverse the Dred Scott decision. The South was sure that these were only the first steps to abolition.

As their candidate for the Presidency the Republicans chose Abraham Lincoln. Lincoln was a moderate but the South could not accept any Republican as President. If he was elected the South saw no alternative to secession, if they wished to live in their own way.

Abraham Lincoln and Secession. Like many brought up on the frontier Lincoln was personally opposed to slavery, but he did not think it right to impose his personal opinion on the whole country. He also thought the Declaration of Independence was hostile to slavery in the long run. The Founding Fathers:

'meant simply to declare the right, so that enforcement of it might follow as fast as circumstances should permit.

'They meant to set up a standard maxim for free society which should be familiar to all, and revered by all; constantly looked to, constantly laboured for, and even though never perfectly attained, constantly approximated and thereby constantly spreading and deepening its influence and augmenting the happiness and value of life to all people, of all colours.'

But a practical solution was extremely difficult. To send Negroes back to Africa was impractical; to free them but not give social and political equality would be no improvement; to give equality was impossible in the short run because, right or wrong, the strength of white feeling could not be ignored. The only alternative left was gradual emancipation. Immediately there were some specific steps to take. Lincoln recognised the constitutional right of the planters to recapture slaves who were their property, but he held that the Fugitive Slave Law was too easily abused. Free men were sometimes made slaves. This would mean at least a change in the Fugitive Slave Law. On the Dred Scott decision: 'We propose so to manage it, as to have it reversed if we can. . . .' And expansion: 'The Republican party think it (slavery) a moral and social and political wrong. Therefore we deal with it so, that in the run of time, there may be some promise of an end to it. . . . We insist on the policy that shall restrict it to its present limits.'

Lincoln realised that no compromise was really possible. It was not a case that could be settled by a committee of inquiry into the facts, it was not a question of misunderstanding but:

'Their thinking it right, and our thinking it wrong is the precise fact on which depends the whole controversy. Thinking it right . . . they are not to blame for seeking its full recognition as being right; but thinking it wrong as we do, can we yield to them? . . . Wrong as we think slavery is, we can yet afford to let it alone where it is, because that much is due to the necessity arising from its actual presence in the nation; but can we, while our votes will prevent it, allow it to spread into the national territories, and to over-run us here in these free states.'

Lincoln was elected. Were the fears of the Southern states justified?

Alabama, Mississippi and South Carolina drew up 'Ordinances of Secession' and five more states joined them. Many southerners did not wish to secede but the extremists were better organised. As President in 1861 Lincoln said that there would be no interference with southern property but that secession was impossible under the Constitution and that he would continue to govern the South as usual. In other words the South would have to fight to get out of the Union.

Notice that the Civil War started to preserve the Union, *not* to free the slaves.

'My paramount object in this struggle is to save the Union, and it is not either to save or destroy slavery. If I could save the Union, without freeing any slave, I would do it; and if I could save it by freeing all the slaves, I would do it; and if I could save it by freeing some and leaving others alone, I would also do that. . . .'

The Civil War was fought then over the right of a state to secede from the Union. As the United States expanded so sectionalism developed and secession was several times discussed. Slavery was the first issue to arouse on a large scale the self-interest and moral indignation of the North and West while at the same time being crucial to the survival of the South. Outnumbered in Congress, with a Republican President, there seemed to be no way except by secession of saving all that the South valued.

Abraham Lincoln in his presidential oath swore 'to preserve, protect and defend the Constitution of the United States'. The War had arrived.

The War

The two sides. Map 23 shows the division of the Union at the beginning of the war. Eleven states joined the Confederacy, twenty-two remained Unionist. The borderline states of Missouri, Kentucky, Maryland and Delaware, where there was less slavery, remained loyal; western Virginia refused to secede (think why) and was later formed into a separate state. Of the South's population of 9 million, 4 million were slaves and only one million eligible for military service, whereas the North had 22 million and 4.5 million who could fight.

In Chapter 4 you saw how the North developed transport, trade and industry, but the South failed to do so. This was a fatal disadvantage. There were only two main east-west railway lines in the South, and no one who could build locomotives. Nor did the South have the metals, the industry or the skills needed to maintain and replace damaged stock and track. This was the first war in which the railways played an essential part. Can you think of any ways in which they would change the conduct of war?

The South had no navy and the North owned most of the merchant ships, so it was difficult for them to get help from abroad or even to export the cotton, on the sale of which they relied to buy munitions for the war. The northern states had 92 per cent of the Union's manufacturing capacity and the war stimulated industry and farming. The demand for large supplies of food encouraged farmers to mechanise. The need for uniforms led to the mass production of off-the-peg clothes. The need for munitions expanded the iron, steel and coal industries, the engineering works and arms factories. It was less

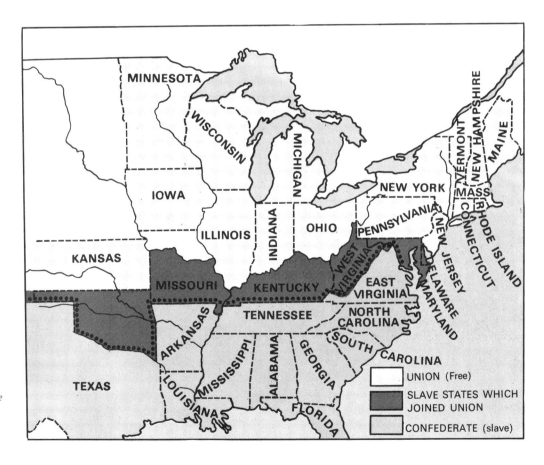

p 23 Confederate Unionist states he beginning of war

easy to increase production by slave labour and plantations could not easily go over to food crops when they relied for their very survival on selling cotton. Table 6 summarises some of these differences for you.

Lastly you will remember that the main reason why the Southern states broke away was to avoid Federal interference with slavery, which they considered the concern of the individual states. Although they formed a confederacy it was more difficult for Jefferson Davis than for Lincoln to get his supporters to cooperate.

Table 6. The Resources of the Two Sides

The resources of the two sides at the beginning of the Civil War

	(million)	(miles)	(million $)	(million $)	(million bushels)	(tons)
	Population	Railway	Value of Manufactured goods	Banking capital	Product of food	Iron bar, sheet etc
Union	22.3*	21,679	1730	345.9	717	482,000
Confederate	9.1*	8,947	156	76	316	31,000
Total	31.4	30,626	$1886m	$421.9m	1033m	513,000

*includes Negro population.

Despite all these material advantages for the North, many contemporaries expected the South to make good its secession. Most of the best officers in the Federal army were Southerners such as Robert E. Lee, 'Stonewall' Jackson and Joe Johnston. The South also had a strong military tradition. The North was critically short of good officers and, if anything, opposed to military discipline. The South therefore was expected to beat the North in the field. To win it had only to avoid being beaten too decisively for long enough for the North to become exhausted or discouraged. Lastly, Southerners were fighting for their own homes and livelihoods and usually on their own soil. That they did stand a good chance is shown by their success in the early stages of the war.

The strategy and course of the war. This section is intended only as an outline. Map 24 will help you to follow the events but you should find out for yourselves the details of the land and sea battles, the campaigns of the generals and the methods of fighting. The Civil War has been called the first modern war: for example, railways, submarines, observation balloons, the telegraph, 'ironclads', Gatling machine guns were all used effectively for the first time in war. In reading the summary and the books we suggest, look out for examples of the use of these inventions.

East of the Appalachians Richmond and Washington, only one hundred miles apart, were the focus of a continuous campaign. Each side hoped to paralyse the enemy by capturing its capital. West of the mountains it was vital to control the Mississippi, Ohio, Tennessee and Cumberland River system and the main rail links with the east at Atlanta and Chattanooga. Look at Map 24 and explain why.

1861   Mainly occupied with recruiting and training armies which the South did more rapidly and efficiently than the North, with the result that on 21 July at the first Battle of *Bull Run*, the half-trained Unionist soldiers ran away.

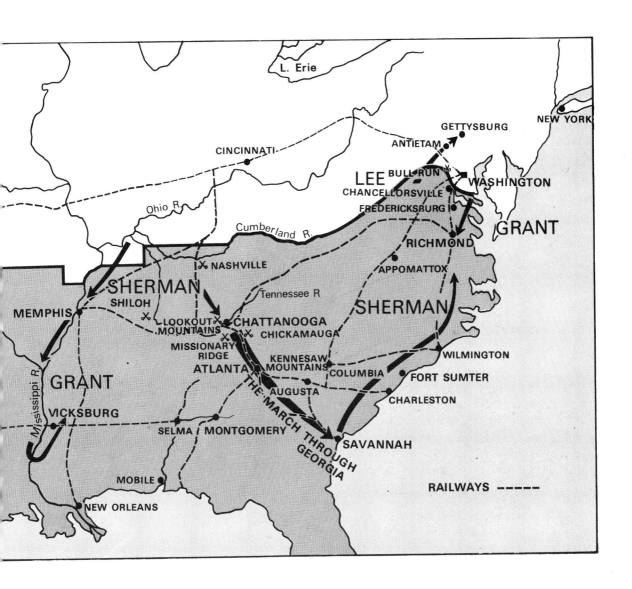

Map 24 The theatre of war, showing main towns, railway lines, rivers and principal battlefields

1862

The Union navy completed the capture or blockade of all important Southern ports except Wilmington and Charleston. It also took *Memphis* on the Mississippi.

In the west: The Union general Ullyses S. Grant was surprised by Confederates at the Battle of *Shiloh* on 6 August. He was only saved by nightfall and the arrival of reinforcements. But the Unionists did clear the Upper Mississippi and a Confederate attack on Kentucky was beaten back to Chattanooga.

In the east: After much delay McClellan attempted to seize Richmond. In a lightning campaign, 'Stonewall' Jackson brought him to a halt, J. E. B. Stuart's cavalry cut his communications and mapped his positions. Robert E. Lee with the main Confederate army closed in for the kill in the *Seven Days Battle* (26 June–2 July) when he inflicted 20,000 casualties. A second Union attack was defeated at *Bull Run* and a Confederate counter attack was only stopped at *Antietam*. The year ended disastrously for the North when General Burnside, despite superior numbers, was heavily defeated at the Battle of *Fredericksburg* on 13 December.

The North's failure to win was making it hard for Lincoln to keep his party united, and he was afraid that European powers might feel encouraged to intervene. So it was almost in desperation that he passed the Proclamation abolishing slavery in the South in 1863. Remember that the war was being fought to preserve the Union, not in order to free the slaves. By freeing them now Lincoln hoped to win the support of Liberal opinion in Europe, to reduce opposition in the North to his own policy and to weaken the Southern war effort. In other words slavery was abolished to win the war, not the reverse.

1863   *In the west*: On 4 July Grant captured *Vicksburg* the last Confederate stronghold on the Mississippi. To do this he had to take the risk of abandoning his supply lines and circling across the river to attack from the South.

   After a Union defeat at *Chickamauga* in September, Grant and Sherman defeated the Confederates at *Lookout Mountain* and at *Missionary Ridge* in November.

   In the east: 'Fighting Joe' Hooker had even less success than his predecessors. Lee and Jackson defeated him at *Chancellorsville* (1–4 May) though they were outnumbered two-to-one. Lee invaded Pennsylvania to destroy Union food supplies and factories but was at last defeated at *Gettysburg* on 3 July.

1864   Grant was now put in charge of all Union forces and for the first time there was an overall strategy and definite objectives. Grant was to hold down Lee by advancing on Richmond; Sherman was to take Atlanta and defeat the western Confederate army. He would then join Grant for the final campaign.

   In the east: Lee repeatedly defeated Grant, inflicting 55,000 casualties in three weeks, but Grant refused to retreat, reaching Richmond and cutting off its communications to the south. Meanwhile General Sheridan devastated the Shenandoah Valley to prevent its supplying Lee. Grant knew that he could always get reinforcement, and that by this time Lee could not.

   In the west: In September after a whole season's campaigning, Sherman at last reached and took *Atlanta*, a most important industrial and railway centre. Having superior numbers he also could allow the Confederates to exhaust themselves in skirmishes. Leaving part of his army to cover the remaining Confederates he started his famous march from Atlanta to the sea. You probably know the song 'Marching through Georgia'. The aim of this was to cut the Confederation in two, destroy its communications and supplies and squeeze Lee between two armies. But it was very dangerous because he might not be able to live off the country in winter, and because the troops he had left behind might be defeated. You can read about the march itself in the next section: and the western Confederates were finally defeated at *Nashville* on 16 December. The war in the west was over.

1865   The remaining Confederates were grossly outnumbered and completely boxed-in. They were cut off from the Deep South by Grant and Sherman. The navy had closed Charleston and cut off all help from the sea. No reinforcements were available, and no supplies could be found from the devastated Shenandoah Valley. On 9 April, after evacuating Richmond, Lee surrendered at *Appomattox* court house.

At his second inauguration as President on 4 March Lincoln had declared a policy of peace and reconciliation.

'With malice toward none; with charity for all; with firmness in the right, as God gives us to see the right, let us strive on to finish the work we are in; to bind up the nation's wounds ... to do all which may achieve and cherish a just and lasting peace, among ourselves and with all nations.'

Abraham Lincoln, April 10th, 1865, notice how the strai[n] of the war has aged Lincoln.

Confederate and Unionist

Hook used by Shermans army for twisting and destroying railroad iron.

Destruction of telegraph and rail communications

Five days after Appomattox Lincoln was shot by a crazed actor. The war to save the Union was over, and the man most responsible for preserving it was dead.

Why did the North win? If you think carefully and re-read the section on 'The two sides' you will be able to list most of the reasons. Think them out under the following headings: population; industrial strength; agricultural production; the navy; the railways; generals; Lincoln.

Extracts from a soldier's diary. Below are some extracts from the diary of Bob Strong, a private in Sherman's army, who enlisted in 1862 and served to the end of the war. They give a realistic idea of what the war was like for those who fought in it. Bob Strong, an Illinois farmer's son, was nineteen when he joined up. Like most of his contemporaries he was used to sporting guns, and when he fought he shot to kill. In the campaign described here one in every four was killed or wounded—50,000 in all.

In the heat of the battle both sides were brutal. The Confederates had killed some prisoners in capturing a certain Fort Pillow. Shortly after Strong's enlistment the Yanks captured a hill. One of their prisoners, a cannoneer, begged for mercy but tattooed on his arm were the words 'Fort Pillow'. The boys . . . yelled, 'No quarter for you! and a dozen bayonets went into him. I shall never forget his look of fear.' Sometimes the dead were never buried, sometimes nothing could be done for several days.

'Our brigade was detailed to bury the dead. . . . It was our first experience, and to carry men to a hole and dump them in was almost too much for me. Some had been dead for three or four days, and the flesh would not hold together to lift them. So we put them in blankets, or tied the legs of their pants and their coat sleeves together and gently dragged them.'

Danger was always present. Once when Strong's group were eating they were alerted, one man jumped up and was shot through the head. Strong commented: 'He fell across my lap, I was still sitting—and his brains and blood ran into my haversack, spoiling my rations. So I took his.'

When possible the wounded and sick were sent back to hospital. Those who died there and were not claimed were dissected by civilian doctors. The remains were supposed to be buried.

'The hospital privies were next to the Dead House. Many times I have seen the intestines of dead men in the vault. More than once I have seen the intestines hanging from the seats, not having been pushed in properly. It was horrible, but we got used to it. And all the while we knew we would be misused in the same way if we died.'

Strong was rarely involved in full-scale battles. After the capture of Atlanta, Sherman cut all communications with the North and East to avoid an attack from the rear. His march through Georgia was intended to destroy Rebel resources, communications and morale. Most of the time was spent in skirmishes, in burning military supplies and ripping up bridges and railway lines. Strong took part in every type of action at one time or another. Here he describes tying 'Sherman's neckties'.

'A hundred or more men would range along the side of the track, stoop, take hold of the ends of the cross-ties, and the word of command, would straighten their backs, bringing up the whole track with them. At the next command, they turned it straight up onto the ends of the ties, and at the next over it would go. The rails would be broken loose from the ties, the ties would be piled on top and burned. As the middle of the rail became red-hot, two or three men would take each end of the rail, lift it off the fire and walk in opposite directions around a tree. . . . Miles of track would be done this way. . . . All this was done by detachments sent to the right and left of the main column.'

Of course the Rebels tried to stop the damage and one rank had to stand guard while the rest worked. Often there would be small-scale battles.

A bummer – drawn by a Yankee soldier

Since it had cut communications, the army had to live off the land, so foragers were sent out, to find food for both the men and the animals. They were also instructed to destroy any supplies useful to the Rebel government. Foraging was dangerous but Strong preferred it to staying with the main column. While the men in the column had to march in strict order:

'The forager, on the contrary, left the camp any time he pleased, day or night, just by making his business known to those in command. He went where he pleased, as he pleased and could rest when he pleased. Men who made good foragers were pretty sure to be detailed for the business, and these men in time came to be called bummers, because they bummed everywhere.'

Naturally the Southerners hid their food and the good forager soon got a nose for ferreting out hidden supplies. On one occasion Strong tells how they came to a large house where the family was in the act of burying a relative who had just died. Finding no food, with apologies, they opened up the grave. The 'coffin' was stuffed with hams, bacon meal flour, etc. 'We loaded the "dear departed" onto our mules and returned to camp, at which point it truly departed for ever.' On another occasion the bummers decided the best way to get food was to capture a town. This they did, and held it until the main

army arrived. If no forage was available they had to live on army rations. These consisted of hardtack

'... baked so hard and dry as to resist all actions of weather and time.... The large ones were as solid as an oak board.... With hardtack went "sow belly", or fat salt pork, and coffee sometimes with sugar, ... we got in addition some beans and rice and occasionally a piece of beef instead of pork.'

Most of the marching was in winter, so cold and wet were added to hunger. Tracks— remember there were few roads—were often so deep in mud that 'corduroy' roads had to be built out of tree boughs or fence rails. Wagons had to be dug out of mud-holes and floated over swollen rivers. To be ready for instant action, they slept without even removing belt or boots. 'It rained a great deal, and for days and days we would not have a dry thread on us. Many and many times I have piled rocks together to keep me out of the water while I slept ... many of us were as good as barefoot.' Since they could rarely wash, they suffered from lice.

'They would get into the seams of our shirts and pants and drawers.... At every leisure moment the boys would pull off their shirts and such a cracking of thumbnails never took place anywhere but in the army. At every opportunity we would strip ourselves and boil our clothes and for a few days we would have peace. Next to fighting and eating and sleeping, and perhaps praying and gambling, came washing.'

Despite their hardships, Bob Strong's corps was never defeated. The men were tough, strong and proud. Their own upbringing and Sherman's organisation of the march made them self-reliant. They became fine soldiers but impatient of unnecessary discipline. Fortunately all the officers of Strong's regiment were kindly and well-liked. 'We thought Put Scott was the kindest of all. He would divide his last cracker or last water in his canteen with the boys. If he got out of water, he would pass down the lines, shaking the canteens until he found one with water in it. Then he would take a drink.'

Some of the other officers were domineering and unfair. Strong himself threatened to shoot a general and a colonel on one occasion, and would have done so too, had they not admitted their mistake. The same men were several times beaten up by Strong's company.

Just as the bummers might capture a town on their own initiative, so there were unofficial truces. After a long day's fighting across a small river 'A Reb sings out, "Say, Yanks, I want to talk to you a minute"... the word passed down, along both sides of the river, for both Rebs and Yanks to cease firing because the boys are going to gas a little.'

The northerners had coffee, the Confederates tobacco 'A number of us from each side laid down our arms, stripped off our clothes, and swam and waded out to the sandbar. There squatting round naked as two tribes of savages, we made our exchange, coffee for tobacco. We told each other stories of the war....' When both sides were back and dressed the cry rang out: '"Hunt your holes, we are going to shoot" so we began again to do our best to kill each other.'

The war did at last end but for the rest of his life Strong suffered from serious bouts of rheumatism from sleeping so often in the wet, and for a long time too he found it difficult to get used to civilian life.

'I remember two things in particular after I got home for good. It was hard for me to sit in a chair or sleep in a bed. For a long time I preferred to sleep and to sit on the floor.'

Reconstruction

The problems of peace. With the Civil War ended and the South defeated, someone had to decide what to do with the Southern states. Bob Strong might think that he could walk off home, but what should happen to the Southern leaders, should they be punished? If the South was forgiven, might she not try to restore things just as they had been before the war, even try to secede again? How was all the damage that had been done to the South to be repaired? The Negroes had been freed but they had no land, no income, nothing; what was to be done with them? To provide the income and employment which the Negroes needed and to break the monopoly of the planters the Southern economy needed rebuilding and reshaping. It required a massive amount of Federal and private investment to drain lands, equip farms, build railways, erect factories and stimulate trade.

The attempt to reorganise the South has been called Reconstruction. Different parties and individuals disagreed about how it should be done. Each side was convinced that the other was wrong, and that it was dishonest and corrupt as well as really interested only in making as much for itself as possible and in getting revenge.

The Southern Democrats. These were the great landowners of the South who had led its forces in the war and been defeated. Their slaves had been freed and they seemed to be faced with ruin. But they were the only class in the South with political experience and wealth. Although they were in a minority they were well organised and were supported by the poorer white classes on the most important single issue—what was to happen to the former slaves? The majority of the Southern whites wanted to see them kept in a thoroughly subordinate position. They considered them inferior in abilities, usually immoral, lazy and incapable of organising their own lives. They were horrified at the idea of having to treat them as equals.

By the end of 1865 the state governments of the South were once more controlled by the planters, not all of whom had sworn an oath of loyalty to the Union. It did not matter: President Johnson tamely pardoned them all.

It was quickly clear what policies the planters would follow. Several of the states clung to the idea of secession and all passed laws against Negro equality. Though free, the Negro was to remain an illiterate, unskilled, landless agricultural worker with no legal protection or rights of his own. These laws became known as the Black Codes. Generally they denied Negroes the vote, introduced segregation (the separation of whites and Negroes) in public places, forbade interracial marriage, excluded Negroes from jury service and from giving evidence against a white man, and revived many of the punishments of the prewar slave codes. In Mississippi they were not to buy or rent farm land: in Louisiana all Negroes had to agree to work for one man for the whole year and were forbidden to leave their workplace for that time; those who refused these terms were made to do forced labour on public works until they changed their minds. Without land or money of their own, the Negroes were at the mercy of their landlords. It was almost as if they were still slaves.

The Radical Republicans. These reactionary policies horrified the Radical Republicans in Congress. Most of these were abolitionists who saw all their efforts in the war being undone. They hated the Democrat planters whom they considered responsible for the war and who they now saw restored to power with exactly the same attitudes as before. The Radicals had fought to free the Negroes. One of them said: 'We must see to it that . . . [the Negro] can go where he pleases, work when and for whom he pleases, that he can sue and be sued; that he can lease and buy and sell and own property real and personal; that he can go into the schools and educate himself and his children; that

THE UNION AS IT WAS.

THIS IS A WHITE MANS GOVERNMENT

THE LOST CAUSE

WORSE THAN SLAVERY.

WHITE LEAGUE

K.K.K.

SCHOOL HOUSE.

the rights and the guarantees of the . . . common law are his, and that he walks the earth proud and erect in the conscious dignity of a free man.'

The North and West had won the war and did not want to lose the peace. When many of the Southern states refused to accept the 14th Amendment to the Constitution recognising Negroes as citizens, the Radicals were able to win the support of the majority in Congress and impose reforms on the South.

The Radicals realised the Negroes would need help to benefit fully from emancipation. Already in 1865 the Freedman's Bureau had been set up to help all the poor in the Southern states. It provided food, clothing and medical care, organised the settlement of abandoned land, provided schools and helped in negotiations with landowners. It issued over 15 million rations and spent 5 million dollars on schools. It drew up labour contracts to protect the Negro and saw that they were enforced, even setting up special courts if necessary to try disputes.

If the Negroes were to vote as they really felt and if they were to receive equal

Restoration of whit power by terrorism

justice in the courts their livelihood would have to be free from planters' control. The Radicals wanted to redistribute planters' lands to the Negroes. How would this help? Unfortunately, Congress would not allow any interference with private property.

But Negroes could at least be legally protected and reactionary Southern governments be destroyed. In 1866 the 14th Amendment and the Civil Rights Act declared that all Negroes were citizens with the same rights as whites in the courts. In the next four years all the Southern governments were abolished and new ones formed which were elected by all citizens including Negroes but excluding the unrepentant white leaders. This right of all citizens to vote was made part of the Constitution by the 15th Amendment in 1869. The new governments had to accept both these amendments.

The failure of the Radicals. The Democrats still believed they were the rightful rulers of the South. They were enraged by the fact of Radical rule and by Negro independence; in particular, by the sight of former slaves in political positions they thought were rightfully theirs. To justify their own attitudes they deliberately built up a false picture of Reconstruction, accusing the Radicals of gross dishonesty and incompetence. The Democrats coined the words 'carpetbagger' and 'scalawag' to discredit Northern Radicals and their Southern allies, the former to describe a Northerner said to have come to the South to 'get rich quick' by dishonest means, the latter a Southerner who helped the 'carpetbagger'. For example, one carpetbagger in Louisiana was accused of embezzling 100,000 dollars from state funds in his first year of office. In Mississippi it was alleged that the state debt was increased by 20 million dollars through extravagant investment. In fact the debt was only half a million dollars.

The Democrats also accused the Radicals of using the Negro vote to keep themselves in power. This was ridiculous since the Negroes obviously voted for the party which wanted to help them. This Democrat fear of Negro votes was not justified by events. Where Negroes were influential they acted only to secure their own independence, not to take revenge on the whites.

Corruption did exist. After the war businessmen tried to win contracts for themselves by bribing Southern politicians. On the other hand the bribery of politicians was common practice, in the North and West as well as the South. We shall say more about this in Chapter 10.

Yet Radicals were not all self-seeking. Many had fought for emancipation long before there was any hope of gain from it. A large amount of investment, and therefore debt, was essential if the Southern economy was to be reshaped. Much money was spent building schools and caring for the sick and handicapped. But expenditure on industry and railways was not enough. The Southern economy was not reshaped and the Negroes did not gain economic independence.

Between 1870 and 1877 the Republican governments were driven out. Negroes were left without help in defending themselves. Democrat propaganda was very successful. The Radicals were inexperienced in government and some were corrupt. Appalled by the real and imaginary mistakes and dishonesty of Radical government the moderates withdrew their support. This support was weakening anyway as memories of the war and its purpose faded. The poor whites had gained by Radical rule. They had received help from the Freedman's Bureau and in South Carolina, for example, they had gained the vote. But since the Negroes were now equal in the courts and in elections the poor whites could no longer feel themselves superior in social status. Thus, the Democrats were able to unite the South against the Radicals. The Radicals were disillusioned by the practical difficulties of government and the slowness with which the Negroes adjusted to their new conditions. They had always been a minority which had to fight for recognition and once their main aims appeared to be achieved, they lost majority support.

The Suppression of the Negro

The Democrat victory. When they returned to power the Southern Democrats were cautious. They feared the North might still interfere. Nevertheless, they could exploit the fact that most Negroes had not been given land of their own. The planters agreed amongst themselves the wages of Negro labour and refused to re-employ any person who left his job. Negro farmers had to renew their land leases each year. All voting was in public and the Negro had to be careful to vote for the Southern Democrats— the party of his landowner or employer. Independent political action by the Negro was stifled from the beginning.

The Negro was made even further dependent when planters set up their own stores for supplying tools, grain, food and fertilizer. Most of the Negroes had to buy on credit and once they were in debt, since they were ignorant of figures, it was very easy to charge sufficient to keep them in debt permanently.

The law was enforced harshly. In Mississippi it was possible to be given five years on convict lease for stealing ten dollars. This was a profitable system. Convicts were leased out as cheap labour and the state was saved the expense of imprisoning them. There were usually no laws governing the hours and conditions of work and the death rate was sometimes as high as one in four persons per year. When Negroes did try to protest there were less subtle ways of dissuading them. Some were mutilated, beaten or driven out of the state by secret societies like the Ku-Klux-Klan. Between 1882 and 1901 there was an average of 150 lynchings a year in the Southern states.

Between the 1880s and the First World War the position of the Negro deteriorated badly. First he lost the right to vote. In 1890 Mississippi rewrote her voting qualifications so as to disqualify Negroes almost completely and between 1895 and 1910 the other Southern states followed suit. They showed ingenious methods of preventing Negroes voting. Only those who paid a poll-tax (a tax on voters) could vote—the Negro could not afford it and even when he could the sheriff often refused to accept it. Voters had to be able to read and to explain a given section of the State constitution but the registrar was given very wide powers to decide whether a voter really 'understood' the clause; another trick was only to allow those to vote whose grandfathers had been able to in 1865 and this automatically excluded most of the Negroes. The results in the state of Louisiana, for example, are below:

	Before 1898	*After 1898*
black voters	130,344	5,320
white voters	164,088	125,437

Once the Negro was deprived of the vote it was easy to pass laws enforcing rigid segregation in practically all public facilities—in schools, on buses and trains, in public parks, cafés, wash-rooms, theatres, swimming baths and even in cemeteries. These were the so-called Jim Crow Laws.

Some reasons for the Southern reaction. These laws were made by the rich landowning Southern Democrats with the support of the poor whites. A main reason for their action was the agricultural depression which swept through America in the 1880s and 1890s. As cotton and corn prices tumbled, the small farmers' debts rose, bankruptcies increased, and more and more people became tenants rather than landowners. The small farmers of the South allied themselves with the Populist Party, protesting about the rich capitalists who were ruining their lives. For a time there was a possibility that these southern Populists would win the votes of the Negro sharecroppers and farm labourers. (Sharecroppers were tenant farmers who worked for the landowners in return for one-third of the crop.) This possibility caused great alarm to the rich landowners who thus took steps to win over the poor whites and suppress the Negroes. This was not too difficult. The poor whites and the Negroes were competitors for jobs, made scarcer by the depression. The Southern Democrats blamed the Negroes for forcing down wages and depriving the white men of jobs. Deep inside, the poor white regarded the Negro as inferior anyway and resented his competition. Thus the agricultural depression and Populism threw the rich and poor whites together. The Negro became the scapegoat for their troubles and the Southern Democrats then deprived him of the vote and enacted the Jim Crow Laws to ensure that he would not threaten them in the future.

In one very real sense these steps taken against the Negro resulted from the failures of Reconstruction. After the destruction of the Civil War and the emancipation of the Negro the South's economy needed rebuilding and reshaping. It required a massive amount of Federal expenditure to drain lands, equip farms, build transport networks, erect factories and stimulate trade. These things would have provided both work and income for the Negro which he needed for his economic and social improvement. Yet the North was unwilling to make such vast investments. This was the age of private, not government, enterprise. Thus the South remained a relatively backward agricultural region prone to depressions. At such times conflicts between whites and Negroes would inevitably increase as they competed for land and jobs. To minimise friction it was therefore in the whites' own interests to relegate the Negro to a distinctly inferior position, politically, economically and socially.

The North failed to interfere for a wide variety of reasons. It had never really been interested in Negro equality. Most Northerners felt that once the Negro was freed, it was up to him to fight for himself. This was the great era of private enterprise and self-made men like Rockefeller and Carnegie. If the Negro could not maintain or improve his status then that reflected his inferiority. This feeling was increased as Negroes moved into northern cities where they crowded into slums, took the poorest jobs, and became associated with crime, gambling and violence. Even the Supreme Court encouraged the Southern Democrats. It upheld the 'grandfather' and 'literacy' tests and in 1883 refused to recognise a Civil Rights Act of 1875. In 1896 it allowed states to enforce segregation, provided that the facilities for each race were of equal quality. In practice this idea of 'separate but equal' turned out to be only half-true—the separation was real enough but equality was not achieved. The Supreme Court recognised this in its 1954 decision. (see Chapter 12).

After the Civil War the attention of America was occupied by the last phase of westward expansion, the rise of big business and vast manufacturing cities with their immigrant populations. The Negro cause was neglected. But racial tension did not disappear. In the twentieth century it has become America's greatest domestic problem.

Further Reading

Allt, A. H., *The American Civil War*, Longman 'Then and There' Series.
Cammiade, Audrey, *Lincoln and the American Civil War*, Methuen, 1967.
Catton, Bruce, *The Penguin Book of the American Civil War*, Penguin, 1966.
Commager, H. S., (ed.) *The Blue and the Grey*, 2 vols., Bobs Merrill, 1950.
Miers, Earl Schenck, *The American Civil War*, Golden Press, 1961.
Strong, Robert Hale, *A Yankee Private's Civil War*, Henry Regnery Co., 1961.

Fiction

Crane, S., *The Red Badge of Courage*, Hutchinson Educational (Unicorn Books), 1960.

8 THE LAST FRONTIER

By about 1860 little trace remained of the great forest wilderness of the east. The vast prairie lands of the Louisiana Purchase, however, remained unsettled by the white man. It was known as the 'Great American Desert', a region unfit for cultivation and suitable only for the Indians and the animals they hunted.

The Great American Desert

The problems of settlement. Why were the prairies called a desert? Why were settlers slow to occupy them? To answer these questions we must remember that down to 1860 the wilderness to be conquered was one of forest. Since Jamestown settlers in America had developed their knowledge, skills, seeds, tools and general equipment to create farms out of forests. They took for granted an abundance of water and timber, a long growing season and a deep rich soil which was easy to plough. While their first crops grew they relied on the forest for game. Produce went to market along rivers, lakes and canals.

The prairies were quite different. Here, the settler faced droughts, a shorter growing season, tough grass with thick matted roots, strong winds which blew away the top soil, exposure and vast distances. Serious fuel and building problems arose from the absence of timber. The transport problem seemed insoluble. The rivers were difficult or impossible to navigate. Canal building was out of the question. Frequent thunderstorms quickly turned dirt roads into bogs. Even hunting was a problem. The buffalo were not in large numbers in the lower plains and killing them required new hunting techniques and much time.

Given these difficulties it is no wonder that the settlers hesitated to cross the Missouri and live on the prairies. Axes, saws, hammers, cast-iron ploughs, wagons and steamboats would be of little use. They needed new techniques and seeds to farm the dry lands and cope with the shorter growing season. Solutions to the problems of building and fuel had to be found. Most fundamental of all, a new form of transport was required before people would venture onto the prairies.

Transcontinental Railways

The coming of the railways. By the 1860s a new form of transport was at hand. Like most settlers before 1860, the railways also stopped at the Mississippi and Missouri rivers. Yet afterwards it was the extension of the railways west as far as the Pacific coast which was the most important single reason for the settlement of the prairies. We cannot stress the significance of railways enough. Nearly everything in the rest of this chapter was the result of railway building on the plains.

Building a railway across the prairies to the Pacific was not easy. There were formidable engineering, financial and economic problems to be solved. Tracks had to be built through the Rockies, an enormous amount of land was needed, and since few people lived in the mountains and prairies a railway company would begin by running at a loss. And who would invest money in a company making a loss? The lack of money was the basic difficulty. It was needed for land, building, rolling stock, wages and salaries, and to subsidise

A good illustration showing a wagon supply train, a construction train, soldier detachment and Indian scouts. Usually, soldiers we not present. The railway gangs had t fight their own batt against the Indians.

the trains until freight and passenger traffic were enough to cover costs. This problem was solved finally by the Federal government which made huge grants of free land and gave large sums of money, between 16,000 dollars and 48,000 dollars per mile, according to the degree of difficulty of construction, to help the companies succeed.

N.B. Federal land grants to the Union Pacific and Central Pacific Railways, for example, took the form of alternate townships on either side of the track.

The Union Pacific Railway Company. The first railway to be built across the prairies was the Union Pacific Railway Company. This was authorised by Congress in 1862, but construction did not begin in earnest until 1866. By then the Civil War was over, the Federal government had more money to spare and demobilised soldiers provided a good source of labour to build the railway.

It has been said that the building of this railway was one of the most rugged undertakings in American economic history. Building materials, equipment and food were brought hundreds of miles by the company. Its men lived in tent cities in very primitive conditions. The prairie Indians were hostile. Construction was done in 100-mile stages. Each stage was graded and the bridges, embankments and cuttings built before any track was laid. On the prairies about seven miles of track were laid each day.

Rivalry with the Central Pacific Company. While the Union Pacific was building westwards the Central Pacific Railway Company was advancing from San Francisco to meet it. The Central Pacific was no easy undertaking either. The Sierra Nevadas presented a formidable building obstacle. Nevertheless, a daily average of three miles a day was made by its

Chinese and Irish labourers. Between these two companies there was an intense rivalry. As they neared each other the competing crews laid their tracks faster and faster. Then an amazing thing happened. The tracks of the two companies did not join. Instead, the two crews passed each other going in opposite directions. Both companies wanted to claim as much land and money as possible from the Federal government. The government was forced to step in and decree a meeting place at Promontory Point in Utah. In May 1869 the two companies joined their tracks. America had its first transcontinental railway.

Other railways. Other railways soon appeared on the prairies. Map 25 shows their positions. The Federal government continued its grants of money and land to help to build railways in the west. Down to the late 1880s the Federal government gave 155 million acres of public land to railway companies. By 1893 six companies had tracks connecting the Mississippi with the Rockies and the Pacific coast.

Cattle Trails and Cowboys

Railways, cattlemen and cattle towns. As the railways penetrated across the prairies they attracted the attention of cattlemen who saw new prospects for trade and profit. In Texas were three million or more lean and hardy long-horned cattle descended from the animals brought by the Spaniards in the sixteenth century. Hitherto they had been left to roam wild on the southern prairies. Now, if they could be rounded up, driven 500 miles north to the railroads and railed to the rapidly growing towns of the Mid-west and the East, they would

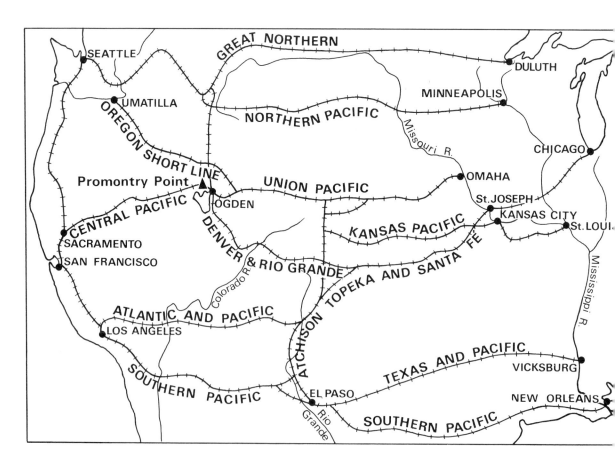

bring high prices and good profits to the cattlemen. Cattle rounded up in Texas could be bought there for four to five dollars a head. To drive a herd of 2500 cattle to the railheads only cost about one dollar a mile. This covered wages and the cost of food and general supplies needed on the trail. The prairies provided free grass for the animals to eat. Stockmen at the railheads bought cattle between twenty and thirty dollars a head. You can calculate for yourself the approximate amount of profit a cattleman could expect to receive.

The first railhead was at Abilene. Its citizens had no objections to dust, smelly cattle or high spirited cowboys. A stock-buyer, Joseph McCoy, persuaded the Kansas Pacific Railway Company to build a spur to Abilene. He sent timber there and built stout cattle pens, offices, a barn and a three-storey hotel called the Drover's Cottage. Texas was pleased. In 1867 36,000 cattle were driven from Fort Worth along the Chisholm Trail to Abilene. In 1868 the number was 160,000, and nearly double this in 1870. Abilene now had three more hotels, ten saloons and ten boarding houses. However, new cattle towns soon sprang up to the west of Abilene. As the farmers ventured onto the prairies their farms blocked the cattle trails. The cattlemen, who were using the prairies without any payment to the Federal government, were forced to move their cattle trails and cattle towns further and further west. After Abilene came Newton, Ellsworth, Dodge City and others. Dodge became the queen of the cattle towns between 1875 and 1885. In this decade about a quarter of a million cattle were sent from Texas to Dodge and then by rail to the slaughter yards at Chicago and Kansas City. Map 26 shows some of the famous cattle trails, cattle towns and railways of the prairies. Between 1866 and 1886 about six million cattle passed along these trails to the cattle towns.

*ap 25 Railways
est of the
ississippi

*or a while
*ichita had the
*eputation as 'the
*ildest and
*ickedest place in the
est'.

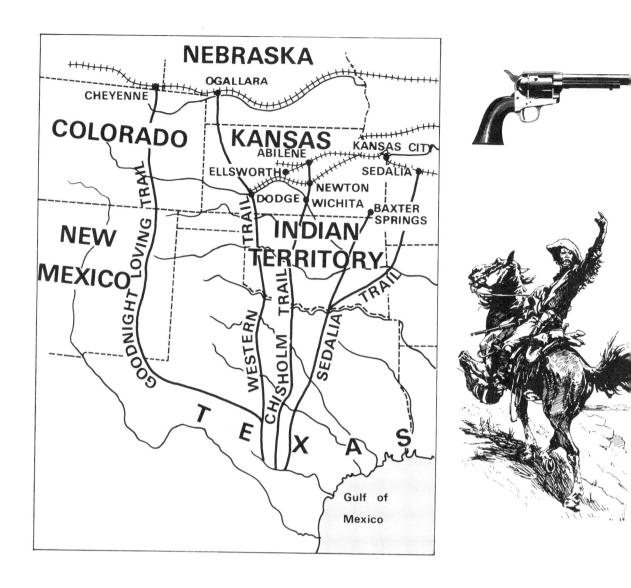

Map 26 Cattle trail North

The cowboys. The men responsible for driving the cattle northwards were the cowboys, most of whom were demobbed Confederate soldiers who had drifted west after the war. The trail drive was the climax of a year's work of riding the range, tending sick animals, round-ups and branding. Like all the cowboy's work the cattle drive was hard, dirty and tiring. The worst position was at the back of the herd, working to keep the stragglers or 'drags' close to the main herd. Teddy 'Blue' Abbot, a trail cowboy, wrote:

'The poorest men always worked with the drags, because a good hand wouldn't stand for it. I have seen them come off herd with the dust half an inch deep on their hats and thick as fur in their eyebrows and mustaches, and if they shook their head or you tapped their cheek, it would fall off them in showers. That dust was the reason a good man wouldn't work back there, and if they hired out to a trail outfit and were put with the drags, they would go to the boss and ask for their time. But the rest of them were pretty nearly as bad off when they were on the side away from the wind. They would go to the water barrel at the end of the day and rinse their mouths and cough and spit and bring up that black stuff out of their throats. But you couldn't get it up out of your lungs.'

Teddy Blue believed the worst hardship on the trail was the lack of sleep. Cowboys often rubbed tobacco juice in their eyes to keep awake. It burned their eyes like fire.

Once at the end of the trail drive the cowboys forgot their tiredness and their hardships. They announced their arrival in town by riding hard along the main street, firing their pistols and yelling Confederate cries. The sleepy town was transformed for a while into a busy and noisy place where the cowboys spent their wages on drinks, cards and women, played pranks on the town citizens and annoyed the sheriff. Sometimes events got out of hand. People were beaten up or killed. Property was badly damaged. The offenders were gaoled or beat a hasty retreat to the open ranges. Most cowboys, however, were not a serious menace. Guns were a necessary part of their life. They used them to stop the charge of a maddened steer, to turn a stampede, to kill rattlesnakes and to defend themselves against rustlers and Indians. Nevertheless, most cowboys were not gunmen and killers.

The real menace came from rustlers, thieves, bank robbers and hired killers—the bad men of the west. Perhaps you can guess why the cattle towns far out on the prairies attracted them? No wonder the citizens of those towns hired men good with guns to act as their peace officers. Abilene's most famous officer was Wild Bill Hickok; Dodge City's was Wyatt Earp. Such men generally were hard fighters and accurate marksmen and they earned the respect of most troublemakers. But books and films have exaggerated their reputations and importance. They were not usually virtuous men. Many gambled in the saloons. Some took bribes. A few even forsook the law and became badmen themselves because it was more profitable. They were never great in number and many towns had to appoint vigilante committees—groups of men who took the law into their own hands—to protect their fellow citizens.

The rise of cattle ranching. Cattle drives and cattle towns were a very temporary feature of the west. The last big drives northwards occurred in 1886. By 1895 they were no more. The main reason for this has been suggested already. Railways across the prairies brought not only the cattlemen but settlers too. As the settlers moved west their farms increasingly blocked the cattle trails. Teddy 'Blue' Abbot himself complained:

'There is no love lost lost between settlers and cowboys on the trail. Those jayhawkers would take up a claim right where the herds watered and charge us for water. They would plant a crop alongside the trail and plow a furrow around it for a fence, and then when the cattle got into their wheat or their garden patch, they would come out cussing and waving a shotgun and yelling for damages. And the cattle had been coming through there when they were still raising punkins in Illinois.'

Not surprisingly the relations between cattlemen, cowboys and settlers were bitter. The settler had a different opinion to the cowboy of course, and you will see this when you read the next section. Inevitably though, the cattlemen and cowboys were forced westwards until there was no more open range left for cattlemen and cowboys to use.

Cattle ranches began to appear in the west of Kansas and Nebraska and in Montana, Wyoming and Colorado in the 1870s. They were encouraged by the boom in beef prices. Many of them were financed by speculators in the east and in Europe who hoped to make large and quick profits from the rising demand for beef. For example, between 1870 and 1890 thirty-seven cattle ranches valued at 34 million dollars were financed by British money—an indication that the Atlantic partnership still persisted. Some of these ranches each covered hundreds of thousands of acres. The land was gained in a variety of ways. It could be bought from the railway companies. Cowboys could be persuaded to claim quarter-sections of land under the Homestead Act and then hand them over to their employers. Sometimes ranchers simply fenced off huge areas of prairie and kept other people out: i.e. they stole part of the public lands. The biggest ranch was the Capitol Freehold Company which in return for the promise to build a state capital received over three million acres of Texas range. The fences enclosing this land were 1500 miles long.

These ranches developed new breeds of cattle. The small, lean Texas longhorn was bred with Shorthorns, Herefords and Galloway cattle to make them yield more meat. The new breeds were less hardy and needed more attention. Water supplies were important. There was much fierce competition for land with running streams. Deep wells were dug. Hay was grown and the cattle fattened on it. When the animals were ready for market they were railed from the ranch. The cowboy's life came to involve fence building and repairs, ditch digging, barn building, mowing and stacking hay, and watering and feeding animals as well as round-ups and branding.

One of the very real dangers of the cowboy's life and the reason why he chose his cow ponies with great care.

The cattle boom collapsed in the 1880s, exports to Europe fell by 50 per cent as America felt the competition from Argentina and Australia. An industrial slump at home and two cold winters which killed thousands of cattle made the crisis worse. Many ranchers went bankrupt but ranching as an industry on the western plains survived. Today it is an important activity of the Mid-West.

The Settlers

On the open plains. Settlers ventured on to the prairies even before the railway companies started to build there. The early farmers kept close to the tree-lined streams but those who came later were forced to settle on the open plains. There they began their new existence in dugouts or sod houses, using dung, sunflowers and straw as fuel, drawing their water from hand-dug wells twenty to thirty feet deep, and ploughing the land with ox-teams and *steel* ploughs. The dugouts were made by digging into the hillsides or banks. They were reasonably dry and storm-proof and kept cool in summer and warm in winter. But dirt continuously fell from the roof. Animals, snakes and birds tunnelled into the walls and roof. Cattle sometimes unwittingly wandered onto the roof and crashed down into the house. Dugouts were unpleasant and Americans soon had the idea of building houses from turf. Sod houses were built from blocks of turf about 15–20 inches long, 12–15 inches wide and 2–4 inches thick. They were laid like bricks, the spaces between being plugged with loose soil. The roof was supported by timber which also composed the window frames and doors. The settlers often travelled long distances searching for

113

suitable timber for these purposes. Sod houses were lighter and better ventilated than dugouts. Inside they were often plastered with a mixture of sand and clay. When dry it was whitewashed and the interior was more pleasant to live in. Nevertheless, dirt and dust filtered through and heavy rain storms could ruin walls and roof and cause their collapse.

The Homestead Act. One factor which explains this migration to the plains was the passing of a new land law—the Homestead Act 1862. This said that all American adults who had not borne arms against the government could claim a quarter-section of 160 acres for settlement and cultivation. After five years of occupation and farming the settler could claim a certificate of ownership on the payment of thirty dollars—a small fee to cover administrative costs. In other words, public land was now virtually free. However, those settlers who could afford to buy the land at one and a quarter dollars per acre received their certificate after only six months.

Free land for settlers had long been discussed. Even the Founding Fathers had not agreed about it. You will remember it was one of the matters which Jefferson and Hamilton disagreed about. The Homestead Act was a victory for those who, like Thomas Jefferson, believed America's destiny to be a country of small, free and independent farmers. Hamilton's objections to such an act had slowly lost their force during the nineteenth century as immigrants continued to flood into America and as American industries developed. Immigrants supplied the labour the eastern states wanted. Growing industries required markets and the expanding west meant a rising demand for simple manufactured goods. Free land would encourage this expansion still further. There was also another important influence too. Land laws had always been a source of dispute between the North and the South. The South opposed the idea of free land. Can you think why? In 1860 it had successfully blocked a Bill in Congress to make land free. The outbreak of the Civil War gave the North a chance to make such a law.

Unfortunately the Homestead Act did not greatly benefit the settler. Most of the prairies were much too far from the railways to be of any use to him. Also, a section of land proved to be too small for prairie farming. We shall return to this point later. In fact, the lands were taken by land speculators who obtained land to sell later at a higher price.

The influence of the railways. The biggest speculators were the railway companies. They owned 155 million acres of land given to them by the government. To make their lines pay these companies had to encourage hundreds of thousands of settlers to live on their prairie lands. Huge advertising campaigns were undertaken by them in the East and in Europe. Largely due to their efforts the prairies were settled and developed. Midwesterners, New Englanders, Englishmen, Swedes, Germans and Norwegians were crowded into special steamships and trains and carried across the Atlantic, the Appalachians and the Ohio and Mississippi valleys to the western plains.

The importance of the railways was not simply that they brought settlers to the prairies. They also sustained them once they were there. The railways carried food, clothing, furniture and timber for barns and houses. Stout wooden houses replaced the sod houses within a generation. New seeds and tools and implements were also carried: steel ploughs, barbed wire, drills, windmills, mechanical reapers and binders, and steam traction engines—the products of American experiments and ingenuity.

Note the fundamental importance of these things. They were the signs that American farmers were adapting themselves to the new environment. For example, wheat seeds more resistant to drought and faster growing than before helped settlers to grow spring wheat not only further west but northwards into the Dakotas too. The steel ploughs turned the tough prairie more deeply and easily. Barbed wire solved a serious fencing

Compare this with earlier modes of westward movement

114

problem. It not only kept animals from trampling down crops but separated the cattle themselves and permitted scientific breeding. The drills and windmills partly solved the water problem. Drilling crews toured the prairies making wells several hundred feet deep. The windmills raised the water to the surface and distributed it round the farms. Mechanical reapers and binders and steam traction engines all saved labour which was scarce and costly on the prairie farm. They also greatly increased the acreage one man could farm. A man with a sickle and flail could harvest seven and a half acres of wheat. One with a mechanical reaper could cope with 100 acres. Thus, these things collectively helped to increase the acreage under cultivation and thus total output. Between 1866 and 1898 the cultivated area on the prairie rose from 15 to 44 million acres and the output of wheat rose from 152 to 675 million bushels. The markets for this wheat were in the East and Europe. The farmers' link with them was by the railways. Clearly, then, the railways were of tremendous importance to the settlement of the prairies.

Table 7. Growth of Population on the Prairies, 1860–1900

State	Statehood	Population in thousands				
		1860	1870	1880	1890	1900
Minnesota	1858	172	440	781	1310	1751
Kansas	1861	107	364	996	1428	1470
Nebraska	1867	29	123	452	1063	1066
Colorado	1876	34	40	194	413	540
South Dakota	1889	5	12	98	349	402
North Dakota	1889	5	2	37	191	319
Montana	1889	21	21	39	143	243
Wyoming	1890		9	21	63	93

Some states had a high proportion of foreigners. In 1890, for example, 45 per cent of the people in North Dakota came from overseas. In Montana the figure was 33 per cent; in South Dakota 28 per cent, and in Wyoming 25 per cent. Table 7 shows you the main direction of movement. Notice that the states which had the most rainfall and the longest growing season attracted most people. The peopling of Colorado, Montana and Wyoming was mainly due to mining and ranching.

The golden West. People moving west continued as always to think of the wilderness before them as the land of promise and opportunity. They agreed that life at first would be a struggle. But given health, strength, hard work, self-reliance and a share of good luck they expected to succeed, to build a new home and life for themselves and to be happy. In the 1880s an English traveller on the prairies wrote:

'To have an immense production of exchangeable commodities, to force from nature the most she can be made to yield, and to send it east and west by the cheapest routes to the nearest markets making one's city a centre of trade and raising the price of its real estate—this ... is preached by western newspapers as a kind of religion. These people ... see all around them railways being built, telegraph wires laid, steamboat lines across the Pacific, projected cities springing up in the solitudes, and settlers making the wilderness blossom like a rose. Their imagination revels in these sights and sounds of progress, and they gild their own struggles for fortune with the belief that they are the missionaries of civilisation and the instruments of Providence in the greatest work the world has ever seen.'

The problems of prairie life. Unfortunately, the West was not so golden as it was painted. Like the settlers of the lands east of the Mississippi those of the prairies faced many problems not mentioned in the advertisements of the railway companies and the writings of travellers. Few people made their lives a real success story. Most experienced setbacks and only slowly increased their wealth and position. Some people failed completely to overcome their problems and lost their money and their hope. They returned east bitter and disillusioned.

We have mentioned the physical problems of the prairies—including drought, winds, blizzards, insect pests—at the beginning of this chapter. There were also economic and social problems. A basic economic problem was the size of the farm. The Homestead Act was based on the experience of farming in the forested areas. It assumed that 160 acres of land was enough to sustain the smaller settler and his family. This was not so. Parts of the prairies were so dry that it required from eight to thirty acres to graze just one cow. Crop yields per acre were lower in the West than the East for the same reason. Crops paid better than animals but to make farming profitable more land and machinery was needed. These cost money which was difficult to earn. Wheat, maize and cotton prices were forced down as more and more farmers began production. The costs of ploughs, harvesters, barbed wire, storage space in grain elevators and rail transport all seemed high to the settler, who complained bitterly about them. He felt himself to be the victim of greedy businessmen out to make big profits at his expense. The only way he could increase the size of his farm and his machinery was to borrow more money at higher rates of interest. Yet all this made his prosperity and independence harder to obtain.

Socially, life on the prairies followed much the same pattern as it had done earlier in the Ohio Valley. People did their best to attend square dances, suppers and church meetings. Drinking, gambling and fighting were common pursuits when men got together. Often, however, farms were not near to the towns. Small market towns were far fewer in the west than further east. The railways meant that buying and selling were no longer done locally but hundreds of miles away in Chicago, Minneapolis, Omaha, Kansas City, or St Louis. Here were the great flour mills, slaughter houses, refrigeration and canning factories. Here, too, many other foods were processed, canned and packeted, clothes made and machines manufactured. These items were all advertised by travelling salesmen and catalogues, ordered by post and telegraph and delivered by rail. The local miller, grocer, butcher, baker, blacksmith and mechanic were no longer needed. All this made farm life more monotonous and lonely. The settler saw few people from one month to the next.

All these problems—physical, economic and social—were to cause very loud protests by the prairie farmers. We shall return to consider this in chapter 10.

The Indians' Last Stand

The Indians' case. The settlement of the prairies made the Indians angry and hostile. Let us try to see their point of view. Before 1860 the Americans had regarded the prairies as a great desert: a land suited only to Indians and wild animals. Within that area the only white men would be Indian agents, army patrols and trappers licensed to hunt and trade for furs. Almost immediately, however, American settlers and miners began to cross Indian Territory on their way to the west coast and the mountains. The Indians were irritated. The American government and its army made no attempt to stop this movement. The miners, in particular, hunted the buffalo on which the Indians depended for their survival. But even more serious, in the 1850s settlers began to build farms on the prairies. The whites were changing their opinion of prairie land. The Indians were asked by the Federal government to sign treaties promising not to attack white men and to give up their claims to part of their hunting grounds to permit the whites to settle there. This was merely the beginning. Soon, railway companies wished to build across the prairies and railways meant more settlers. The Indians were asked to sign even more treaties. Their resentment against the white man grew. The American government was not keeping its promises. It helped and protected the whites but not the Indians.

The most important single reason for the growing resentment of the Indians was railway building across the prairies. The railways brought the destruction of their way of life. In 1840 there were perhaps forty million buffalo roaming the prairies. By 1890 only about a thousand remained. Railway construction crews and miners began the mass slaughter. It was continued with far greater vigour by trainloads of wealthy westerners and Europeans who shot the animals to satisfy their sporting instinct and by professional hunters who sought profits from buffalo hides. Armed with heavy calibre repeating rifles a good marksman could slaughter 100 animals in one stand. A hunter named Tom Nixon was said to have killed 120 buffalo in forty minutes. In thirty-five days he killed 2173. William Cody is another example. Employed by the Kansas Pacific Railway Co. to supply meat to the construction crews he killed 4280 animals in seventeen months. He earned the nickname of 'Buffalo Bill'. This near extinction of the buffalo is the greatest animal slaughter the world has ever seen. With its disappearance the Indian tribes could no longer support themselves. Many more Indians died of disease and starvation than the 5519 killed in battles with the U.S. Army between 1865 and 1890.

The Americans felt differently about the prairies. They had bought the land in 1803. The West offered them wealth and opportunity. The railway companies, miners and settlers had little sympathy for the prairie Indians. They expected the Indians to stand aside, abandon their nomadic life and settle down on reservations as small farmers.

Inevitably, conflicts between whites and Indians arose. The army was used increasingly to protect the whites and subdue the Indians. To make its job easier the army encouraged the slaughter of the buffalo. This embittered the Indians even more.

The anger of the Teton Sioux. Against this general background let us now study the fortunes

118

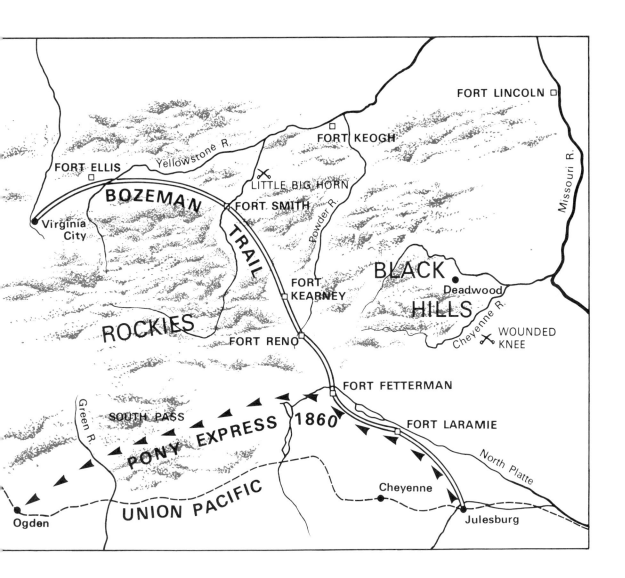

of the Teton Sioux who by this time numbered about 10,000 people spread across the northern plains. Well before 1860 they had gained horses and guns and had become the most powerful of the prairie Indians.

In 1863 miners opened the Bozeman Trail to carry supplies from Julesburg on the South Platte River to Virginia City in the Montana goldfields. This trail passed through the valleys of the Yellowstone River and its tributaries—the heart of the Sioux hunting grounds. About the same time the Union Pacific Railway Company began to build across Nebraska, their southern hunting grounds. Map 27 shows these developments and it will help you to follow the story below.

Red Cloud, the most important Sioux chief, resented these intrusions. He objected particularly to the Bozeman Trail and demanded its closure. During the next few years travel along the trail became very unsafe. The Sioux attacked miners, settlers, soldiers and the forts they built.

The American government was in a quandary. The Sioux were a serious menace to life

and property. To defeat them would require many more soldiers and supplies in the West. *Sitting Bull*
Somehow the Sioux had to be confined to a reservation. In 1869 General Grant became
President. He decided to invite the Sioux chiefs to Washington. Red Cloud agreed to
peace only if the whites left the Yellowstone and closed down the Bozeman Trail and its
forts. Grant agreed to these terms. In return Red Cloud and the chiefs with him agreed
to leave Nebraska, to allow the creation of a reservation in South Dakota west of the
Missouri River and to a four-year period during which they were to be fed and trained
for a farming way of life by the Indian agents. Do you think Red Cloud was wise to accept
these terms? Discuss it with the class. Whether the Sioux nation as a whole would accept
the treaty was another matter, of course. Remember that chiefs spoke for themselves.
Their warriors were not bound to support them.

In fact the treaty did not work very well. Many warriors agreed with Red Cloud.
They felt their numbers were too small and their traditional hunting grounds too extensive
to defend them against the flood of white men with their railways and guns. Many more
did not agree. They followed Crazy Horse and Sitting Bull who refused to surrender to

120

the white man. Food was short on the reservation. During the hunting season even the friendly Indians left the agencies and roamed far to the west. It became difficult to know which Indians were friendly and which were not. The peace which followed the treaty was an uneasy one.

Then in 1874 gold was discovered in the Black Hills by members of an army scouting expedition under George Custer. Within a year there was a wild rush of miners to South Dakota who ignored the fact that the Black Hills were part of the lands given to the Sioux in the treaty of 1868. In 1875 the richest strike was made in Deadwood Gulch and by the summer of 1876 Deadwood was a city of 25,000 miners, thieves, gamblers and murderers. The Indians were insulted and some were killed. Miners offered 200 dollars per scalp. To the Federal Government the only solution seemed to be to confine the Sioux strictly within their reservation. In December 1875 an order was issued that all Indians who were not on the reservation by 31 January would be considered hostile. Some did as they were told: some never heard the order. Others, like Crazy Horse and Sitting Bull, prepared for war. In alliance with them were the Cheyenne.

Custer and the Battle of the Little Big Horn. The army was now told to enforce this order. The hostile Sioux were reported to be in the region of the Yellowstone. It was rugged terrain and the Indians would be hard to find. Three army columns were sent to the area. They were to meet at the mouth of the Powder River. The first column, under General Crook, moved north from Fort Fetterman. It twice engaged Crazy Horse and his warriors but failed to defeat them. Crook was forced to return to his base and he took no further part in the campaign. The other two columns met as planned. One under General Terry, had moved west from Fort Abraham Lincoln. The other, under Colonel Gibbon, had come from east Montana. At the rendezvous scouts reported Indian trails along the Powder River. Terry decided to send 400 infantry under Gibbon up the Big Horn River, and the much faster moving 7th Cavalry under George Custer up the Powder River. Custer was told to assess the direction of the Indian trail and if it went up the Little Big Horn to swing south to the Tongue River and then advance northwards to meet Gibbon who would cut off the Indians' retreat if they were camped in the Little Big Horn valley. The Sioux would be caught between the two army forces.

Custer was thirty-seven years old at this time. He was known to the Indians who called him Yellow Hair. The 7th Cavalry had been trained by Custer himself, who thought it could outfight any band of Indians. Custer was an ambitious man. Recently his reputation had suffered a blow when evidence he gave about greedy Indian agents had involved President Grant's relatives and friends. Afterwards he said: 'I am going to clear my name or leave my bones on the prairie.'

It is known that Custer pushed his men very hard up the Powder River valley. His scouts reported an Indian encampment in the valley of the Little Big Horn. No one knew how many warriors it contained. Custer did know he had been spotted by an Indian lookout. He decided to make a frontal attack. He split his men into three groups. One company under Captain Benteen was sent to the left to scout the ridges. Another under Major Reno was sent forward. Custer led the third group along the right of the valley. Reno met fierce resistance and was forced across the river to high barren ground where he was pinned down for the next day. Later he was reinforced by Benteen's company and together they fought off the Indians. Meanwhile, Custer pushed ahead to the top of a ridge overlooking the Indian camp. There he was charged by Sioux and Cheyenne warriors led by Crazy Horse and other war chiefs. Custer and his 225 men were all killed.

Since that battle in 1876 people have argued endlessly about it. Some say Custer was a hero. Others say he disobeyed the orders, acted foolishly and rashly, disregarded the safety of his own men and sought glory for himself. His defenders say Terry did not give clear instructions. Read this account again and give your opinion.

The defeat of the Sioux. The Americans were thunderstruck. It was the most serious defeat the Indians had ever imposed on them. They regarded the battle as a massacre. Sitting Bull had a different opinion: 'Let no man say this was a massacre. They came to kill us and got killed themselves.'

Despite this victory the Sioux lost. General Terry defeated Sitting Bull's warriors and escorted them back to the reservation. Sitting Bull himself escaped to Canada but he returned to the reservation in 1881 and surrendered. Conditions there remained bad. Crops failed, cattle died and epidemics of measles and whooping cough broke out. Many Indians became resentful. They heard that a messiah was coming to save them. The whites would die and the Indians would be free of disease and hunt the buffalo again. This messiah craze became a new religion. The Sioux danced the ghost dance and prayed:

Father, have pity on us   *We have nothing to eat*
We are crying for thirst   *Father, we are poor.*
All is gone!   *We are very poor.*

122

The buffalo are gone,
They are all gone.
Take pity on us, Father,
We are dancing as you wished
Because you commanded us.
We dance hard,
We dance long—
Have Pity.

Father, help us
You are close by in the dark
Hear us and help us.
Take away the white men
Send back the buffalo
We are poor and weak
We can do nothing alone
Help us to be what we once were—
Happy hunters of buffalo.

The agents became frightened and in 1890 called in the army. Most of the Indians ran away. Sitting Bull was killed. Soldiers pursued the fleeing Indians and killed many men, women and children. The Americans called it the Battle of Wounded Knee. The Sioux called it a massacre. The remaining Sioux finally surrendered to the army in 1891.

Other Indian tribes shared similar fates. Eventually all the tribes were confined to reservations. The Indians had to be taught to live a settled life. This was an enormous problem for the future. We cannot discuss it here.

The Close of the Frontier

The American census report of 1890 said that no more large areas of empty land suitable for the small settler existed. The continent was conquered. The West was won. In fact the westward movement continued. There remained many small areas to be settled and huge areas of very dry land remained empty. Such was the land hunger of Americans that many tried their luck. Bankruptcies were numerous. Yet the peak year for claims under the Homestead Act was as late as 1913. Even in the 1920s and 1930s lands on the prairies were being settled for the first time.

Nevertheless the year 1890 is symbolic. By then agriculture had ceased to be the main activity of America and the west was no longer the centre of attraction. Enormous industries and cities were rising in the east. The days of the frontiersman, the settler, the cowboy, the Indian, the marshall and the outlaw were over. Taking their place were inventors, scientists, bankers, merchants, industrialists and factory workers. To this aspect of American history we now turn.

Further Reading

Breihan, Carl W., *The Day Jesse James was Killed*, John Long, 1962.
Chapel, Charles E., *Guns of the Old West*, Coward-McCann, 1961.
Collinson, Frank, *Life in the Saddle*, Univ. of Oklahoma, 1963.
Gribble, Leonard, *Famous Stories of the Wild West*, Arthur Barker, 1967.
Hawgood, John A., *The American West*, Eyre & Spottiswoode, 1967.
O'Connor, Richard, *Wild Bill Hickok*, Redman, 1960.
Paine, Lauran, *The General Custer Story*, Foulsham, 1961.
Sandoz, Mari, *The Buffalo Hunters*, Univ. of Oklahoma, 1962.
Longman 'Then and There' Series Currie, Barbara, *Railroads and Cattlemen in American West, 1860–90*.
Heineman fiction 'New Windmill' Series
    Schaefer, Jack, *Shane*
    Prebble, John, *The Buffalo Soldiers*

9 THE RISE OF BIG BUSINESS, 1860–1920

The completion of the great westward movement coincided with a tremendous industrial revolution in the northeastern and mid-western states of America. The country was transformed in a few decades from a rural land of small farmers and tradesmen to a modern industrial state dominated by vast sprawling cities, giant companies and multimillionaire businessmen. By 1913 America produced 36 per cent of the world's total industrial output. Thus the longstanding argument between Jeffersonians and Hamiltonians was finally resolved.

Some Main Features of the Industrial Revolution

The basic industries. The centre of this industrial revolution lay in the dirty coal mines, the smoking chimneys, the glowing blast furnaces and forges and the smelly coking plants in and around the cities of Pittsburg, Chicago, Cleveland, Toledo, Milwaukee and Birmingham. Before 1860 the main forms of power for industry and transport were water, wind and muscle. By 1900 coal in the form of steam or electricity supplied 90 per cent of all the power used in America. Subsequently, petroleum, natural gas and hydroelectric power grew more important, but even in 1920 coal still gave 80 per cent of the country's power needs. Coal therefore powered the great industrial revolution. It also helped to feed America's greatest single industry—iron and steel. Each year the furnaces, forges and rolling mills of the Mid-west thrust out millions of tons of iron and steel on which the new America was built. Iron and steel rails laced the various parts of the country even more tightly together. Iron and steel bridges stepped across even the broadest of rivers. Steel frames supported the growing number of skyscrapers in the eastern cities. Everywhere iron and steel were part of the countless machines, tools and weapons that America increasingly used.

Not that other industries were unimportant. Textile production continued to expand although the centre of activity tended to move away from the northeast to the South where labour was cheaper and raw cotton closer to hand. Much further west, in Chicago, Minneapolis, Cincinnati, St Louis and Louisville giant food processing industries developed based on the cereals and cattle of the midwest and the far western plains. These cities contained the greatest flour mills, slaughter yards and meat packing factories in the world. We have mentioned this development already in the previous chapter.

More spectacular was the rise of the oil industry. In 1860 the output of oil was negligible. By 1910 annual production was 200 million barrels. Oil not only lubricated and greased machinery of every kind but was burnt in kerosene lamps and stoves in countless American homes, particularly in the West. It was the westerner's main source of domestic heating and lighting. The introduction of the motor vehicle after 1900 provided another fast-growing market for the oil industry.

None of these industries would have grown so quickly at this time without the railways. Growing industries and towns need easy, cheap, quick, reliable and daily deliveries of raw materials, food and finished goods. The railways met these needs far better than steamboats and horse-drawn vehicles. Can you say why? Discuss this in class. The superiority

90,000 people lived in Pittsburg in 1878. 150 factories produced machinery and agricultural tools, 8 plants made 50,000 tons of steel per year, copper manufactures totalled 3 million dollars per year and glass 11 million dollars.

of the railways is shown clearly in the extension of lines in this period. In 1860 there were nearly 31,000 miles of track in America, mostly east of the Appalachians. By 1920 this figure had jumped to 254,000 miles. Much of this extra mileage lay between the Appalachians and the Rockies but every part of America was accessible by railway at this date. Along these tracks travelled most of the nation's grains, animals, timber, coal, iron ore and manufactured goods.

The period after 1850 has been given a number of labels. It has been called the age of coal, the age of steel and the age of railways. It has also been called the age of the machine. By 1920 America was easily the most mechanised country in the world. Locomotives, blast furnaces, windmills, typewriters and motor cars are all obvious examples of machines. Machines were everywhere. They sawed timber and cut coal. They processed food and tinned it. Clothes for men's wear were machine-cut into a wide variety of standardised shapes and sizes and then sown together at speeds of up to 2800 stitches a minute. Iron ore was loaded into trains by giant steam shovels, railed a thousand miles east to Lake Superior, shipped to a Lake Erie port and then railed again to Pittsburg. Machines loaded and unloaded it at every stage until the ore was finally tipped into the top of a blast furnace. The use of machinery was so widespread that examples of it would fill the chapter.

A striking feature of all this industrial activity was the production of many standardised goods based on interchangeable parts. In other words, many firms would each make hundreds, thousands or even millions of goods which were exactly the same as each other. For example, any one Winchester Model 73 rifle was identical to any other. The same part in any one Model 73 would fit in any other. The making of identical parts depended on precise measurements involving thousandths of an inch and the planing and boring of perfectly smooth and accurate metal surfaces. In turn this rested upon the invention of machine tools capable of such fine precision. The invention and manufacture of these tools progressed rapidly in America after 1850.

Trusts and multimillionaires. Two other very striking features of this industrial revolution were the rise of trusts and the growing power and control of very rich businessmen. The trusts were giant firms or groups of firms cooperating with each other to fix prices and outputs and thereby to control a particular industry. These trusts were very powerful. The Standard Oil Company controlled 90 per cent of the total output of the American petroleum industry in 1879. The Carnegie Steel Company made about one-third of the country's steel output in 1900. Its successor, the United Steel Company, made one-half of America's steel after 1901. Powerful trusts also rose in beef, cottonseed, oil, lead, sugar, tobacco and rubber. In 1904 a survey showed that more than 5000 previously independent companies had been merged into 318 trusts.

Huge fortunes were made from this big business. Individuals each made millions of dollars out of timber, milling, meat-packing, mining, railways, steel, copper and oil. Before 1860 America's biggest fortune was that of John Jacob Astor who amassed about twenty million dollars from the fur trade and the sale of property on Manhattan Island. Only about one hundred men had become millionaires. By 1900 there were over 4000 millionaires—mostly merchants, railway operators, manufacturers and mine owners. At least twenty men had fortunes worth 100 million dollars. Andrew Carnegie, the richest of them all, was said to be earning an annual income of 20 million dollars just before he sold his steel company for 450 million dollars.

The growth of towns and cities. The nerve centres of America's industrial revolution were its towns and cities. Here were the country's mines, factories, mills, foundries, slaughter yards, granaries, banks, railway stations and sidings, docks, wharves and many other buildings which were the visible signs of the revolution. These towns and cities grew rapidly. Between 1860 and 1890, for example, Philadelphia and Baltimore doubled their populations, Detroit and Kansas City grew fourfold, Cleveland sixfold and Chicago tenfold. In 1860 no city in America had a million people. Indeed only sixteen cities had populations over 50,000. The population of New York reached a million by 1880. Both Philadelphia and Chicago had followed suit by 1890. In this year fifty-eight cities now had populations over 50,000. By 1920 the number was 144.

When America won its independence only about 5 per cent of its population lived in urban areas. In 1860 the figure was 20 per cent. By 1920 it was 51 per cent—over half the population. These urban dwellers either came from abroad or from the countryside. In many cities the immigrants were very conspicuous. New York, Boston, Philadelphia, Cleveland, Cincinnati and Chicago, for example, had numerous tenements and cheap boarding houses crammed with Irish, Germans, Jews, Poles, Greeks, Ukrainians, Italians and other races. It was said that New York contained more Italians than any other city except Rome, more Irish than in any other city except Dublin, more Germans than in any other city except Berlin, and more Jews than in any other city in the world.

These were some of the main features of the industrial revolution in America between 1860 and 1920. Now we must suggest some reasons for this revolution and America's rise to world industrial supremacy.

Some Reasons for the Industrial Revolution

Natural resources and a continental market. One very obvious and fundamental reason was the fabulous wealth and diversity of the country's natural resources which in the nineteenth century seemed boundless. The Americans conquered a huge land mass with vast lowland areas enjoying a variety of soils and climates. These features gave them hundreds of thousands of farms and extensive forests which not only supplied them directly with many foods but provided industries with an expanding flow of raw materials for processing—wheat, maize, fruit, cotton, timber, hides, furs and skins. America's great mountains, rivers, lakes and waterfalls offered an abundant volume of water for the generation of hydroelectricity, a rapidly increasing source of industrial power by 1920. Beneath this huge land mass was an untold mineral wealth the Indians neither knew nor cared about. Locked away in the continent were about half of the world's coal and iron ore deposits, two-thirds of its copper and one-third of its lead. In abundance too were petroleum, natural gas, gold, silver, sulphur, salt, zinc and many other minerals too numerous to mention.

American industries were the most fortunate in the world for another reason as well. America itself provided the world's largest and richest single market. The opportunities facing the enterprising businessman were both very diversified and very profitable. Between 1860 and 1920 the American population grew from 31.4 million to 105.7 million. In this same period the average yearly income of each person nearly doubled. Thus more and more people had more and more money to spend. Moreover, this lucrative market was largely denied to British and European industries because the American government placed heavy taxes on imported manufactured goods and so protected its own industries from serious foreign competition. American industries had a virtual monopoly over the home market. This market was one huge free trading area knit together by the railways. This was the greatest single benefit the railways bestowed on America in the nineteenth century. The railways themselves made a tremendous demand on American industries. To build and operate about 225,000 miles of track between 1860 and 1920 meant a huge market for the coal and steel industries. Can you think why?

The role of the frontier and immigration. Two more features of the American market deserve notice. First, the western movement of ranchers, settlers and miners meant a great need for products such as ploughs, combine harvesters, guns, barbed wire, drills and mining machinery. The moving frontier, then, was a great market for American industry. But its effect was more than this. Subduing the wilderness was a hard task. Life was often a grim struggle for survival. The urgent need was for cheap and reliable tools and weapons which would do the job in hand and meet the basic needs of the pioneers. If tools or weapons broke they had to be repaired or replaced easily. The frontier was no place for expensive or fancy goods. Thus, the frontier not only supplied a great market for industry but was one main reason for the development of interchangeable parts and the large-scale production of standardised goods. Remember, too, that even when the wilderness had been subdued and the frontier pushed back many families would be slow to change their ideas about the sort of goods they needed. Frontier habits died hard. During the nineteenth century large numbers of families were at, or near, a frontier at some time or other. Thus many Americans tended to accept standardised goods because these were what they were used to.

The second noticeable feature of the American market was the large numbers of immigrants within it. Between 1860 and 1920 about 28 million immigrants settled in America. Here was another huge market for standarised goods. Those who came to live in America sought a better life. They wanted to become American, to forget their past. Naturally they tended to copy the Americans and thus bought many of the same goods. And since they arrived with little money and took up jobs for low wages they could afford to buy only the cheap goods.

Historians think that this immigration had other effects on American industry. Perhaps you will remember that before the Civil War American industries faced a serious shortage of labour, particularly skilled labour. We argued that this was a very important reason why businessmen encouraged the use of labour-saving machinery. Some historians argue that this situation continued after the Civil War. They say that the West still drew too many Americans with skilled knowledge away from the industrial areas. Although the number of immigrants rose heavily, the number of skilled industrial workers entering America was still limited. Thus the urge to invent and use labour-saving machinery remained very strong. Other historians say that American businessmen would have introduced just as many machines even if immigration had been small. They emphasise the size of the market and the frontier. Nevertheless, they think immigration was important. The heavy immigration of labour tended to reduce the level of wages. This meant that costs were lowered and profits increased. Thus more money was available for investment and so even more machinery could be introduced.

Inventions, Investments and Enterprise. The introduction of machinery depended also on inventions and discoveries. The industrial revolution was impossible without them. America borrowed many ideas from Britain and Europe. Both the iron and steel and the motor car industries, for example, leaned heavily upon overseas inventions—the Bessemer converter, the Siemens-Martin open hearth, the basic process of Gilchrist-Thomas and the internal combustion engine. Find out about these inventions for yourselves from the library. Nevertheless Americans themselves made important inventions and discoveries. They pioneered, for example, the dynamo, electric telegraphy, the telephone, the typewriter, the adding machine, the electric light bulb, railway refrigeration trucks and cold storage packing plants. The Americans also made noteworthy contributions to the manufacture of machine tools.

The industrial revolution also depended upon investment—that is money to pay for factories, steel works, mines, railways, machines, ranches and so on. There were three main sources of this money. First, the Atlantic partnership remained important. Funds from Europe and Britain helped to finance American business expansion. In 1913, for example, British investment totalled between £750 and £800 million—about a third of all foreign investment there. Second, American governments—Federal, state and municipal—supplied huge sums of money to help finance the railways. Third and most important, money came from Americans themselves. They financed the great manufacturing industries. We shall mention some of their names below.

A final reason we must emphasise is business enterprise. Individual enterprise was crucial in this period. Upon businessmen fell the great task of encouraging inventions and discoveries, raising capital, introducing machinery, recruiting labour, finding and developing raw materials and markets, and meeting the competition of rivals. The government imposed few restraints upon the individual businessman. He was allowed to build his firm as he saw fit with little interference or direction from the government of the day. Such a government policy has been called one of *laissez-faire*. The Republican Party in particular believed this to be a sound policy. In this period the Republicans were strong champions of private enterprise and big business.

Before the Civil War industry remained relatively backward and manufacturers were not very important people in America. The war changed that. Industrial strength became the key to the North's victory. Manufacturers now began to influence both politicians and laws. Abraham Lincoln, for example, complied with the manufacturers' demands for tariffs on imported industrial goods. Together with bankers, railway operators and mineowners the manufacturers grew increasingly important. No longer were they held back by the seaboard merchants and Southern planters and by Jeffersonians who believed in a rural America of small farmers.

The new millionaires were called the 'captains of industry'. They were of mixed origins. Some began rich, others poor. Some were immigrants, others were American. Some were farmers' sons, others were townsmen. It is most difficult to generalise about them. Most were ruthless, aggressive and vigorous in their enterprises and competed their rivals out of business or gained control in one way or another over their companies. They were a new breed a conquistadors. Men like Pierpont Morgan, John D. Rockefeller, Andrew Carnegie and the Vanderbilts were responsible for the rise of the trusts. Indeed, by the early 1900s Morgan and Rockfeller and their close business associates together held 341 directorships in 112 banks, railroads, insurance and other corporations. The value of these assets under their control was said to be over 22 billion dollars. These men really controlled American business.

We have chosen one of the great captains of industry to study in more detail.

John D. Rockefeller, the Standard Oil Trust and Monopoly

Rockefeller began his working life in 1854 as a bookkeeper for a Cleveland produce merchant at fifteen dollars a month. He soon proved to be excellent at his job and his monthly salary was raised to fifty dollars. In the next three years he earned 1800 dollars and saved nearly half of it. He liked reading the Bible, rarely going out except to the local Baptist church where he always left money in the collection box.

The making of Standard Oil. In 1858 Rockefeller pooled his savings with an Englishman called Clark and they began a produce business. It flourished and out of its profits they invested in an oil refinery with a man called Andrews who boasted that he could extract more kerosene from a barrel of crude oil than anyone else. Rockefeller pruned costs to the minimum. Andrews produced the best refined oil. Their refinery made good profits. So engrossed in oil did Rockefeller become that in 1865 he sold his share in the produce business to Clark and bought Clark's share in the refinery.

This was a very risky thing to do. In 1865 the oil industry was a free-for-all. In the oilfields thousands of small prospectors each dug their own wells and hoped for a big strike and an overnight fortune. Eager for quick profits they ruined farmland, sank wells in the wrong places and caused numerous fires, explosions and deaths by their carelessness and ignorance of drilling techniques. Sometimes they had too much oil to sell and at other times too little. Prices went up and down erratically. Each producer undercut his neighbour's price when sales were bad and forced a hard bargain with the refiners when oil was scarce. About 250 refineries competed for the oil. Some, like Titusville and Oil City, were on the oilfield itself. Many more were in New York, Philadelphia, Erie, Pittsburg and Cleveland. The refiners bid up prices when oil was scarce and tried to persuade producers to sell to them rather than to their rivals. City rivalled city and railway companies took sides too. Keen to secure oil freight for its own lines each company tried to undercut the rates of its competitors. In this business there seemed to be no rules: it was every man for himself.

Rockefeller and Andrews soon needed more money for expansion. They adopted a new partner and received 70,000 dollars which was used to build a second refinery. Their firm then became the biggest refinery in Cleveland. Secret negotiation now began between Rockefeller and the Michigan Central Railroad Company about railway charges. Rockefeller complained that refineries in other cities enjoyed lower charges than he did and this made it difficult for him to compete with them. Probably he hinted that he might have to remove his refineries from Cleveland unless his own freight rates were lowered. Since Rockefeller's firm was the biggest and best firm in Cleveland the railway company stood to lose good business if it went elsewhere. It agreed to charge the firm lower rates on its

e early American industry

oil freight. This victory further reduced Rockefeller's costs. His firm increased in size and competitive strength and as its use of the Michigan Central Railroad increased it won further reductions for its freight charges. Rockefeller's rivals in Cleveland were furious, but since they were less important customers of the railway they received no rebates. By 1870 Rockefeller's firm was the biggest refinery in the world. It now became known as the Standard Oil Company and it was worth one million dollars.

The fight for monopoly. The oil industry remained a cut-throat business. The supply of oil tended to run ahead of demand. Producers faced falling prices and refineries worked below full capacity. Rockefeller believed the industry was being strangled by ruinous competition. Somehow the intense rivalry between producers, refiners, cities and railways must be stopped and the small inefficient firms put out of business. His Standard Oil Company must dominate the industry. Competition must be replaced by monopoly.

Very secretly Rockfeller bought an unknown company, the South Improvement Company, one which would arouse no suspicions. He then asked the railway companies to charge lower rates for all oil freight owned by members of his new company and increased rates on the oil of their rivals. In return, Rockefeller's Company would give the railways substantial and regular cargoes and therefore higher profits. Each railway would receive equal treatment. The railways were not told how many refineries had joined the South Improvement Company. In fact, there were none so far. Next Rockefeller saw each of his rivals in turn. Each rival was informed of the railway agreement and very bluntly told that unless it joined his scheme it would soon have no business left because its freight rates would be too high. Rockefeller then offered to buy the firm either for cash or its equal value in Standard Oil Company stock. Once more, no firm was told which other firms had joined the scheme. It did not know the strength of Rockefeller's hand.

The trick worked very well. The railway companies agreed and within three months all the twenty-five Cleveland refineries had sold out to Rockefeller who now controlled one-fifth of America's total output of refined oil. But he did not stop there. Rockefeller then extended his scheme to take in refineries in other cities. Unable to compete against him they too sold out. By 1879 he controlled 90 per cent of the oil refining business. Never before had any single American wielded so much power over an industry. Rockefeller became America's first supreme monopolist.

Opposition and victory. This was done despite tremendous opposition from oil producers, refiners, lawyers and statesmen. They said Rockefeller was a monster intent on devouring all his enemies. He was destroying Jefferson's America where every man had the right to be independent and to work on his own account. They said he was cruel, ruthless, corrupt and consumed by greed. The producers complained that he dictated prices to them and destroyed their profits. Many of the refiners who sold out to him for cash protested that he paid them less than their business was worth. Not that they gave up without a fight. For example, in 1878, to avoid the high railway rates, oil producers built their own pipeline to the east coast. Rockefeller built his own pipelines and bought out more of his rivals. The producers countered by building their own refineries. Then they found that Rockefeller, probably by using a false name, had bought one-third of the shares of their pipeline company and become the biggest shareholder. They were defeated.

In 1882 Rockefeller streamlined the oil industry still further. At this time there were thirty-seven refiners who rather than sell out to Rockefeller for cash had chosen to accept shares in the Standard Oil Company. All these men helped to manage the industry. Rockefeller felt the number was too big. It took too long to make decisions. He now persuaded them to give their shares in trust to nine trustees of whom he was the most important. In return they received trust certificates equal to the value of their shares. This meant that nine men headed by Rockefeller now had direct control over more than forty companies.

He could carry out his business plans more quickly and effectively. Thus the Standard Company became a trust. It was valued at 70 million dollars. In 1886 its yearly profit was 15 million dollars. By 1899 it was 45 million dollars and Rockefeller's own fortune 200 million dollars. Once the example was set, other industries adopted the trust idea. Small groups of very powerful men came to dominate, for example, the sugar refining, biscuits, whisky, telegraph, electrical appliances and steel industries.

Hated as he was, Rockefeller felt no regret for his actions. In his view he created order, efficiency and progress in an industry where once there had been chaos and waste. To those who said he bought out refineries for less than they were really worth he replied that every man was given the chance of taking shares in the Standard Oil Company. His favourite advice to each refiner was to take shares not cash. With shares no family would ever become poor. Such was Rockfeller's confidence in the future profits of the Standard Oil Company.

It has been said that by about 1880 the American oil industry was the most efficient large-scale manufacturing business in the world. Rockefeller carefully scrutinised every aspect of his company and tried to cut costs and improve quality wherever possible. He made the world's best kerosene and he sold it on every continent. It has also been said that since his profits rose considerably his prices could not have been pruned all that much. The customer could have been offered much lower prices. Standard Oil pursued monopoly and profits above anything else.

After his retirement in 1896 Rockefeller invested his money increasingly in other activities like railway, coal and iron mines, banks and insurance companies, and he increased his fortune. Yet by his death he had given 550 million dollars to American and world organisations like universities, colleges, hospitals and research centres which benefit mankind.

Perhaps there can be no final opinion on Rockefeller. What do you think about his aims, methods and achievements? Would you praise or condemn him?

Further Reading

Allen, Frederick Lewis, *The Big Change*, Harper, 1952.
Burlingame, Roger, *Machines that Made America*, Signet, 1953.
Josephson, Matthew, *The Robber Barons*, Eyre & Spottiswoode, 1962.
Kouwenhofen, John A., *Adventures of America*, Harper, 1938.
Walker, Robert H., *Everyday Life in the Age of Enterprise 1865–1900*, Batsford, 1967.

10 THE AGE OF PROTEST

World industrial supremacy was not gained without cost. The industrial revolution had its black side. American workers, farmers and professional people all found themselves increasingly protesting about the evils of industrial and urban growth.

Workers and Trade Unions

The workers' lot. In its relentless pursuit of greater outputs, profits and power big business undoubtedly took steps which many workers opposed. Employers installed machinery which replaced labour skills and lowered men's status and wages. They encouraged immigration because this increased the workforce, lowered wages and supplied reserves of men who could be used as blacklegs to defeat strikes. Indeed, businessmen were ruthless in dealing with strikes. Not only did they bring in men from outside the strike area but they employed spies recruited at the Pinkerton detective agency to mingle with the strikers, provoke trouble and pinpoint the ringleaders. Blacklists were published regularly and circulated to other employers. In the textile and clothing industries women and children were used wherever possible because they accepted lower wages than men. At all times the businessmen reserved the right to hire and fire men at will and to cut wages if they deemed it necessary. Thus when trade was bad, wages were slashed and men laid off. Workers were not only insecure because they could be sacked on the spot. Often they worked in dangerous and unhealthy places. If they were killed, injured or sick, neither they nor their families received any compensation from their employers. Even in safe jobs men worked long hours with no holidays. Many workers rightly felt they should not be slaves either to an employer or a machine. There was more to life than toil and sweat.

Craft and industrial unions. Workers began to organise trade unions even before 1860. The two main types of organisation were craft unions and industrial unions. A craft union consisted of skilled men each engaged in the same craft or trade. An industrial union included skilled and unskilled men in all kinds of jobs but within the same industry. The craft unions tried to protect the wage levels, skills and status of their members. The industrial unions sought to prevent wage cuts, unemployment and long hours.

Union federations. After 1860 craft and industrial unions often joined together to form federations. The Knights of Labour began in 1876, the American Federation of Labour in 1886, and the International Workers of the World in 1905. The aims and methods of these federations differed considerably.

The Knights wished to unite skilled and unskilled men and women of all races and religions from all trades and industries. All workers had a common cause. The Knights stood for equal pay for men and women doing the same job, no employment of children under fourteen and an eight-hour day, the settlement of disputes by arbitration and not strikes, and the abolition of the practice of contracting labourers abroad and bringing them to America. Ultimately it wanted public ownership of all utilities, particularly railways, and the creation of workers' cooperatives to control most of the country's industry and trade. Big business would be destroyed by ending private ownership of property. The leaders

*...en workers went
strike at
...ssachusetts shoe
...tory in 1870 the
...ployer brought in
...inese labour from
...n Francisco 3,000
...les away.

...scuss the content of
...s cartoon in class.
...at is it saying? Do
...you think it is a
...od cartoon?*

of this movement set the example by buying up coal mines and running them on cooperative lines. To achieve real success, however, they urged all workers to use their votes to elect men to state and Federal governments who understood and backed their ideas.

The American Federation of Labour tried to unite the craft unions and to champion the interests of the skilled workers. It aimed to improve their wages, hours and working conditions not by cooperatives, votes or strikes but by winning the confidence and friendship of their employers by peaceful collective bargaining. It did not want the abolition of private enterprise.

The International Workers of the World appealed to the unskilled worker and the new immigrant. It wanted all workers to combine into one big union to fight the employers by violent methods. Socialist in its thinking it said that employers and workers were eternal enemies. Its members must destroy big business by sudden and aggressive strikes and acts of sabotage. The I.W.W. would then take control of all industry and trade.

Big business v. trade unions. From the outset businessmen were against trade unions and relations were far from peaceful. Between 1881 and 1900, for example, when the trusts and giant firms were making their appearance, there were nearly 24,000 strikes and lockouts involving over 127,000 workplaces and over $6\frac{1}{2}$ million men. The workers lost nearly 307 million dollars and the employers nearly 143 million dollars. Some of the biggest strikes involved gun battles, sieges, burnings, looting, killings, hangings, Pinkerton agents and spies, and Federal troops.

For example, in 1894 came the Pullman strike in Chicago. Pullman housed many of his workers but charged high rents. In 1893 he made a profit of 25 million dollars from the Chicago World Fair. The following year was a bad one so he cut wages by 20 per cent, but not many rents or salaries, and dismissed many workers. The American Railway

Union called a strike and its members refused to handle trains pulling Pullman cars. Twenty-seven states and territories were involved. Federal troops intervened, twelve people were killed, many were injured and 575 arrests made. The leaders were prosecuted under the Sherman Anti-Trust Act. This was a great blow to the workers. The Act had said 'that every contract, combination in the form of a trust or otherwise, or conspiracy, in restraint of trade or commerce among the Several States . . . is hereby declared to be illegal'. It was supposed to be against big business. Yet now in 1894 a trade union was said to be a conspiracy in restraint of interstate commerce.

The results of trade union activity. By themselves the workers did not make much headway against big business between 1860 and 1920. Important industries like steel and textiles were still not organised in 1920. Steel workers continued to work twelve hours a day and seven days a week even after this date. The Knights of Labour gained over 700,000 members by 1886 but subsequently it declined and was virtually dead by 1900. the I.W.W. met a similar fate in the early 1920s. The failure of many industrial unions and the I.W.W. meant that the unskilled workers—the largest section of the workforce— achieved no permanent organisation by 1920. Indeed, in that year only about one-fifth of all wage earners were organised into unions.

On the other hand some gains had been made. In coal mining the United Mine Workers had organised over half the workers in an industry which sprawled across many states. In the Mid-west coalfield labour conditions were determined by conferences of employers and workers drawn from four states. Skilled men in the railway industry had formed themselves into various craft unions after the failure of the Pullman strike and had made gains for themselves. The third federation, the American Federation of Labour, grew in size and importance throughout the period. By 1920 it had 4 million members and it was recognised by the employers as the spokesman for skilled workers.

The unions also gained some important laws. In 1885 employers were stopped from contracting for labour abroad. Several acts from 1882 onwards placed other restrictions on immigration, particularly from China and Japan. By 1920 many states had passed laws regulating child and female labour and providing workmen's compensation. However, many of these laws were passed after 1900 and were the result of more pressure from the middle classes than from the workers. We shall write about the middle-class protest later.

Some obstacles to trade union progress. Why did the workers make only slow progress before 1920? Throughout the nineteenth century they faced not only hostility from the employers but from the government, the law courts and the general public as well. Remember that Americans had always regarded their country as the land of opportunity, the place where individuals could begin life anew and improve themselves by their own efforts. The captains of industry were the best example of this but there were millions of Americans in farming, lumbering, mining, trade and transport, manufacture and the professions all working for themselves and increasing their incomes and property. These people had little sympathy for trade unions which tried to restrict the individual businessman's activities, and particularly those which proposed to actually destroy private enterprise. Understanding this basic idea helps to explain why the Knights of Labour and the I.W.W. failed and the American Federation of Labour survived. It helps also to explain why the Sherman Anti-Trust Act was turned against trade unions. Discuss these points with your teacher.

This thinking even extended to many workers. As industries grew and mechanisation increased skilled men frequently became foremen, overseers and managers. Their wages and status grew without the help of trade unions. Many workers too saved as hard as they could and dreamed of the day they would move west or begin their own business. They did not think they would be workers for long. Thus until the end of the nineteenth century trade unions swam against the general tide of ideas and beliefs.

The Farmers, Granges and Populism

The farmers' grievances. The Western farmers also had grievances and, like the workers in the East, formed political organisations to protest about them and to win reforms.

We have discussed the problems of prairie farming in Chapter 8. If you cannot remember them turn back and re-read pp. 117 to 118 before you continue here.

A basic theme of this book is that the wilderness was a magnet to millions of people who wanted to make a better life for themselves. They saw the West as a land of opportunity, a place where they could lead richer, freer and happier lives. Unfortunately, those who went west started out ignorant of the problems there. Their dream of a better life often either never came true at all or took a very long time to materialise.

With his hopes and dreams shattered the western farmer began to blame other people for his distress. Faced with mounting debts he hated those who lent him money—the bankers and speculators in the far-off eastern cities and in Europe. In his opinion they deliberately raised the rate of interest to line their own pockets. To him they were parasites growing rich at his expense and robbing him of a better life in the West. Faced also with rising freight charges and rising prices of manufactured goods the farmer felt bitter towards

137

the railways and big business. Isolated on the prairie, living a lonely and monotonous life, the farmer realised that the life of the nation no longer revolved around him but around the city, its industries and workers, who increasingly were immigrants from central and south-eastern Europe. He complained that:

'We have become the world's melting pot. The scum of creation has been dumped on us. Some of our principal cities are more foreign than American. The most dangerous and corrupting hordes of the Old World have invaded us. The vice and crime which they have planted in our midst are sickening and terrifying. What brought these Goths and Vandals to our shores? The manufacturers are mainly to blame. They wanted cheap labour; and they didn't care a curse how much harm to our future might be the consequence of their heartless policy.'

You can see that the farmer hated big business and all that it stood for. In other words he clung to the ideas and beliefs of Thomas Jefferson who wanted America to be a land of happy and contented farmers and tradesmen. The farmer believed he was the backbone of America, that he had made the country what it was. He resented the interference and

A Farmer's Grang

profiteering of the bankers, the industrialists and the railway companies and believed that the growing vice and crime in America was the result of immigration.

The Granges. As early as the 1870s farmers in Minnesota met together to talk about their problems and the solutions to them. The farmers' associations were called Granges and they were allied to others in Wisconsin, Iowa and Illinois. The Granges had some success. In Minnesota, for example, a community of Swedes began farming on a cooperative basis. They created their own creamery, stores, bank, insurance, telephones and grain elevator and thus reduced their costs. The Granges also tried to persuade the state governments to pass laws controlling railway charges but here they had limited success. Indeed the real solution to their problems lay in diversifying their farming—relying less on grains and more on dairying—a change which began in the 1870s.

The Populist Party. Farther west, in the Dakotas, Nebraska and Kansas, grains remained the chief money earner. It was here that the physical, economic and social problems were the most serious. Grain prices had fallen since the 1860s. In the late 1880s the fall became more pronounced. Many farmers went bankrupt and were forced to sell their

*This cartoon reflec[ts]
the opposition of th[e]
Grange to the high
rates charged by th[e]
railways*

farms. Some trekked back east. In 1891, for example, 18,000 wagons entered Iowa from Nebraska. Their land became wilderness or grazing grounds for cattle farmers who stepped in and bought up the cheap farms. Others remained but became tenants on land they had once owned. Their status was lowered, their independence was lost and their pride greatly hurt. Depression was widespread.

In the South the small cotton farmer found himself with similar economic problems. Prices for his crop were tumbling. His debts were rising. He joined with the grain farmers of the prairies to protest about his difficulties.

In 1892 farmers in the West and South combined to form the Populist Party. The party opposed the railways and rich businessmen. It demanded Federal ownership of the railways and action to stop the speculator grabbing lands under the Homestead Act. Most important, however, it attacked the money and banking system and demanded higher prices and lower rates of interest. The Populists said that prices were low and interest rates high because gold was in short supply. They demanded the use of silver as well as gold in the nation's money supply. The mines in the Rockies were providing ample quantities of silver at this time. The use of silver would increase the amount of money in the country. More money meant more spending and therefore higher prices for all goods, including farm produce. More money meant easier borrowing and therefore lower rates of interest and smaller debts. With silver as their main cry the Populists tried to win the elections of 1896. They stood against the Democrats and the Republicans. However the Democrats were persuaded to support the introduction of silver and the Populists lost the initiative. Unfortunately the Democrats lost the elections and the farmers did not win their demands.

The money supply was not the main cause of the farmer's troubles. The root cause was too much production of grain and cotton. Grain production in particular rose rapidly.

140

*is cartoon shows
railways riding
*ghshod over the
erican economy

Farmers in Canada, Argentina and Australia were also growing more and competing for the markets in Europe. These markets were not growing fast enough to absorb all the extra produce. The depression of the 1880s and early 1890s checked output. This stopped the price fall. By the mid-1890s prices were rising. For the first time in many years the farmers' prospects looked promising. Their rising incomes helped them to pay off their debts and improve their farms. With this recovery their support for Populism faded away. As we shall see this new period of prosperity only lasted to about 1920.

The Urban Middle Classes and the Progressive Movement

The muckrakers. From 1850 onwards a small but growing group of middle-class people tried to combat the mounting evils of urban life. They crusaded against slums, saloons, poverty, drunkenness, vice and crime. From the 1890s the middle classes were aroused by a series of books and magazine articles written by people known as the muckrakers. These people were convinced that American industry had become too powerful and that businesses, cities and governments had become rotten and corrupt. These writers earned the name of muckrakers because they raked up evidence to show the badness of businessmen and politicians. They wrote to expose these men, to shock the American public and to make the middle classes demand reforms in business and politics.

What the muckrakers said. Here are some of the findings of the muckrakers. The 4000 multimillionaires—only one-two-hundredth of one per cent of the total population—owned 20 per cent of all America's wealth. One per cent of the total population owned 54 per cent of the country's wealth and about 12 per cent owned 85 per cent of the wealth. Over half of the population owned practically nothing. This grossly unequal distribution of wealth was very unfair. The muckrakers gave the captains of industry another name—

141

THEY HATE THE LIGHT, BUT THEY CAN'T ESCAPE IT.

the great robber barons. Morgan and Rockefeller were the greatest of these. Together with a few close business associates these men controlled America's leading banks, insurance companies, railways, steamship companies and public utilities as well as the steel and oil industries. It was estimated they controlled businesses whose total value was $22\frac{1}{4}$ billion dollars. Here was tangible proof of a great money power dominating America. The muckrakers were not afraid to criticise businessmen by name. Rockefeller was branded a liar and a conspirator, a man with no pleasures save that of 'seeing his dividends come in'. The robber barons enriched themselves by plundering America's vast natural resources. 'Great timber grabbers swept away vast timber lands of Michigan, Wisconsin and Minnesota, often carelessly setting fire to what they did not themselves cut off for lumber. . . . What was done by the timber grabbers was also done by the coalmine grabbers, and by the men who fenced the public lands.' In Montana, Marcus Daly mined 50 million dollars' worth of copper from Butte Bill, 600 acres of land he had bought from the Federal government at five dollars an acre. America had bought Alaska for $7\frac{1}{2}$ million dollars. Rockefeller, Morgan and other plunderers had moved in, bought the land and made hundreds of millions of dollars from gold, timber, copper, land, coal and fisheries. 'The domain should not be a grab bag, but a treasure house in which the nation shall hold vast store of riches to be developed economically for the public's good.'

Colossal fortunes were made in other ways too. Inland transport was virtually monopolised by the railways, which used their position to push up charges and exploit the customer. In the meat packing industry in Chicago businessmen like Armour flouted the public health laws. Not only was meat canned in foul conditions but pigs with tuberculosis were made into sausages; old, crippled and diseased cows covered in boils became canned meat; and potted chicken was really made from tripe. Some meat products were found to contain ground-up rats, refuse and even workers who had fallen into the giant mincing machines. Patent medicine manufacturers claimed their products would cure all sorts of ailments and diseases. In fact their medicines contained coloured water, alcohol, drugs and even poisons. Many people became alcoholics and some died from poisoning. The great American people were being swindled, cheated and deceived by cranks and profiteers.

The workers suffered heavily too. The muckrakers said over half a million workers were killed or maimed every year in American industries. They made careful enquiries into particular firms. In one plant of the United States Steel Corporation forty-six men had been killed in 1906—killed by burning, dynamite, electric shocks, suffocation, falling objects and railways. 'But what happens to the widows, to the orphans? They do not evaporate. But society pays—in crime, poverty, demoralisation and vice.' The company escaped. It paid no compensation at all. Investigations were made into the employment of children. In 1900 America employed 1.7 million children in factories, mines, workshops and textile mills. Conditions of work were exceptionally bad in the textile industry. The muckrakers said that no Indian ever asked a child to work yet Christian white men employed child slaves in a country which had rejected slavery. Beginning at 4.30 in the morning these children trudged to the textile mills to work for twelve to fourteen hours a day. They were not so well fed, well housed or well clothed as the Negro slaves had been.

This was not the end of it. Big business controlled the Federal, state and city governments and the law courts. The Senate was bossed by a man called Nelson Aldwich who was connected to Rockefeller by marriage. 'Thus the chief exploiter of the American people is closely allied . . . with the chief schemer in the service of the exploiters.' The Senate was guilty of treason. It passed laws favourable to big business and considered hardly at all the interests of the consumer, the farmer or the worker. Similarly, state governments were bossed by men in the pay of the great trusts and other robber barons. American government was corrupt. Businessmen chose their own candidates to stand for office as senators, governors and judges and secured their election by expensive political

is tenement housed
hty people. In
ch an environment,
ewn with filth
d waste and
errun by vermin,
hus, smallpox
d diphtheria were
e.

fantastic photo-
aph and one which
lped to stir the
unicipal authorities
to action to clear
e muck from the
eets.

campaigns, meetings and advertisements. Others were persuaded to serve the business interest by the payment of bribes.

Bribery and corruption were rife even in the great industrial cities. Each city had its Republican or Democratic boss and political machine. The machine, financed by businessmen and party supporters, was an army of people whose job it was to win votes for the boss and put him into office. Active in every part of the city, the machine offered business to lawyers, shopkeepers and tradesmen, free soup to tramps, beer to alcoholics and release from gaol for petty criminals. In particular, the machine chased the immigrants. It offered them jobs, provided accommodation, lent them small sums of money, got them out of trouble, attended their christenings, marriages and funerals and did anything else in return for just one thing—their votes. Usually these people gave the machine what it wanted. It was in their interests to do so. Flooding in from central and southeastern Europe they arrived penniless, friendless and jobless. They spoke no English. In return for a vote the machine befriended each immigrant and started him off on his new life. To the immigrant who had never possessed a vote in his own country, it all seemed too good to be true. He often did not realise that he was aiding bribery and corruption and he resented it when he was criticised about this.

Once elected the boss and his followers profited from their position. They awarded city contracts for things like gas and electricity, railways, water works and sewage disposal to businessmen who offered the highest bribes. Licences were sold to saloon keepers, gamblers, race track operators and prostitutes for the privilege of starting their businesses in the city. These same people often paid protection money to the boss if he promised to keep the police away. Honest policemen were often sacked and the remainder bribed by the boss or a businessman either to encourage gambling, drinking and prostitution or to ignore them altogether.

The muckrakers investigated many cities. In Chicago, for example, in 1906 there were 7300 licensed saloons and their takings exceeded 100 million dollars. The average amount of beer drunk per person in a year was said to be seventy gallons—three and a half times the national average. Gambling dens took 15 million dollars. They paid 200,000 dollars to the boss for protection from the police. The police force itself was bribed easily and it contained many criminals. In 1904 and 1905 half the Chicago police force was charged with burglary, shoplifting and other offences. Indeed, in a city where gambling and drinking were encouraged and where the police force was so corrupt, there were plenty of opportunities for organised crime. Gangs operated from the wharves and slums of the city and robberies and murders were common. The city was renowned for its large number of street hold-ups.

The birth of the Progressive movement. These were some of the things the muckrakers wrote about. They certainly succeeded in shocking the middle classes and steering them to

Far left:
This cartoon show
the powerful railw
interest in Congre
opposing the
proposed Interstat
Commerce
Commission.

action. Their writings coincided with a general rise in prices starting in 1896 and as peoples' living standards were squeezed they became even more willing to believe that the trusts were exploiting the American people. Thus was born the Progressive movement which lasted from about 1896 to 1916. It was supported by workers and farmers but it was really an urban middle class movement.

The aims and ideals of the Progressives. This movement is important in American history. Let us explain what the Progressives really wanted. Quite simply, they wished to preserve the tradition of America as the land of freedom, the land of economic opportunity and political democracy. America must remain the country where even the poorest person had a chance to make a better and richer life for himself, where every man had the vote and the opportunity to take an active part in political affairs. Such ideas should remind you of the promise of 'life, liberty and the pursuit of happiness' contained in the Declaration of Independence, and the ideas of people like Thomas Jefferson and Andrew Jackson. Big business and political bosses greatly endangered these ideals. The small man in business could not possibly compete with the giant trusts which had an iron grip on forests, minerals, lands, water supplies, transport and manufacturing, and which were in alliance with the party bosses. Competition was being destroyed. Similarly the powerful machines were destroying democracy in political affairs. The ordinary American had less and less to do with the running of his town and state. The Progressives wanted a fairer deal for themselves and their supporters. The power of these great organisations had to be curtailed. Like the makers of the Constitution the Progressives were fearful of too much power in too few hands whether this was in government, business or politics.

Progressivism and Populism compared. You will see that the Progressives had much in common with the Populists. Both groups spoke out for those decent, hard-working Americans who wanted to improve themselves and to take part in political affairs. Both wanted a better deal for such people. At bottom, however, the Populists yearned for a rural America like Jefferson did. The Progressives were realists. They saw the industrial revolution was inevitable and they welcomed the prosperity it gave them. They accepted industries and towns as part of their life but they wished to purify them, to weed out their bad features while retaining their good ones. Somehow the ideals of economic opportunity for all and political democracy forged when America was a rural country had to be kept alive in the new industrial nation.

Progressive action. What actions followed these protests? The Progressives realised that the only organisation strong enough to stand up to big business was the Federal government. Most Americans had always hated the idea of a strong Federal government but it now seemed necessary. After 1900 the Progressives found two presidents sympathetic to their cause. These were Theodore Roosevelt, a Republican, and Woodrow Wilson, a Democrat.

Teddy Roosevelt and 'The Square Deal'. Teddy Roosevelt was an ungainly and bespectacled figure yet he won the confidence of the ordinary man. Born of a wealthy family and well educated, Teddy Roosevelt was a writer, politician and soldier. A one-time rancher he loved the outdoor life and enjoyed sailing, bird-watching and big game hunting. He read widely, talked to anybody and gave opinions on everything. A firm believer in democracy and eager for reform, he promised Americans honest government and a square deal.

Roosevelt achieved several important reforms. Look at Table 8. He began the policy of conservation of natural resources. Railway rates were regulated successfully for the first time. In 1906 the first laws were passed to combat the adulteration of foods and the sale of dangerous drugs.

He felt that the answer to the rise of big business organisations was to form big counter-

Table 8. The Progressive Legislation of Roosevelt and Wilson, 1902–16

1. ROOSEVELT

Act	Purpose of Act
Reclamation Act 1902	To provide Federal irrigation schemes to overcome drought in the plains and deserts of the far West.
Elkins Anti-Rebate Act 1903	To prevent railway companies giving rebates to certain firms and not to others.
Department of Commerce Act 1903	Set up a Department of Commerce and Labour with a subsidiary Bureau of Corporations to investigate into organisation, conduct and management of corporations.
Hepburn Act 1906	To strengthen the powers of the Interstate Commerce Commission in the investigation of railway affairs. Gave Commission the right to lay down 'just and reasonable maximum rates' chargeable by railways.
Pure Food and Drug Act Meat Inspection Act 1906	Two acts to force food and drug manufacturers to sell unadulterated products.
National Conservation Commission 1908	To conserve America's remaining forests, mineral deposits and power sites from further privateering.

2. WILSON

Act	Purpose of Act
Federal Reserve Act 1913	To set up twelve regional banks as the Federal Reserve System. All national banks compelled to be members of their Regional Federal Reserve Bank. Both national and regional banks forced to hold a certain percentage of their deposits in reserve.
Underwood Act 1913	(a) To reduce the general level of duties on imports from 40 to 26 per cent; (b) to increase the range of imports allowed into America duty-free.
Clayton Anti-Trust Act 1914	Forbade price discrimination, interlocking directorates and tying agreements—in which manufacturers compelled retailers to sell only their products and not those of their rivals.
Federal Trade Commission Act 1914	Set up Federal Trade Commission to investigate questionable business practices with powers, if necessary, to issue 'cease and desist' orders.
Federal Farm Loan Act 1916	To make Federal long term loans available to farmers at low interest rates.
Workmen's Compensation Act 1916	Financial assistance given to Federal civil servants absent from work because of disability.
Adamson Act 1916	Gave an eight-hour day and extra pay for overtime to railway workers engaged in interstate commerce.

1906 twenty-six such schemes undertaken. Of great lue to those who were affected by the schemes.

oosevelt used this act to successfully prosecute the andard Oil Co., and the Chicago meat packers.

e activities of the big corporations were to be opened public scrutiny. Act opposed by big businessmen who sented Federal government interference.

creased Federal control over railways. An important w departure in railway policy—Federal government w could influence railway charges *in the future*.

e first acts of their kind. They contained many loop- les. Muckrakers attacked them, saying they were not ective in stopping profiteering from patent medicines

he culmination of six years' close attention to the need r conservation. Roosevelt the first President to make e nation realise the importance of conserving its tural resources. This was his greatest achievement.

nerican banking remains privately owned but (*a*) one central bank—banking was decentralised to oid build-up of a money trust; (*b*) members of deral Reserve Board, which supervised the system, re elected by President. The Act made the supply of oney more flexible and reduced risk of bank failures.

e first real reduction in tariffs since the Civil War. merican industry now less protected from foreign mpetition. Consumers, particularly farmers and orkers, enjoyed a fall in their cost of living.

m was to strengthen Sherman Anti-Trust Act.

mmission could enforce its orders via the courts t they did not prove very cooperative.

elped to satisfy a very long standing demand by rmers for cheap money.

e of the few pieces of social legislation by the deral government up to this time.

elcomed by 1.7 million railway workers. Opposed big business.

organisations. The Federal government must be the main one but he also encouraged individuals to combine together into political associations like trade unions and farmers' organisations. Teddy Roosevelt was prepared to use the Federal government to supervise and even coerce big business. This was well shown in 1902 when he told the coal owners that unless they agreed to arbitration he would take over the mines and run them with soldiers. His threat worked and the miners gained shorter hours and higher wages. In the same year the President launched a law-suit against the Northern Securities Co; two years later the Supreme Court decided the case in his favour. This Company was a giant holding company worth 400 million dollars, created by Pierpont Morgan who merged the Northern Pacific and Great Northern Railways. This trust was now broken. Later he acted successfully against the Standard Oil Company and against trusts in meat-packing and tobacco. These were sensational victories and earned Teddy Roosevelt the title of 'the trust-buster'. Notice that Roosevelt's policies forsook the traditional ones of the Republican Party. We have already said that the Republican Party was the champion of free enterprise and big business. It was opposed to government intervention in economic activity.

Woodrow Wilson and the New Freedom. Woodrow Wilson was a southerner and a Democrat. As Governor of the state of New Jersey he showed himself to be no puppet of the party political bosses who had given him his position. He drove through a series of reforms which democratised New Jersey and gave him a national reputation. In 1912 he opposed Roosevelt and Taft for the presidency of America. His election speeches appealed to the hearts and minds of the Progressives even more than did Roosevelt's. Wilson said he was making 'a crusade against powers that have governed us—that have limited our development—that have determined our lives—that have set us in a straightjacket to do as they please.' He continued: 'This is a second struggle for emancipation. . . . If America is not to have free enterprise, then she can have freedom of no sort whatsoever. . . . Anything that depresses, anything that blocks, discourages and dismays the humble man is against all the principles of progress.' Wilson sided with 'the beginner', 'the man with only a little capital', 'the new entry' in the race, the 'man on the make'. Unlike Roosevelt who accepted the idea of monopoly Wilson sought to restore and regulate competition. He promised the ordinary man a New Freedom from the authority and power of big business. Wilson won the presidential election of 1912.

He soon showed he meant business. Look at the table again. Wilson felt that high tariffs bred monopoly and the tariff reform of 1913 was the first real reduction since the Civil War. Like Andrew Jackson, Wilson was suspicious and afraid of money trust, and his Federal Reserve Act decentralised banking and rejected forever the idea of a strong central bank. He helped the farmers and railway workers too and extended Roosevelt's conservation programme.

State and municipal reforms. The Progressives also won important reforms at both the state and the municipal levels. Political reforms were won almost everywhere. Candidates for political office were to be nominated now by the people—not the railways or some other big business. Everywhere voting was made secret. Important issues were to be decided by referendums. In these and other ways the Progressives hoped to give back to the ordinary citizen the control of state and city governments. In some states and cities the power of the political bosses was smashed completely. Wisconsin led the way under its new governor, Robert M. la Follette. The legislature regulated railways, broke up monopolies, set minimum wages and maximum hours, made up workmen's compensation schemes, passed factory and child labour acts and protected the area's natural resources. Many other states passed similar legislation. By 1915 twenty-five states had passed laws on workmen's compensation and between 1908 and 1913 twenty states passed acts on pensions. Most states had laws regulating child labour by 1920. In many cities attempts were made to improve the honesty of the police forces and to control gambling, vice and crime. Many cities received better public services and more parks and schools.

The success and failure of the Progressives. You can see that the Progressives won many victories against big business and political machines. These benefited the workers and the farmers as well as the middle class. Indeed the protest of the Progressives was much more effective than that of the trade unions or the Granges and the Populists. Big business and political machines were forced to take notice of the muckrakers. They were thrown into the defensive. No more could they afford to ignore completely the welfare of the ordinary American citizen. Some industries voluntarily improved their working conditions and tried to improve the relations between employers and workers. A few even began their own pension and profit-sharing schemes.

Yet despite these triumphs the Progressives did not really break the powerful grip of the trusts and machines on American society. Roosevelt was *not* a trust buster. He did nothing to strengthen the Sherman Anti-Trust Act and the number of trusts actually rose during his presidency. Even the trusts he broke reformed under a new guise. He said: 'Our aim is not to do away with corporations: on the contrary these big aggregations are a necessary part of modern industrialism. . . . We are not attacking corporations but endeavouring to do away with any evil in them.' Some trusts were good, others were bad. He wished simply to root out those which had gained their position by unfair means. For this purpose he created the Bureau of Corporations, whose job was to investigate the trusts and publish reports on them. Wilson seemed to take more positive steps than Roosevelt. The Clayton Act and the Federal Trade Commission were new weapons used against the trusts. Yet despite the speeches in favour of the small man and competition Wilson admitted that: 'We shall never return to the old order of individual competition because . . . the organisation of business upon a grand scale of cooperation is, up to a certain point, itself normal and inevitable.' He supported the idea of free competition but recognised that this could lead to monopoly. Monopoly gained by fair methods was a good thing. It was bad if it resulted from unfair ones. Wilson's difficulty was to say what was fair or unfair. Only by thorough investigation of each monopoly could he decide. This took time and meanwhile new monopolies were forming.

Think carefully. The Progressives wanted both the benefits of big business and the continuance of America as the land of promise, the land of opportunity for the plain man. Yet these aims conflicted with each other. Roosevelt and Wilson were right. Big business had come to stay. It could not be made little again. Inevitably it greatly reduced the chances of the ordinary man to start from scratch, work hard, buy and sell and win for himself an independent economic status and respected social position. The Progressives *failed* in their basic aim to revive the traditions of old America because it was impossible to do such a thing. The rise of big business shattered Jefferson's ideals once and for all.

Similarly, the Progressives failed to smash the bosses and the political machines. The main reason was simple. None of the political reforms we have mentioned—secret ballot, referendum, the choice of candidates by the people and so on—altered the relationship between the bosses, the machines and the new immigrants. The bosses still suggested the candidates for office and the immigrants voted for them. The immigrants voted as they were told to do by the machines. As in business, so in politics. Times and conditions had changed. The immigrants were in America to stay. Their presence meant that the Progressives were bound to fail in their attempt to revive Jacksonian ideas of popular democracy.

Other Protests

The Temperance Movement and Prohibition. As Progressivism faded a movement to prohibit the manufacture and sale of alcohol to the general public reached its climax. Ever since colonial times Puritans had opposed the drinking of alcohol which they linked with idleness, poverty, crime and vice. In the nineteenth century such evils became associated particularly with the urban immigrant. As early as the 1820s Puritans saw their Sabbaths ignored by drunken Irish navvies fighting, swearing and gambling in the slums of Boston and New York.

As immigration increased the Puritans attracted the support of rural areas and women's organisations. In the 1870s members of the Women's Christian Temperance Union marched into saloons, sang psalms, read from the Bible, poured 'the Devil's Brew' into the streets, and tried to persuade their audience never to drink again. In 1893 the Anti-Saloon League was formed. It was 'an army of the Lord to wipe out the curse of drink'. The muckrakers gave the movement more backbone when they exposed the monstrous profits of the breweries, the alarming number of town saloons, the evil licensing system and the corruption of the cities and their bosses. By 1916 cities and states, containing 68 per cent of the population, had outlawed the saloon.

The war against Germany stirred American patriotism and allowed the Temperance movement to win its cause. Americans at home were asked to give moral support to their soldiers abroad by making sacrifices. Giving up alcohol was one of them. In 1918 the League and the W.C.T.U., backed by millions of voters, pressed Congress to adopt the 18th Amendment to the Constitution. This prohibited 'the manufacture, sale or transportation of intoxicating liquors' even in peacetime.

Americans v. the 'new' immigrants. If you have read this chapter carefully you will have noticed that workers, farmers, the urban middle classes and the Temperance movement all made complaints about immigrants. From about the 1880s there grew up a demand for the restriction of further immigration. The main reason for this was the change in the character of immigration after about 1880. Before then the bulk of immigrants came from northwestern Europe—from Britain, Germany and Scandinavia. In other words most Americans were members of the Celtic and Anglo-Saxon races which were mainly Protestant in their religion. Between 1880 and 1920, however, over 40 per cent of the immigrants were Slavs, Jews and Latins from central and southeastern Europe. They were not Protestants. It was these 'new' immigrants in particular whom the Americans identified with blacklegging, strikes, militant unions, socialism, the slums, drunken-

ness, vice and crime, the boss and the political machine. Such activities were thought to debase American life, to undermine a nation dedicated to liberty, free enterprise and democracy. But the demand for a curb on immigration implied a fundamental change of policy. Ever since the founding of Jamestown there had been virtually no restrictions on people entering America.

During the 1914–18 war, however, there were groups of Germans, Irish, Poles, Czechs and other people recently arrived in the New World who were much more interested in supporting the policies of their homelands than those of America. In their instincts and thoughts they were European, not American. After the war the collapse of governments and economies in many parts of Europe threatened to cause a renewed heavy migration of Poles, Jews, Slavs and Latins to America. Meanwhile, American industry and trade suffered a postwar depression which caused much unemployment, many strikes and violent clashes between 'new' immigrants and American workers.

In 1917 came the first significant departure from the policy of freedom of entry. Immigrants now had to pass a literacy test before they could enter the U.S.A. Four years later a new Immigration Act was passed. Two more Acts came in 1924 and 1929. The effect of these three Acts was to limit the total number of immigrants in any one year to 150,000 and to admit a greater proportion of people from Britain, Germany and Scandinavia than from central and southeastern Europe.

This drastic change of policy was one of the important results of the age of protest. We hope you can see its great significance. The great New World experiment of gathering together in the wilderness peoples of mixed origins and moulding a new race of Americans was now considered to be over. The American character and its way of life had been decided. The 'new' immigrant had nothing good to offer. To continue to allow his free entry into America was to undermine its Anglo-Saxon heritage. This Americans did not want.

Further Reading

Allen, Frederick Lewis, *The Big Change*, Harper, 1952.
Dodd, John W., *Everyday Life in Twentieth Century America*, Batsford, 1965.
Hofstadter, Richard, ed. *The Progressive Movement, 1900–1915*, Prentice-Hall, 1963.
    (Contemporary documents.)
Kouwenhofen, John A., *Adventures of America*, Harper, 1938.
Regier, C. C., *The Era of the Muckrakers*, Peter Smith, 1957.
Walker, Robert H., *Everyday Life in the Age of Enterprise*, Batsford, 1967.

11 PROSPERITY, DEPRESSION AND THE NEW DEAL, 1920–41

The 1920s were a golden era for big business and the Republican Party. Surviving all the attacks made on it big business further increased its power and prestige as industrial output reached unprecedented heights. The problems of the trusts, the slums and political corruption now seemed less pressing as the economy prospered as it had never done before.

The Golden 'Twenties

The business boom. During the 1920s the output of American manufacturing industry rose by over one-third and by 1929 America produced about 46 per cent of the world's industrial goods. (In 1913 the figure had been 36 per cent.) This great business boom was led by three new industries—motor vehicles, electricity and chemicals—which achieved spectacular increases in output. For example, between 1920 and 1929 the annual production of motor vehicles rose from 1.9 to 4.5 million and that of electricity from 43 to 96 billion kWh.

These three industries had enormous effects upon other industries, employment, international and domestic trade, and the American way of life. Rapidly rising motor production required growing amounts of rubber, plate glass, leather upholstery, petroleum, copper, iron and steel and other goods. In 1928 the motor industry consumed 80 per cent of the country's processed rubber, 65 per cent of its leather upholstery, 50 per cent of its plate glass, 11 per cent of its iron and steel, and 8 per cent of its copper. Such was the demand for rubber, oil, tin and copper that America was forced to import more and more of these products. The 1920s saw new oil rushes to Texas and Oklahoma, and the petroleum industry received a new lease of life. By 1928 the annual consumption of petrol by motor vehicles was about 7 billion gallons. The growth of electric power encouraged a much more widespread use of electric lighting and electrical goods like irons, ovens, washing machines, vacuum cleaners, refrigerators, radios and telephones. Associated with the growing chemical industry were the manufacture of cosmetics and synthetic plastics such as bakelite, cellophane and rayon.

All these goods had to be sold. Advertising now became an important industry. Products were advertised in newspapers and magazines, on billboards and over the radio. Americans were told that their favourite products were not only good and cheap but also that they made life more glamorous, romantic, exciting and happy. In 1923 a car called the Jordon Playboy was advertised like this:

'Somewhere west of Laramie there's a broncho-busting steer-roping girl who knows what I'm talking about. She can tell what a sassy pony, that's a cross between greased lightning and the place where it hits, can do with eleven hundred pounds of steel and action that's going high, wide and handsome. The truth is—the Playboy was built for her. . . . She loves the cross of the wild and the tame. . . . Step into the Playboy when the hour grows dull with things gone dead and stale. Then start for the land of real living with the spirit of the lass who rides, lean and rangy, into the red horizon of a Wyoming twilight.'

Intensive advertising was backed up by slick salesmen in showrooms and at the front door. Full of praise for the products they sold, very persuasive, reluctant to take no for an answer, alert to any opening given, they too made themselves a power in the land. Both ad-men and salesmen often sold their wares on hire purchase terms. Payment by instalment became an integral part of the American way of life.

All this was a tremendous stimulus to the building industry. The 1920s witnessed the construction of many new factories, generating stations, chemical plants, telephone exchanges and communications, and radio networks both local and national. Once more the motor industry was a major stimulus. Mud tracks became concrete highways lined with garages, petrol stations, hot dog stalls, chicken dinner restaurants, tearooms, camping sites, rest centres and traffic signs and signals. Town centres were rebuilt to accommodate the motor traffic and new housing suburbs sprang up remote from city centres. As oil boomed in Texas and Oklahoma, skyscraper cities appeared almost overnight. Holiday

NEW

Kissproof

the waterproof rouge . . . in a startling jade green case

50¢

New! Different! Exquisitely modern! Daintily thin! Never before has a Compact Rouge been offered in such a strikingly original case! Luxurious gold and brilliant jade green! An Exclusive Compact Rouge for Particular Women —yet costs but 50c! And its genuine Kissproof!

Waterproof it stays on !

Kissproof — the modern rouge — stays on no matter WHAT one does! A single application lasts all day! The youthful NATURAL Kissproof color will make your cheeks temptingly kissable—blushingly red—pulsating with the very spirit of reckless, irrepressible youth! Your first application of Kissproof will delight you!

Your dealer, if up to date, has this striking new rouge. Get it today! Look for the rich gold and jade green case—and be sure it's stamped Kissproof! If your dealer cannot yet supply you, send direct or

Send for Kissproof Beauty Box

It contains a week's supply of this new, natural Kissproof Compact Rouge, a dainty miniature Kissproof Lipstick, a whole month's supply of Delica-Brow, the original liquid dressing for the lashes and brows, and a week's supply of Kissproof, the Extra Hour Face Powder. Send the coupon now—you'll be glad Kissproof is what it IS after you start using it!

Kissproof *is waterproof it stays on !*

Kissproof Lipstick 50¢

Kissproof Compact Rouge 50¢

Kissproof Face Powder $1.00

resorts mushroomed inland and along the coasts, particularly in California and Florida, to cater for the more wealthy and more mobile American. Everywhere land values boomed, particularly in New York, where the motor revolution and the general prosperity created the famous skyscraper outline so familiar to us today. King of the skyscrapers was the Empire State Building, eighty-six storeys and 1248 feet high, begun in the 1920s and finished in 1931.

Inevitably new giant firms and holding companies appeared on the scene. There were 89 mergers in 1919 and 221 in 1928. The electric power industry was controlled by a powerful trust which by 1928 caused Americans new concern about the trust problems. In 1930 the American Telephone and Telegraph Company became the biggest holding company in the world. In the motor industry there were dozens of small firms competing with each other in the early 1900s. By 1929, however, industry was dominated by the three giant firms of Ford, Chrysler and General Motors. This last firm was controlled by the firm of Dupont which dominated the chemical industry. The money power of big business was as strong as ever.

Changes in social life. Clearly, the face of America was slowly changing. More and more Americans lived in mortgaged surburban houses or in newly-built rented flats and apartments. Their homes contained several labour-saving devices and outside stood their car paid for on an instalment plan. The radio gave them a continuous contact with the rest of America. Manners and morals also changed, particularly amongst the teenagers. They attended cocktail parties, smoked cigarettes, drank gin, danced the foxtrot to saxophone music until the early hours of the morning, and went for all-night car rides. The young ladies began to cut their hair very short and to wear lipstick, skirts just below

l Boom in Texas

the knee and high heeled shoes. Bearing all this in mind no wonder the 1920s has been called various names like the Jazz Age, the Era of Wonderful Nonsense, the Roaring Twenties, the New Era, and the New Freedom.

The new industries rested not only on American and European inventions of the late nineteenth and early twentieth centuries, a massive investment of money in new plant, high pressure advertisement and salesmanship and hire purchase finance, but also on the technique of mass production—sometimes called the American System. The pioneer of this technique was Henry Ford.

Henry Ford, mass production and the motor car. Henry Ford was the son of an Irish pioneer farmer and his Dutch wife. He was born near Detroit just after the great battle of Gettysburg. From an early age Henry's great interest lay not in farming but in tools and machines. When he was thirteen he saw his first steam engine. So struck was he by the idea of a 'horseless carriage' that soon it became the consuming passion of his life. He read about the work of Otto and Daimler on petrol engines and vehicle propulsion and he spent countless hours experimenting for himself. In 1896 Henry built and drove his first motor car. Three years later he became the superintendent of the Detroit Automobile Company. He built twenty cars in two years but the company failed. Other firms made sturdier and simpler cars. Ford then built a powerful but lightweight racing car which won several races and gave him the reputation and the financial backing he needed to start his own firm. The Henry Ford Motor Company was born in 1903.

This time he did not fail. In five years he made eight different models and sold them all successfully. His factory floor space rose five-fold and he built a hundred cars a day. But Ford was not satisfied. He did not want to be 'a quiet respectable citizen with a quiet respectable business'. By now he held the majority of the company's shares. In 1909 he announced that henceforward only one model would be made—the Ford Model T. This was to be a car for the ordinary man, large enough for his family but small enough

for him to care for. It was to be built by the best workmen using the best materials and the simplest designs. Above all, it would be very cheap to buy and run. His success was phenomenal. Between 1909 and 1928 15 million Model T's were built. For most of this period one out of every two American cars was a Model T. By 1913 the new Ford factory at Highland Park in Detroit was turning out one car every three minutes of the working day. Later, it was one car every minute. In the 1920s at the River Rouge plant in Detroit, one car was turned out every ten seconds of the working day. At first its price was 1200 dollars. By 1928 it was 295 dollars. The model was ugly and black but it was sturdy, extremely reliable and built with interchangeable parts. Any man could dismantle it with a monkey wrench and pliers. Defective parts could be taken to the nearest Ford garage and given in part exchange for new ones. The car could then just as easily be rebuilt.

Before 1909 the car was the toy of the very rich. Ford's great achievement was to make it the possession of the ordinary man. He did this by reorganising his factory methods and producing on a vast scale. Ford's practice of mass production was the large-scale manufacture of a standardised car made of interchangeable parts. The product was assembled largely by unskilled labour in a mechanised factory using complex and accurate machine tools and moving assembly lines. It was cheap production aimed at a giant single market. Of course there was nothing new about standardised goods, interchangeable parts, machine tools or moving assembly lines in 1909. But no one before Ford thought about using all these methods together within one factory. Ford's great contribution to industrial practice was this combination of separate methods into one complete, continuous and integrated process. This is very important. Let us look at it in more detail.

At first Ford had made cars like any other firm. Each chassis stood in its place while labourers brought the various parts to it from the stores. The skilled mechanics then fitted them in place. But when Ford conceived his idea of a car for the ordinary man he realised that this method was not capable of producing millions of cars.

In the first place it was too slow. Time ticked by while men fetched parts. Too many men stood idle while they waited for parts or for each other to finish their particular task. In the second place there were not enough skilled men available to make so many cars. Even if there were, think of the space all the chassis would need and the vast problem of supervising them all. A new method was needed which would save time, reduce the waiting periods, employ skilled men and keep production under one roof. Ford did not devise it overnight. He pieced it together slowly. But the final result was fantastic. First he used his skilled men to build specialised machines which at the pull of a lever or the press of a button could speedily and accurately perform tasks like drilling twenty holes at once in four different directions or exert ten ton pressures to shape metal as it passed by. Unskilled men could then be used simply to pull the levers and press the buttons: their machines did the rest. Next he installed giant conveyor belts and gravity slides which moved all the materials and interchangeable parts from one end of the factory to the other. No more waiting. Engine parts came down one subsidiary conveyor; transmission parts down another; rear axle differential parts down another and so on. Men and machines lined the conveyor belts and as the materials and parts moved by them at a slow steady speed they were processed and fitted together. Each man had his own task to do hundreds or thousands of times a day. Often it was as simple as drilling a hole or tightening a screw. Assembled engines, transmission units, rear axle differentials and so on then moved on to the main assembly line where they were fitted to the chassis and wheels to make a completed car.

Mass-production of the Model T

Such was Ford's creation. As he perfected the practice of mass production his car prices fell, his workers' wages rose and his profits multiplied. Most of his profits were used to build bigger and better equipment which lowered prices and raised wages still more. Soon he was copied by the rest of the motor industry and firms making electrical and household goods, cigarettes and foods who made their own amendments to the method to suit their own particular needs. Despite these benefits to the customer and the worker the new method attracted bitter criticism. It is said that mass production makes men slaves to machines. They are taught no skills. The tasks they do are so simple and monotonous that workers have no pride in their work and are bored by their jobs. What do you think about mass production? Do you think on balance it is a good or a bad thing?

Poverty in the midst of plenty. Despite all we have said so far the 1920s was not a golden decade for everyone. Coal-mining, the railways and the New England textile industry all began to decline. Farmers of grains, sugar and cotton in the Midwest and the South faced falling prices after the war. They tried to maintain their income by producing more crops but this tended to destroy or exhaust the soils and make prices fall even faster. Their falling incomes were not matched by falling expenditures. Taxes and mortgage payments still had to be paid, farm wages tended to rise, and the prices of the manufactured goods they bought fell more slowly than their own farm prices. The farmers took out new mortgages worth 2 billion dollars in an attempt to stave off disaster. Many,

armers' problems, 920s.

however, were so indebted that their farms passed to their creditors and the farmers became tenants on the land they once owned. Very real poverty continued to exist amongst the unskilled 'new' immigrants in the big cities and the Negroes both in the North and the Deep South. These were the second-class citizens—low paid, under-nourished, badly housed, and very restricted in their economic and social opportunities. They represented a grim contrast to the majority of Americans enjoying the new prosperity of the 1920s.

Prohibition and crime. Prohibition was intended to stop the liquor trade, drunkenness and crime in the towns and cities. It failed in this aim. Most Americans ignored the law. Alcohol prices rocketed upwards, supplies fell and drunkenness declined, but Americans did not stop drinking. Some Americans cities became even more corrupt. Prohibition undid much of what the muckrakers and the Progressives had achieved. The manufacture and sale of alcohol fell into the hands of bootleggers, moonshiners, rum-runners, hi-jackers, gangsters, racketeers, gunmen and speakeasy operators. The boot-leggers sold redistilled industrial alcohol, the moonshiners made their own home brews, and the rum-runners smuggled liquor into America by ship, speedboat, car and lorry from Europe, the West Indies, Canada and Mexico. The hi-jackers were modern highway-men who stole the alcohol-laden boats, cars and lorries of the bootleggers and the rum-runners who soon hired professional gunmen to protect their interests. Every city and

Al Capone

A Moonshine Still

162

town contained its speakeasies where alcohol was sold illegally to customers who quietly spoke the right passwords at the door. Gangsters operated protection rackets to shield those in the trade. Many judges and policemen not only received bribes from gangsters and racketeers but were bootleggers, moonshiners and rum-runners themselves. Some operators made millions of dollars profit from the illegal alcohol trade. They have been called the barons of booze. It is not surprising to learn that the 1920s have also been labelled 'the Lawless Decade'.

Al Capone. The most notorious gangster was Al Capone—known as Public Enemy Number One. Born in Italy, Capone spent part of his early life in the gangs of the New York slums. He called himself Scarface Al Brown. In 1920 he moved to Chicago to work for Johnny Torrio. This man was the leading figure in the Chicago underworld. He had organised most of the gangs in the city into a crime syndicate and had made racketeering big business. Capone's new job was to intimidate Torrio's remaining rivals and force speakeasy operators to buy liquor from the Torrio organisation. In 1925 Torrio was almost killed by the North Side gang and he decided to get out while he still could. He handed over his empire to Capone who within six years graduated from a 75 dollars a week gangster's bodyguard to America's leading bootlegger and racketeer. By 1927 Capone's earnings from alcohol sales reached 60 million dollars while an extra 45 million came from gambling saloons, dancing halls, race tracks and other rackets.

His expenditures, however, were almost unbelievable. It is said he spent 75 million dollars bribing politicians and policemen and maintaining his own private army of gunmen. Capone controlled both the city of Chicago and the state of Illinois. 'He was the Mayor, Governor and Machine Boss all rolled into one.' At election times his hoodlums watched the polling booths to see that people voted the right way. Thus in 1927 Capone's man Big Bill Thompson defeated the reformers' candidate in the election for mayor. Big Bill said: 'We'll not only reopen places these people (the reformers) have closed, but we'll open 10,000 new ones.' (speakeasies, etc.) Nevertheless, Capone had many enemies. There were rival gangs like the O'Banions, the Gennas and the Aillos. He always had a bodyguard and he drove an armour plated limousine which weighed seven tons and cost him 30,000 dollars. Gang warfare was rife: 227 hoodlums were killed in four years. On St Valentine's Day, 1929, seven O'Banions were machine-gunned to death by men dressed as policemen.

Capone himself was never convicted of murder but the Federal government finally caught up with him in 1931. He was found guilty of tax evasion and sentenced to eleven years' imprisonment. Gaol ruined his health and on release he retired to his Florida mansion where he died in 1947. He had been America's most powerful and formidable gangster. Gangsters and violence have remained a marked feature of American urban life and today are one of the most serious domestic problems.

Izzy Einstein and Moe Smith—prohibition agents. Passing a prohibition law was one thing, enforcing it was another. The Federal government created 1520 prohibition agents to ensure Americans obeyed the law. Later the number was increased. By 1930 there were 2836 agents. The most famous and successful of these agents were Izzy Einstein and his friend Moe Smith. Neither man looked like a detective. Izzy was only five feet five and weighed sixteen stones. He was shaped like a cigar. Moe was two inches taller than Izzy and weighed about seventeen stones. They became so famous that their pictures hung in many speakeasy bars. Masters of disguise and pretence they usually gained access to the speakeasies and stills. Once inside they ordered beer or whisky, poured it into little flasks to keep as evidence, showed their badges and told the men behind the bar that their game was up. In five years they confiscated 5 million bottles of booze worth 15 million dollars and thousands of gallons in kegs and barrels. They closed down hundreds of stills and breweries. Together they made 4,392 arrests and nearly every person was convicted.

The reasons why Prohibition failed. Despite the great personal success of Izzy and Moe the prohibition agents faced an impossible task. Not only had they to keep a watchful eye on those who sold alcohol for industrial and medicinal purposes but they had to patrol 18,700 miles of coastlines and borderlands, police a population of 125 million, fight very well-armed and mobile gangsters, outwit the well-planned and well-organised crime syndicates, resist the bribes offered them, and overcome public apathy. The public consumed the alcohol. It paid the money which gave the crime syndicates their profits. Sometimes, as in Chicago, the public even voted the racketeers into political power. Inevitably, the prohibition agents failed. Nevertheless the Federal government took a long time to end Prohibition. It continued until 1933.

Crash and Depression, 1929–33

Meanwhile legitimate big business and the economic prosperity of the 1920s had collapsed. On 1 September 1929 the total value of stocks and shares in the Wall Street money market of New York was 89 billion dollars. The great crash began a few weeks later. On 24 October over 13 million shares were sold in Wall Street. Five days later another 16 million were traded. These were black days indeed but the sale of shares and the fall in their value continued until 1932. On 1 June 1932 the total value of stocks and shares on the Wall Street market was down to only 15 billion dollars. This loss of 74 billion dollars was borne by millions of investors. Many people lost all they possessed.

Side by side with the Wall Street crash came the enormous collapse of American national income, production, trade, employment, wages and prices. Between 1929 and 1933 American national income fell by about 44 per cent, industrial production by 46 per cent, farm prices by 60 per cent, wholesale prices generally by 38 per cent and wages by as much as 50 per cent. Retail trade declined by one-third. Over 5000 banks closed—they had too much money tied up in securities.

Unemployment. Very disturbing too was the high rise in unemployment. During the 1920s unemployment never exceeded about 2 million. In 1930 it was double this and by early 1933 it was at least $13\frac{1}{2}$ million and perhaps as high as 16 million. Jobless workers in New York, for example, became bootshine boys and sellers of apples, vegetables, rubber

*employment in the
eat Depression*

balls, newspapers and ties. In many cities there were men, women and children who slept in the street, on fire escapes, in warehouses or on park benches. Some deliberately got themselves arrested. Gaol meant warmth, shelter and food. Undernourishment was widespread. One-fifth of all the children in New York were underfed but the proportion was even higher in coalfield areas and some industrial towns. Thousands of boys and girls became tramps, living in railcars and on camp sites near the tracks, travelling from place to place in or under freight wagons. The problem of relief was enormous and insoluble. Private charities, religious bodies and municipal and state governments tried hastily to organise temporary homes, supply food and clothes and offer jobs. Bread lines and soup kitchens became familiar sights in American cities. In 1931 alone 1 billion dollars was spent on the relief of poverty. It was nowhere near enough.

The farm problem. While people in the East stood in bread lines or hunted for waste food in dustbins wheat remained unharvested in the Midwest, fruit rotted along the west coast, and sheep were slaughtered and burnt on their hilly pastures. Prices for farm products tumbled so low that thousands of farmers could not afford to market their produce. The Great Depression aggravated the distress of the farmers particularly in the Midwest and the South who had suffered hardship since the end of the war. In these areas overproduction persisted and the destruction, exhaustion and erosion of the soil continued on millions of acres of land. As farm incomes plunged down, debts

165

piled up. Many more farmers now went bankrupt. They were either evicted from their land or retained by their creditors as tenants. Gone were their lives' work, their independence, their social status—gone were the things prided most by people reared in the Jeffersonian tradition.

The attitude of big business. In October 1929 the country's leading financiers met at the House of Morgan to pool 240 million dollars. They bought shares and thus tried to stop the panic selling and to restore the investors' confidence. Big business stepped in too. At the height of the panic John D, Rockefeller said: 'There is nothing to warrant the destruction of values that has taken place in the past week, and my son and I have for some days past been purchasing sound common stocks.' President Hoover, leader of the Republican Party and champion of big money and big business, declared: 'The fundamental business of the country, that is the production and distribution of commodities, is on a sound and prosperous basis.' Indeed, throughout the slump Hoover continued to insist that the economy was fundamentally sound. Together with bankers, industrialists, economists and politicians Hoover kept saying the worst seemed over and that prosperity was just around the corner. He believed big business would recover its drive and lead America out of the depression. Everyone waited for the recovery. It did not come. National income, production, trade prices and wages continued to fall. Worst of all, unemployment rose higher and higher. The country began to lose faith in big business and Republican government. Disillusionment turned to anger and bitterness. The wealthy bankers and businessmen seemed untouched by the unemployment, the poverty and the loss of homes and farms.

Republican measures. In 1929 the Republicans had made drastic cuts in Federal government expenditure. No attempt was made to relieve poverty and unemployment although the Farm Relief Act tried to encourage farmers' to form cooperatives. The worsening slump and the falling popularity of the Republicans, however, forced Hoover to adopt other policies. He reduced taxation, expanded public works to create more jobs, passed a Home Loans Act to help people in difficulty with mortgage payments, and created a Reconstruction Finance Corporation which made loans to ailing firms. Yet such efforts were not enough. Farmers, workers, the middle classes—all wanted more action. A drastic situation required a dynamic new leader and determined new policies.

Franklin D. Roosevelt

Roosevelt and the New Deal, 1933–41

Franklin D. Roosevelt. A new leader was at hand. In the presidential elections of November 1932 Franklin Delano Roosevelt, a Democrat and a distant cousin of Teddy Roosevelt, was voted into office by 472 votes to 59, the biggest majority ever recorded in American history up to that time. Like Jefferson, Jackson and Wilson he stood as the champion of the common people. As one of them said: 'Roosevelt is the only president who ever cared for people like us.' He raised their hopes and promised immediate action. His pledge was 'a new deal for the American people'. So powerful was Roosevelt's political magnetism that the common people voted him President three more times. This remarkable man, crippled by poliomyelitis but patient, firm and resolute in mind was to dominate American politics until his death in 1945.

The New Deal. Franklin D. Roosevelt promised action and he gave it. Between 1933 and 1938 numerous laws were passed, many new government bodies were created and billions of dollars were spent by the Federal government to help businessmen, bankers, trade unions, farmers, workers, the unemployed, the homeless and those in debt. Indeed, there was a New Deal for everybody. It is impossible here to describe the entire New Deal. Table 9 summarises some of the main features of Roosevelt's programme. Study it carefully, section by section. Discuss each section in class in the following way. Begin by recalling the main problems of the farmers, the businessmen, the trade unionists, the unemployed and so on. To do this you may have to reread earlier sections in this or previous chapters (the index will give you the page references). Once you are clear about the problems study the government's measures to deal with them, read the comments about them in the final column of the table, and then try to explain to each other which problems each measure was concerned with and how it hoped to overcome them.

It has been said that the New Deal was concerned with relief, recovery and reform. Now that you have studied the table carefully perhaps you can rearrange its contents under those three headings. Ask yourself which government measures were designed to bring relief, which were taken to promote recovery, which were aimed at reform? Make up your own table to summarise your classification.

One last exercise is worth doing. Compare Table 9 with Table 8, showing the work of Teddy Roosevelt and Woodrow Wilson. Do you notice any similarities between the programmes of Progressivism and the New Deal? Can you see any differences between them?

Let us try to summarise the nature of the New Deal and explain its significance in American history. Like Progressivism it was a reform programme based on action by the Federal government. However, unlike Progressivism, the New Deal was *not* an attempt to restore free competition and popular political democracy to a nation otherwise very healthy and prosperous. Roosevelt left the urban machines undisturbed and he regarded the trust problem as a secondary issue. The nation was certainly not healthy and prosperous. No, the New Deal was a series of practical experiments designed to cure a very sick economy, to promote economic recovery, to restore a lost prosperity, and to provide security for the ordinary citizen. It involved Federal government to an extent undreamed of by previous generations of Americans. Even the Progressives did not picture such a powerful use of central government. Measures like the enormous public works schemes, the Tennessee Valley programme—which aimed at nothing less than the complete economic and social development of the valley based on hydroelectricity and the navigability of the river—the Wagner Act and the Social Security Act were unknown in America before the 1930s. Never before had Federal government been so powerful a force in economic and social affairs. Between 1933 and 1938 dozens of new government agencies were created, the number of civil servants rose from half a million

Table 9. Some Major Details of the New Deal Programme

Act	*Purpose of Act*
Banking Act 1933	Federal government insured people's deposits in banks against losses caused by financial panic.
National Industrial Recovery Act 1933	Three aims: (1) to set up a *Public Works Administration* to build public works of all kinds (2) to set up a *National Recovery Administration* to make rules or 'codes' for each industry dealing with hours, wages, unfair competition and outlawing child labour; (3) to give trade unions the *legal right* to bargain with employers.
Agricultural Adjustment Act 1933	Set up the *Agricultural Adjustment Administration* to pay subsidies to all farmers willing to reduce their yearly output. Money for subsidies to come from taxes placed on producers like millers and cotton spinners who used the farm products.
Tennessee Valley Development Act 1933	Set up *Tennessee Valley Authority* to re-develop community life in the Tennessee Valley—a region spanning seven states and over 40,000 square miles.
National Labour Relations Act (Wagner Act) 1935	To force employers to recognise and deal with trade unions. To give workers the right to form and join trade unions and to engage in *collective bargaining*. Set up a National Labour Relations Board to punish employers who failed to recognise workers' rights.
Social Security Act 1935	Set up the first *national* scheme of *old age pensions*. Employers and workers to pay into Federal pension fund. Also provided a plan of unemployment insurance, each state to work out its own details.
Soil Conservation Act 1936	(1) Federal government now paid subsidies to farmers who agreed to leave their lands fallow or to plant them with leguminous crops. (2) Federal government began *scientific research into soil conservation*.
Fair Labour Standards Act 1938	Aimed to reduce *maximum working hours* and raise *minimum wages* for workers engaged in inter-state manufactures and trade.
Agricultural Adjustment Act 1938	Federal government now prepared to *subsidise the prices* of many farm products, the amount of subsidy to be raised gradually until farm prices had reached their prewar levels.

168

gether with other banking acts this restored public
fidence in the banking system.

PWA spent over 7 billion dollars and employed mill-
s of men. (2) Codes came to cover 16 million workers.
ild labour prohibited. Workers got 8-hour day and
nimum weekly wage of 12½ dollars. In 1935 N.R.A.
clared unconstitutional by the Supreme Court (3)
embership of trade unions now began to rise.

rm prices rose and farmers' income nearly doubled,
33–37. Act declared unconstitutional 1936. Federal
vernment no right to interfere with agricultural output
a state or to impose such taxes.

very ambitious and very large experiment involving
droelectric stations, flood control, soil conservation,
w communities and industries.

e principle of collective bargaining firmly established.
ade union membership rockets from 3.6 million in
35 to 8.6 million in 1941. A new trade union feder-
on—the C.I.O.—is now born.

ach opposition to this from Conservative Republicans
o regarded it as a measure of socialism. Yet act came
cover 35 million people. After 1945 came further
cial Security Acts.

is was not unconstitutional. Federal government
s a duty to conserve land. Leaving land fallow or
nting it with these crops would improve fertility.

timately gave protection to over 13 million people.
chieved a 40-hour week and a minimum hourly
ge of 40 cents.

is was an attempt to guarantee a minimum income
farmers and to eventually make them as well off as
ey had been just before 1914.

Agency	Purpose of agency
Civilian Conservation Corps	To employ jobless single men aged 18–25, for six-month periods in camps in the mountains and forests. Men taught forestry, flood control, fire prevention.
Works Progress Administration	To coordinate all schemes of public works.
Reconstruction Finance Corporation	To lend money to state and local governments for relieving the poor—'dole' money—and to lend money to firms and banks in debt or for investment.
Farm Credit Administration	To use Federal money to pay off farm creditors and save farmers from bankruptcy.
Home Owners Loan Corporation	To use Federal money to pay off house mortgages and prevent house buyers from losing their homes.

to over 850,000 and many new government buildings appeared in Washington D.C.

This vast extension of Federal government activity horrified the Republicans, big business and the Supreme Court, which declared several acts unconstitutional. This is very understandable. Remember that the American Revolution in 1776 was a protest about over powerful central government; this was what the Founding Fathers tried to prevent when they drew up the American Constitution with its checks and balances. Fear of strong Federal government was deeply implanted in the American mind. Most Americans thought of their country as a land of *minimum* governmental interference with the individual who remained free to shape his own life and destiny in a country which offered tremendous economic and social opportunities for all who could grasp them. Remember, too, that American industry had grown up in an environment of high tariffs, low taxes and weak trade unionism. The New Deal, with its enormous extension of Federal power, seemed to conservatives to undermine the whole American tradition of individualism. To them the New Deal was Socialism.

Looking back now it is perhaps safe to say that the New Deal was not Socialism. The New Deal was a gigantic effort to restore business confidence and thus to revive big business and individual enterprise. It aimed to end the depression and restore prosperity. Once prosperity returned the need for the New Deal vanished. Indeed, to this day America remains the home of private enterprise. The compensation and relief schemes of the 1930s have not formed the basis of a Welfare State. In America today the individual still largely depends upon his own privately arranged insurance schemes to safeguard himself against unemployment, accident, sickness and old age.

How successful was the New Deal in reviving the American economy? This was the main aim of the massive government spending during the 1930s. Federal expenditure created employment and put money into people's pockets, thus increasing their spending on goods and services. Roosevelt hoped that in turn this increased demand would revive business confidence, encourage more output of consumer goods, and stimulate new investment in manufacturing plant, power and transport. A revival in industrial output would further increase employment, wages and spending and boost business

arly 3 million men took part in the scheme, 1933–41.

ent over 10½ billion dollars of Federal money and *mployed* 3.8 million men, 1935-41. Amongst other *ings* built 122,000 public buildings, 77,000 bridges, *5* airports, 664,000 miles of roads, 24,000 miles of *wers.*

confidence, output, employment and income still more. The idea was that the economy would spiral itself upwards to prosperity once government spending created the initial momentum. Try to get this idea clear in your mind. We return to our question: did the New Deal achieve economic recovery?

Perhaps you can work out your own answer to this. Look at the graphs on national income, investment, the output of consumer goods, unemployment, wages and prices. By comparing their levels before and after the period 1929 to 1932 you can make some conclusions about the degree of success of the New Deal. Compare the level of national income in, say, 1921, 1929, 1932 and 1939. What do you conclude? Now do the same for the graphs on investment, consumer goods, unemployment and wages and draw your own conclusions. Put all your findings together and answer these two questions. Did the American economy revive at all between 1933 and 1939? Was the economy as healthy in 1939 as in 1929? Give reasons for your answers. Finally, make your own assessment of the success of the New Deal. Was it completely or only partially successful or a failure? What do you think?

Perhaps you will agree that the New Deal did not restore the American economy to full vigour by 1939. Some historians have said that this was because big business grew to hate the New Deal and therefore did not give it their full support. Others have argued that government spending was *not* massive enough. This meant that as a whole the demand for goods and services in the 1930s remained lower than that of the 1920s. The country's industries coped with it without need for the enormous new investments like factories, roads and power stations, which had greatly encouraged the 1920s boom.

We must remember, however, that the depression between 1929 and 1933 was the greatest slump in American economic history. The road back to prosperity was long and uphill. Undoubtedly, the New Deal at least began America's climb back to recovery. Remember, too, that the Tennessee Valley authority has proved to be very successful and that the New Deal brought relief, employment and hope back to millions of Americans—the jobless, the homeless, the farmers and businessmen. To these people Roosevelt's programme was of direct importance. The farmers, in particular, received

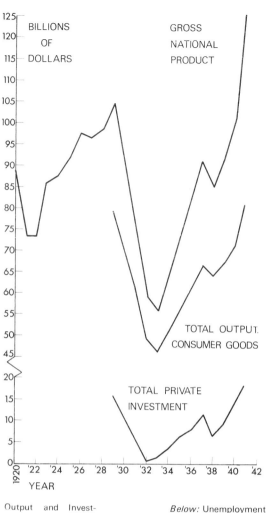

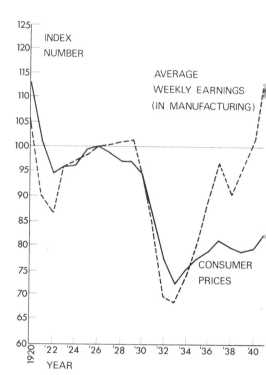

Output and Invest-
ment 1920–41

Below: Unemployment
in the United States
1920–1941

Earnings and Pri■
1920–1941

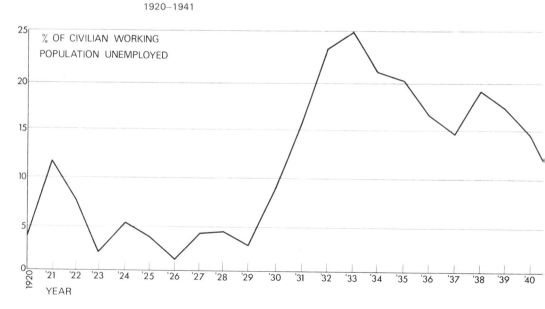

much benefit from the New Deal. Over-production of farm products continued, despite the benefit payments, but farm prices now not only turned upwards but more quickly than those of manufactured goods. By the late 1930s American farmers nowhere faced the distress so common in agriculture between 1920 and 1933. Indeed, farming had become relatively profitable. The social life of farmers no longer was distinct from that of urban dwellers. Roads, cars, electricity, telephones, radio and films became important features of country life. Politically too the farmers had progressed. Encouraged by the agricultural measures of the New Deal American farmers formed a strong and permanent bloc to press the Federal government to protect their interests. Since the 1930s the farmers have remained a forceful political group in American politics.

Labour also greatly benefited from the New Deal. Trade unions had not made much headway in America before 1933. Suddenly, in the National Industrial Recovery Act of that year, the Federal government declared collective bargaining by labour to be legal. The Wagner Act 1935 was a positive encouragement to labour. Workers became free to join unions without any interference from their employers. Big business now had to recognise the unions to which the majority of their workers belonged and to bargain with them in disputes over hours and wages. The workers were given protection from unfair treatment by their employers by the National Industrial Relations Board. Membership of the American Federation of Labour jumped from about 2.1 millions in 1933 to over 4 millions in 1939. But more spectacular and significant was the birth of a new federation of unions—the Congress of Industrial Organisations. By 1939 its membership was about equal to that of the A.F.L. This new federation consisted of industrial unions composed of unskilled men drawn mainly from the ranks of the 'new' immigrants. The mining, transport, construction and mass production manufacturing industries were the ones mainly affected by this new unionism. This was a most important development. Many unskilled men now joined industrial unions which were to remain a permanent feature in American life. Big business could no longer ride roughshod over the working man who now had a voice in his own economic destiny.

In summary we think that the New Deal was only partly successful in reviving the American economy but that it brought great benefits to organised groups like big business, farmers and workers. Indeed, in a very real sense the New Deal strengthened democracy in America.

The New Deal strengthened the Americans' belief in themselves and their great experiment of building a new nation out of a wilderness. Roosevelt's aim was to revive not only big business but all free enterprise. He stood for the welfare of the plain man as well as the profit-making businessman. America was for Americans, both rich and poor. All had a 'right to life, liberty, and the pursuit of happiness'. The day when the robber barons could plunder the continent for their own benefit without concern for the public good was finally over. They were forced to consider the wishes of workers and farmers and to accept that the Federal government was stronger than big business. At the same time even the government had to work within the framework of the American Constitution. The Supreme Court remained the guardian of the Revolutionary ideal.

Further Reading

Allen, Frederick Lewis, *Only Yesterday*, Harper & Row, 1957.
Allen, Frederick Lewis, *The Big Change*, Harper, 1952.
Dodd, John W., *Everyday Life in Twentieth Century America*, Batsford, 1966.
O'Callaghan, D. B., *Roosevelt and the United States*, Longman, 'Modern Times' Series, 1966.
Sann, Paul, *The Lawless Decade*, Arco, 1958.
Sinclair, Andrew, *Prohibition: the Era of Excess*, Faber, 1962.

12 MODERN AMERICA: RICH AND POOR

The Affluent Society

The arsenal of democracy. Japan bombed the American base at Pearl Harbour on 7 December 1941. America went to war against Japan the following day. Germany and Italy, the allies of Japan, declared war on America on 11 December.

Earlier in 1941 Congress had approved of Roosevelt's programme of 'Lend Lease'. By this scheme America volunteered to lend arms and equipment to all nations fighting Hitler until they defeated him. So even before Pearl Harbour America had chosen sides. Roosevelt had made his country 'the arsenal of democracy'.

Between 1941 and 1945 the first priority of the American economy was arms and equipment. In this period American industry produced over 86,000 tanks, 297,000 planes, 17.4 million rifles, carbines and side arms, 64,500 landing vessels, and thousands of ships of various kinds. This huge production required not only labour but materials of every kind, the conversion of factories from peacetime to wartime goods, and the building of new factories and plants.

The war completed the economic recovery begun by the New Deal. In 1940 the total output of America had still not reached the level of 1929. By 1945 it was more than double the 1929 figure. At the time of Pearl Harbour there were still $5\frac{1}{2}$ million people unemployed. By the end of 1942 the figure was down to $1\frac{1}{2}$ million. From then to the end of the war unemployment fell about one million or less—under 2 per cent of the total civilian labour force. In these war years the total numbers employed rose from 51 to 63 million, a figure which included 4 million women and many old or partially handicapped people previously without jobs. Real incomes on average rose about 30 per cent.

When the war ended the world looked with envy at America. It had suffered no war damage. Its economy had benefited enormously from the war effort and its industries were more than a match for their foreign competitors. The ordinary American citizen enjoyed the highest standard of living ever known to mankind. But Americans feared that the end of the war would mean the end of prosperity, full employment and high wages.

The age of high mass consumption. American fears of an end of their prosperity proved unfounded. With peacetime came another great boom in economic activity which lasted until the 1960s. The total product of America rose by over one and a half times from 314 billion dollars in 1945 to over 492 billion dollars in 1963. Its economy still dominated the world. In 1964 America produced over a third of the world's total of electrical energy, about a quarter of the world's coal, crude petroleum and steel, and more than one-sixth of its iron ore.

Most American families and individuals shared in this new round of prosperity. Table 10 summarises the general upward trend in peoples incomes between 1947 and 1965. Discuss the main features of it with your teacher.

174

Table 10. The Distribution of Family and Personal Incomes: 1947–65

Percentage figures: constant 1965 dollars

1. FAMILIES			2. UNRELATED INDIVIDUALS		
Income $	*1947*	*1965*	*Income $*	*1947*	*1965*
Under 3000	30	17	Under 1500	52	39
3000–4999	31	16	1500–2999	24	22
5000–6999	19	18	3000–4999	17	17
7000–9999	12	24	5000–6999	4	12
10,000–14,999	8	17	7000–9999	1	7
15,000 and over		8	10,000 and over	2	3
	100	100		100	100

A cruder but simpler way of showing the rising prosperity of the American is to use a statistic called average real income per head. You can see from the graph that in 1945 the average American received an income after tax of 1642 dollars. By 1966 his income was 2294 dollars – almost double that of 1929. This present income is also bigger than that of the average citizen in other industrial countries and enormous compared to people in undeveloped and over-populated countries. Here are a few comparisons selected from a table compiled by the United Nations.

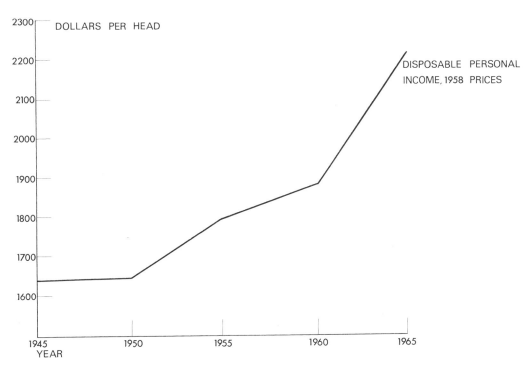

Table 11. Relative Incomes per head in 1965: Ten Selected Countries

(figures in American dollars)

Country	Average income per head of population
America	2893
Canada	1825
New Zealand	1706
Australia	1620
United Kingdom	1451
West Germany	1447
Japan	696
Mexico	412
India	86
Malawi	38

Foreign demand for American goods, a rise in the American birth rate, another housing boom based on a large-scale movement of people to the suburbs, a further increase in Federal expenditure, the continuing revolution in motor and air transport, a high demand for standardised and mass-produced goods—these were just a few of the reasons for this great postwar prosperity. This prosperity centred around cars, superhighways, suburban houses filled with electrical labour-saving gadgets, supermarkets, frozen and processed foods, high pressure advertising, slick salesmanship, radio and television, the forty-hour week, long summer holidays and tourism. These today are marked features of

The high standard of living which most American families enjoy is often made possible by the mother of a family returning to work once her children are growing up

the American way of life. The next paragraph contains some facts and figures about these things to help you to see their importance in American life and to show you why the postwar years have been called 'the age of high mass consumption'.

Most American homes contain labour-saving gadgets. In 1929, the peak year of the golden twenties, the value of electrical household appliances in the country was 160 million dollars. In 1963 they were valued at 9 billion dollars. Such gadgets include electric ovens, washing machines, dishwashers, clothes driers, refrigerators and, more recently, appliances like electric blankets, shavers, toasters, shoe cleaners, hedge shears, coffee grinders, coffeepots and tin openers. The refrigerator is standard equipment for Americans. Their consumption of frozen foods is outstanding. Frozen foods had barely been introduced in 1929 but in 1962 10 billion pounds in weight were eaten. Radio and television are other standard items in the American home. Radio sets numbered 176 million in 1962—almost one set for each person. Television has shown a spectacular increase. There were only 4 million sets in 1950. By 1962 the number was over 56 million. Nearly every home has at least one television set. Americans own half the total number of television sets in the world.

Even more staggering is the number and importance of motor cars in American life. There is one car for every three Americans and many families now have at least two cars each. In 1964 there were 84 million cars in America—over one half of all the cars in the world. The car has meant a renewed flight to the suburbs. In the 1950s 16 million Americans joined those already in suburban homes. It has also given people great freedom to travel. Americans can visit the West during their long holidays. The national parks and the national forests each received over 100 million visitors a year in the 1960s and picnics, fishing, hunting, ski-ing, camping and swimming provide outdoor pursuits for the mobile Americans.

This high mass consumption of goods depends in part upon the willingness of Americans to accept mass production, and the cheap, standardised products associated with it. Americans still retain the habits of the frontiersman and the immigrant who, as we have explained in Chapter 9, each had his own reasons for buying these products. This willing acceptance means that most Americans, despite their different incomes, have very similar patterns of life. For example, a Ford factory worker may have the same kind of car, wear the same styles of suits, use the same kind of central heating and kitchen labour-saving devices, watch the same television programmes, and eat the same brands of packaged food as a Ford executive or a Detroit banker. Conformity in the mode of living has become a marked feature of American society.

A rich society with problems. Despite its great wealth and prosperity modern America faces serious domestic problems. Responsible Americans realise that their society is still far from perfect. The rapid growth of population, cities and industries has meant great wastes of natural and human resources. In the past the American was prodigal. He moved ever west, ransacking the wilderness of its products as he went. Not so today. Soils have to be carefully conserved and kept fertile, forests preserved by huge reforestation schemes, and flood waters contained by dams and irrigation projects. Densely populated cities and suburbs have created enormous problems of waste disposal, water supplies and air pollution. Motor vehicles clog streets forested with traffic signs. Parking is a nightmare. By 1965 more Americans were dying each year in road accidents than were killed in the Korean War between 1951 and 1954. More disturbing are the high rates of crime and violence, drug addiction, juvenile delinquency and divorce which prevail, particularly in huge urban areas like New York and Chicago. There is no room in this chapter to consider these problems. Instead we shall concentrate on the two most fundamental domestic problems in America today: poverty and racial prejudice. These two problems of course are very closely linked to the last group of problems we have just mentioned.

Poverty and Racial Prejudice

Poverty in the land of plenty. That poverty is a fundamental problem in modern America appears very surprising. We picture America as the land of plenty. Yet for 10 million families or more poverty is a hard fact of life. It is not merely that they possess fewer of the things that most Americans have—one battered old car instead of two new ones, one television instead of several. Many are poor in the absolute sense of the word: they do not receive enough of even the basic things in life. Their housing is dilapidated and unhealthy, their food inadequate in quantity and quality, their education poor or non-existent, their choice of employment very restricted, and their jobs insecure and irregular. In 1947 the poorest fifth of Americans received only 5 per cent of the total income earned by the entire population. This proportion was still the same in 1965. The national wealth is very unequally shared. Poverty then is a serious and persistent problem; a national disgrace.

Who are the American poor? The short answer is the small farmer, black and white farm labourers in the Deep South, Negroes and immigrants in the urban slums, Indians on reservations, Eskimos in Alaska, and Spanish-Americans in Texas. They are the jobless and the under employed.

The reasons for their poverty are many: old age, ill-health, oversized families, low mental ability, poor general education, the lack of appropriate skills or knowledge, unequal opportunities for employment because of discrimination based on sex, race, religion or colour. Before reading on discuss in class in general terms how and why these various factors affect employment and income.

The poverty of the Negro. The Negroes are the largest single group of the American poor. Look carefully at the following table and say what you conclude.

Table 12. The Distribution of Family Incomes by Race and Region: 1966

Percentage figures based on 1965 income levels

Income $	North and West		South	
	White	*Negro*	*White*	*Negro*
Under 1000	1.9	3.2	4.1	11.3
1000–1999	4.1	7.4	8.1	20.6
2000–2999	5.9	11.6	8.3	18.3
3000–3999	6.6	13.3	8.6	15.6
4000–4999	7.1	11.4	9.4	10.2
5000–9999	45.1	38.8	42.4	20.0
Over 10,000	29.3	13.3	19.1	4.0
	100	100	100	100

The poverty of the Negro is now mainly an urban one and as much a feature of the North as the South. Before the First World War nine-tenths of all Negroes lived in the rural South—once the area of slavery. Since then they have moved in large numbers from the land and agriculture to the centres of industrial and commercial towns throughout the country. By 1966 69 per cent of all Negroes lived in the large cities of America. 45 per cent lived in the North, concentrating particularly in the slums or ghettoes of New York, Chicago, Detroit, Philadelphia, Baltimore, Cleveland, Milwaukee and Washington D.C.

These ghettoes occupy the oldest parts of the town. The Negro quarter in New York, for example, is called Harlem. Here a quarter of a million Negroes are crammed into an area of three and a half miles where the tenements are rat-infested and the streets full of refuse. In 1964 an official report on the conditions in Harlem said that at least 90 per cent of the living accommodation was built before 1921 and 40 per cent before 1901. The houses and tenements were generally 'unsafe, deteriorating and overcrowded'. The average yearly income of Negroes in Harlem was 3480 dollars. For the rest of New York it was 5103 dollars. One out of every five males over the age of fourteen was separated from his wife. Two out of every seven females over fourteen were living apart from their husbands. At school Harlem children in the third grade were a year behind the standards of other New York children; those in the sixth grade were two years behind. Juvenile delinquency was twice as common in Harlem as in the rest of the city; similarly, drug addiction was five times and the number of murders six times as frequent there.

Most Negroes find it impossible to escape from their poverty. Many white Americans argue that the basic reasons for this are idleness and lack of initiative. They say that America is the land of opportunity, the place where hard work brings its material rewards. A recent report on Negro poverty takes a different view. Born into large families living usually in slum surroundings, badly cared for and poorly educated compared to the white man, the Negro becomes an unskilled worker. Unskilled work is irregular and low paid. As automation and mechanisation increase, the number of unskilled jobs falls. In the past, railways, coal mines, steel mills and packing houses all employed large numbers of Negroes but today jobs here are dwindling. Unemployment is much higher amongst Negroes than whites. In 1966 3.4 per cent of white workers were without jobs: the Negro figure was 7.5 per cent. In some ghettoes, however, unemployment amongst young male Negroes is as high as 50 per cent. Unemployment means humiliation, a sense of failure, a loss of pride. Such feelings are often increased amongst male Negroes because their wives are more regularly employed as white collar or domestic workers and become the breadwinners of the family. Humiliation and failure lead to divorce, drunkenness, drug-taking, crime and violence. The Negro family becomes unstable and poorer. The children see little hope for themselves, make little effort at school, and like their fathers enter the adult world as unskilled workers. The vicious circle starts all over again. Before you read on, discuss this vicious circle with your teacher.

Negro poverty and racial discrimination. Negro poverty is rooted in racial discrimination. If you re-read the later parts of Chapter 7 you will see that despite the Civil War the South remained convinced that the black man was subhuman, a creature not entitled to the political and economic rights which the whites enjoyed. This racial prejudice remains almost as strong today as it did a century ago.

In 1963 Martin Luther King, the Negro civil rights leader, described the life of a black person in Birmingham, Alabama, in these terms:

'You would be born in a jim-crow hospital to parents who probably lived in a ghetto. You would attend a jim-crow school. . . . You would spend your childhood playing mainly in the streets because the "coloured" parks were abysmally inadequate. . . . If you went shopping with your mother and father, you would trudge along as they purchased at every counter, except one, in the large or small stores. If you were hungry or thirsty you would have to forget about it until you got back to the Negro section of town, for in your city it was a violation of the law to serve food to Negroes at the same counter with whites. . . . If you wanted a job in this city—one of the greatest iron- and steel-producing centres in the nation—you had better settle on doing menial work as a porter or labourer. If you were fortunate enough to get a job, you could expect that promotions to a better status or more pay would come, not to you, but to a white employee regardless of your comparative talents. On your job, you would eat in a separate place and use a water fountain and lavatory labelled "Coloured" in conformity to citywide ordinances.

'. . . You would be confronted with every conceivable obstacle to taking that most important walk a Negro American can take today—the walk to the ballot box. Of the 80,000 voters in Birmingham, prior to January, 1963, only 10,000 were Negroes. Your race, constituting two-fifths of the city's population, would make up one-eighth of its voting strength.'

Similar conditions existed everywhere in the South and are disappearing only very slowly.

In the great cities of the North the Negro long since gained the vote and has never had segregation imposed upon him by state or city laws. Nevertheless he has been the real victim of racial prejudice. As he moved to the city centres seeking work white people moved out to the suburbs. In part this was because the whites felt that the presence of the Negro in their district would mean a fall in the value of their houses, a lowering of standards in the schools, and violence and danger in the streets. Gradually, the Negro has found himself living in a neighbourhood inhabited only by people of his own colour. If he became better off and tried to move into the white suburbs he found that white property owners refused to sell or rent accommodation to him. Social segregation had arisen: not because the law demanded it but because the Northern whites desired it and took steps amongst themselves to create it. Once the wealthy whites deserted the central districts of their cities they took little further interest in their planning and development. They became reluctant to see their city governments spend money to improve facilities there. The Negro areas became neglected and more and more squalid. The ghettoes became slums.

The economic position of the Negro worker in the North has been an inferior one. Unskilled white workers resented his intrusion and competition. Many trade unions refused to admit him. The northern employers showed a similar prejudice against the black man as their counterparts in the South. For example, in 1963 only 2 per cent of all Americans involved in apprenticeship training were Negroes. Even the Federal government practised racial discrimination in its employment of labour.

The Response of the Federal Government, 1945-68

All the postwar Presidents expressed their concern about the problems of poverty and racial prejudice. Each one has proposed a programme of action to overcome them. The programmes had different names. Truman's was called 'the Fair Deal', Eisenhower's 'the New Republicanism', Kennedy's 'the New Frontier', and Johnson's 'the Great Society'. These slogans show that the basic aim of the Presidents was to reshape American society, to make opportunities for all more equal so that America was more truly democratic. All these programmes proposed measures to improve minimum wages, health, housing, education and social benefits, and to guarantee civil rights. Truman urged a compulsory health service. Kennedy and Johnson urged free medical care for the old. The Fair Deal also called for schemes in the Missouri and Columbia Valleys similar to the one created in the Tennessee Valley. Kennedy wanted particularly large funds for schools and colleges providing basic and vocational education and retraining schemes for the poor and unemployed.

The failure of the Presidents. Despite all these hopes and promises there was no Fair Deal. The New Frontier was not reached. The Great Society remained a dream. In 1968 the problems of the unemployed, the sick, the aged, the small farmer, the slum dweller and the Negro were at least as acute as they had been in 1945. Efforts were made but they fell far short of success.

The biggest single attempt to reduce poverty came in 1965. President Johnson's Economic Opportunity Act was backed by a Federal grant of one billion dollars. The act created an Office of Economic Opportunity to direct work training problems for young people. One of its projects is the Job Corps. Young people between sixteen and twenty-one attend conservation camps and training centres to improve their literacy and receive vocational guidance. In 1965 100,000 people were involved. Yet there are millions of people in need of this kind of help—Negroes, Indians and recent immigrants as well as whites—who will never receive it.

The racial problem is more acute now than ever before. The Federal government has helped the Negro to win certain civil rights but these have not given him the economic and social opportunities to become the white man's equal.

The Civil Rights Act 1964 outlawed the segregation of whites and Negroes in all public places. Henceforth it was against the law to prevent Negroes mixing with whites in places like hotels, restaurants, sports arenas and places for public amusement. It also prohibited racial discrimination in employment and trade unions. Finally, and very important, it standardised the literacy test and banned any practices which prevented Negroes from voting. At the same time a new amendment to the Constitution prohibited the poll tax. (To understand this you may need to re-read p. 104 in Chapter 7.)

In the Southern states, however, the Negro still found it difficult to vote. President Johnson himself said in 1965 that:

'The Negro citizen may go to register only to be told that the day is wrong, or the hour is late, or the official in charge is absent. And if he persists and if he manages to present himself to the registrar, he may be disqualified because he did not spell out his middle name or because he abbreviated a word on the application. And if he manages to fill out an application he is given a test. The registrar is the sole judge of whether he passes this test. He may be asked to recite the entire constitution, or explain the most complex provisions of state laws. And even a college degree cannot be used to prove he can read and write.'

In 1965 the Voting Rights Act was passed to stop any device used to prevent a person from voting. Today the right of the Negro to vote is now widely accepted in the South although

Mississippi, Alabama and South Carolina continue to evade the law as much as they can.

The Southern states have also been very slow to give the Negroes the same educational opportunities as the whites. In 1954 the Supreme Court ruled that states must mix whites and Negroes in the same schools so that they could enjoy equal facilities. This had to be done with 'all deliberate speed'. In 1957 the Central High School at Little Rock, Arkansas, wanted to admit its first coloured pupils. Governor Faubus intervened, placed National Guardsmen round the building, and ordered them to prevent Negro children entering it. He ignored both a Federal Court order and a command from President Eisenhower to remove the National Guardsmen. An angry white crowd gathered round the school in support of Faubus. Eisenhower then sent 1000 Federal troops to Little Rock to disperse the mob and protect the Negroes as they used the school. This important episode showed, on the one hand, the determination of the Federal government to achieve desegregation and, on the other, the delaying tactics of a Southern state. As late as 1967 90 per cent of all Negro children in the Deep South states still attended all-black schools. Even today Negro parents who try to send their children to white schools are intimidated by white Southerners, who fire bullets into their houses or threaten them with the sack or eviction from their homes.

There is little educational equality even in the North. The Negroes live quite apart from the whites. They remain in the ghettoes with their slum housing and outdated, decaying schools. Still poorly educated and untrained, the better paid jobs remain beyond their reach. They continue to be victims of the vicious circle we spoke of in the last section.

ung men receiving truction in electri- wiring under the *b Corps pro-* *amme.*

Conservative Republicans and Southern Democrats. Why have the postwar Presidents achieved so little of their Programmes? The most important single reason is the strength of the Conservative Republicans and Southern Democrats in Congress. We have already spoken of the alliance of these two groups earlier in the book.

On the one hand the Conservative Republicans cling to their old belief that America is the great land of opportunity, the place where hardworking and enterprising people can win themselves a good full life. To them America is built on private enterprise. Those who remain poor have only themselves to blame. The Conservative Republican resists the extension of government enterprise as hard as he can. He resents Federal money being spent on social security services. He is against ideas like minimum wage rates, pensions, Medicare, subsidised housing. He calls this Socialism and considers it a real threat to the American way of life. Powerful in Congress, he tries hard to stop social legislation like this, or at least, to cut the amount of Federal money available for such reforms.

On the other hand the Southern Democrats cling to their longstanding belief that the white man is superior to the Negro. This belief goes back well before the time of the American Civil War. The Southern Democrat flatly opposes the Negro's demand for civil rights; his aim is to keep the Negro in a position of inferiority. Even when civil rights laws have been passed, the Southern Democrat has disobeyed them and intimidated Negroes by burnings, bomb-throwing and killings.

You can see that by working together these two political groups can stop, delay or water down bills introduced into Congress by the presidents.

The Negro Protest

Background. Negroes have protested about their position in American society since the very first days of slavery. Yet until modern times those who protested were a small minority: most Negroes remained silent, suppressed first by the greater physical force of the slave-owner and later by the 'Jim Crow' laws. In the present century, however, more and more Negroes have been willing to express their anger, to participate in the movement for civil rights: i.e. the possession of the same rights and opportunities as the white man.

There are many reasons for this swelling protest. Negroes have fought and died for their country in two world wars and in Korea and Vietnam. They have fought to defend democracy and personal freedoms. Yet at home democracy is not complete. The Negroes have fought for freedom but they are not free themselves. White Americans, so eager to protect and promote democracy in the world, are reluctant to give it to the Negroes of their own country. Meanwhile the Negroes in Africa had achieved a political revolution. Martin Luther King wrote:

'The American Negro saw, in the land from which he had been snatched and thrown into slavery, a great pageant of political progress. He realised that just thirty years ago there were only three independent nations in the whole of Africa. He knew that by 1963 more than thirty-four African nations had risen from colonial bondage. The Negro saw black statesmen voting on vital issues in the United Nations—and knew that in many cities of his own land he was not permitted to take that significant walk to the ballot box. He saw black kings and potentates ruling from palaces—and knew he had been condemned to move from small ghettoes to larger ones.'

Caught up in the vicious circle of poverty and unemployment the American Negroes have grown increasingly bitter and resentful. By walking along city streets and gazing in shop windows, by watching films and television, by reading books and magazines they can see how much wealthier the whites are than themselves.

American Negroes first seriously tried to help themselves in 1910 when, with the help of white liberals, they formed the National Association for the Advancement of Coloured

People (N.A.A.C.P.). Its main aim was to give Negroes legal protection and to bear the costs of fighting test cases before the Supreme Court. Partly due to its efforts the Supreme Court has made several decisions favourable to the Negro cause: for example, the 1954 ruling in favour of desegregation in education which we mentioned earlier.

The slowness of the legal victories won by the N.A.A.C.P., the snail pace of educational desegregation, and the shortcomings of the policies of the Federal government have been additional reasons why in recent years the Negroes have rallied together in huge numbers to win equal rights and opportunities.

Martin Luther King and nonviolent direct action. In 1955 in Montgomery, Alabama, Rosa Parks refused to give up her seat on a municipal bus to a white person. She was promptly arrested. Angry Negro women urged their local leaders to act. They called a boycott of the city buses. For the next six months none of the 17,000 Negroes of Montgomery used them. Despite violence from white hooligans and the imprisonment of many boycotters on trumped-up charges, the Negroes kept off the buses. The life of the Deep South now came under a glaring spotlight. The rest of America and the world followed the events on television and radio and in the press. They saw the Negroes for the first time win a significant victory over their white tormentors—not by physical violence but by peaceful and orderly mass protest led by black clergymen. Faced with an alarming fall in its bus revenues the city government gave way and desegregated its public transport.

The Montgomery boycott produced an important new leader, Martin Luther King, and encouraged the tactics of nonviolent direct action in other cities and states.

Martin Luther King was born in Georgia in 1929. He became a Baptist minister and a writer. As President of the Montgomery Improvement Association he directed the bus boycott of 1955–56. The following year, together with clergymen from other Southern cities, he formed the Southern Christian Leadership Conference (S.C.L.C.) to fight against racial segregation.

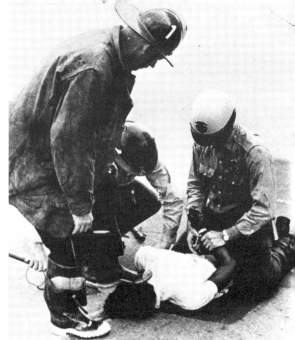

*Nonviolent Direct
Action*

He said that the Negroes were tired of 'three hundred years of humiliation, abuse and deprivation'. They were tired of racial discrimination, poverty and segregation.

'The Negro wants absolute and immediate freedom and equality, not in Africa or in some imaginary state, but right here in this land today. . . . It is because the Negro knows that no person—as well as no nation—can truly exist half-slave and half-free that he has embroidered upon his banners the significant word NOW.'

How were the Negroes to make their demands felt? King believed that physical violence was not the answer. The Negro was 'unarmed, unorganised, untrained, disunited'. More important, as a Christian he had been taught to oppose bloodshed. On the other hand, fighting legal battles in the courts was very slow. No, the best form of protest was nonviolent direct action, a method used by the first Christians against the Roman Empire and very recently by Ghandi to drive the British from India.

Nonviolent direct action meant a mass turnout of Negroes in public places. It meant the turnout of the lame, the crippled and the blind as well as all those of sound mind and body. It meant that Negroes would stand up before the white man, look him straight in the eye and dare him to do what he will. It meant listening to insults and jeers, getting soaked by water hoses and manhandled by police, being thrown into gaol without due cause—and not retaliating with anger and violence but with moderate language and courtesy. It meant that Negroes would fight with their hearts, their consciences, their courage, and their sense of justice. Nonviolent direct action gave Negroes confidence and pride in themselves as people: it gave each of them a chance to take part in winning his own freedom.

'An important part of the mass meetings was the freedom songs. In a sense the freedom songs are the soul of the movement. . . . We sing the freedom songs today for the same reason the slaves sang them, because we too are in bondage and the songs add hope to our determination that We shall overcome, Black and white together, We shall overcome someday.

'I have stood in a meeting with hundreds of youngsters and joined in while they sang

A Negro demonstrator is held face down on the ground by a police officer and a fireman's boot as he is handcuffed after his arrest during massive protest marches in Birmingham Alabama. A Third officer, truncheon in hand, helps to hold the man down

186

"Ain't Gonna Let Nobody Turn Me 'Round". It is not just a song; it is a resolve. A few minutes later, I have seen those same youngsters refuse to turn around from the onrush of a police dog, refuse to turn around before a pugnacious Bull Connor in command of men armed with power hoses. These songs bind us together, give us courage together, help us to march together.'

Re-read this section and then discuss in class whether or not nonviolent direct action was easy for people to do.

Nonviolent direct action simply draws public attention to the Negro's claim for equal rights and opportunities. But how are civil rights to be really achieved? Martin Luther King called for full civil rights legislation which must then be obeyed throughout America. The Negro must be allowed to vote, to attend integrated schools, to have an equal chance when seeking employment. The President must wholeheartedly support the Negro movement for freedom, the Federal government must allow no state or region to ignore or distort the laws, the Negroes must vote as a bloc and use their political power as a tool to win liberation.

Yet 'the struggle for rights is at bottom a struggle for opportunities'. Economic and social opportunities for the Negro must be created and he must be given the means to exploit them. King wanted large-scale investment in public works by the Federal government and in private works by big business. At the same time he called for massive Federal expenditure on the housing, education and training of the Negro: for example, cheaper house mortgages, plentiful loans from the banks to begin businesses, good grants and subsidies to pay for school, college and apprenticeship courses. In other words, preferential treatment for the Negro so that he could catch up with the white man. Such schemes, said King, would transform Negro life and give the prosperity, the satisfaction, the pride, the hope that the black man needed.

The Birmingham Demonstration, 1963. After the success in Montgomery the Negroes tried other peaceful demonstrations in Alabama and won new victories. The big effort came in 1963 in Birmingham where, as we have seen, segregation was rigidly enforced. The Negroes began to protest on 12 April, led by King and other members of the SCLC. Those taking part had been carefully trained in the tactics of nonviolence. 'Jim Crow' stores were boycotted; sit-ins were held in lunch counters, churches and libraries; the campaign to register Negro voters was intensified. In the first march on the City Hall forty-two were arrested. On 2 May, 1000 children suffered the same fate. King himself spent eight days in gaol. By now the Birmingham police were using dogs, clubs, electric cattle prods, and powerful water hoses used at a pressure sufficient to tear bark off trees.

The demonstration lasted a month. The Negroes won their demands. All lunch counters, fitting rooms, fountains and rest rooms were to be desegregated within ninety days. Employment in Birmingham was to be put on a non-discriminatory basis within sixty days.

This was not quite the end of the affair. The Ku Klux Klan bombed King's headquarters—luckily he was not at home. Negroes leaving bars at midnight heard the news and began rioting. The police were stoned, cars overturned and stores set on fire. King said: 'Whoever planted the bombs had *wanted* the Negroes to riot. They wanted the pact upset.'

President Kennedy now sent 3000 Federal troops to Birmingham to quell the violence. Meanwhile the Birmingham Board of Education expelled 1000 students for taking part in the demonstration. The courts ruled this unconstitutional and the students returned. Next day Bull O'Connor, the Birmingham boss, was taken from office.

The Birmingham demonstration sparked off rallies and marches in support of civil rights in other cities. Negro leaders now called for a mammoth march on Washington where Congress had just been asked by President Kennedy to pass new civil rights legislation. Nearly a quarter of a million people responded to the call, coming from all over the country in cars, trains, buses and planes to take part in the march. White people took part as well as Negroes. Many churches and trade unions also supported the march.

1963 was a momentous year in the history of the civil rights movement. It was marred by the assassination of President Kennedy but his death helped the Civil Rights Act of 1964 to pass through Congress.

Race riots and Black Power. Until his assassination in 1968 Martin Luther King continued his nonviolent campaigns for civil rights. For example, in 1965 he was very active in Selma, Alabama, trying to register Negro names on the voters' lists. The following year he led a march from Memphis to Jackson (sometimes called the Mississippi March) to encourage the Negroes in Mississippi to register themselves as voters. Later, in Chicago, he headed a demonstration against racial segregation in housing.

In these same years, however, Negro support for the aims and methods of King's SCLC weakened considerably. Scores of American cities suffered serious race riots between 1964 and 1968. In 1967 the race riots were said to be 'more widespread, more violent, and more destructive than in any previous year'. The riots took place in the South and in the North, in small towns as well as big cities. For the first time the police authorities had to face guerrilla tactics. People armed with rifles sniped from rooftops, and mobs in the streets threw Molotov cocktails. As in previous years, the riots were sparked off by allegations of police brutality or injustice towards Negroes and murders of Negroes by whites.

The worst riot in recent American history took place in Detroit between 23 and 27 July 1967. It started in the slums where between 6 and 8 per cent of the Negroes were jobless. A police raid on an illegal bar led to seventy-three arrests. A brawl began between police and Negroes and a riot soon developed. During the first two days a thousand shops and stores were ransacked. Nearly 300 fires were started. A state emergency was declared: 8000 National Guardsmen were mobilised to help the 4000 police. Later 5000 Federal troops moved into the city. At one point sniping was so serious that the police and troops had to use helicopters, tanks and machine guns to flush out the snipers. In the four days of the riot forty-three people died, 1500 were injured, and 5000 were arrested. The damage to property was estimated at 45 million dollars.

An increasing number of Negroes now sympathise with militant organisations like SNICK (the Student Nonviolent Co-ordinating Committee) or CORE (the Congress of Racial Equality). Some have become members of the Black Muslim sect. SNICK, as its name implies, began as a student organisation seeking racial integration through non-violent means. Its emblem was a black hand and a white hand clasped in friendship. In the early 1960s it worked closely with the SCLC. In the mid-1960s its aims and methods underwent a radical change. Its chairman, Stokely Carmichael, rejected the aim of integration and substituted that of Black Power. This was to be achieved by violence and revolution. The emblem of the organisation now became a black panther. Its student membership declined but it won growing support from young Negroes born and raised in the ghettoes of America.

Stokely Carmichael believes that the basis of Black Power is black pride, black consciousness. Negroes must learn to believe in themselves as individuals, and as a people with a history and culture of their own. They are not 'lazy, apathetic, dumb, shiftless or good-timers'—as the white man says they are—but 'energetic, determined, intelligent, beautiful and peace-loving'. They are not 'Negroes' or 'niggers'—white man's words—but black people whose origins are in Africa. They are Afro-Americans.

This black pride and black consciousness was possessed by the Black Muslim sect well before Carmichael became a Negro leader. This sect began in 1930 when a mysterious pedlar appeared in the Negro sector of Detroit. Some said he was of Arabic origin. His name was Farrad Mohammed and he sold raincoats and silks to the black women, telling them that the silks came from their home country. Soon he became well-known and a hall was hired so that Mohammed could tell his stories to larger audiences. In 1934 the

Race riots in the 1960s

pedlar disappeared as mysteriously as he came. Since then the organisation started by him has become a nationwide religious sect about 100,000 strong. The Negroes who have become Black Muslims believe that Farrad Mohammed was really Allah, the God of the Religion of Islam, who came to earth as a man to deliver his people from bondage. They believe that the present leader of their organisation, Elijah Muhammed, is Allah's representative on earth and knows the truth about the world. Those who become Black Muslims reject Christian teachings and the ways of the white men. They pray to Allah five times a day. Before prayers they rinse out their mouths and wash their hands, feet and forearms. They eat one meal a day, refuse to eat pork and corn, and promise not to smoke or drink. At all times they must work hard and be self-reliant. In the house the woman must be wife, mother and homemaker. She must not go out to work. All Black Muslims use the letter X for their surname. They reject the surnames given them by the

Christian slave owners because these names are not their proper ones. Their real surnames are lost in the distant past.

The truth about the world, say the Black Muslims, is that the black man is the descendant of the World's first man; that in very early times he lived along the banks of the Nile where the first civilisations grew up; that the white man enslaved the black by force, trickery, lies and deception; and that the Day of Judgement is coming when Allah will revenge these wrongs by sweeping the white man from the face of the earth.

Meanwhile, the Black Muslims hate the white man and tell him so at every opportunity. They say the white man has no intention of making the Negro a free and equal partner in society. The white man is the root cause of the Negro's problems. The white man is the devil, the force of evil. The Negro could not obey Martin Luther King, who asked him to forego violence and hatred and love his enemies as Christ had taught. Malcolm X, a former leader of the sect, said: 'It is not possible to love a man whose chief purpose in life is to humiliate you.' The Black Muslims demand the total separation of whites and blacks in America. They want the Federal government to give them land, tools and money to set up a separate black state within the U.S.A. The black man must fend for himself. He must not feel inferior to the white man but be proud of his achievements. He must change his own image. Land is the key to total independence. 'We must become as a people, producers, and not remain consumers and employees. We must be able to extract raw materials from the earth, manufacture them into something useful for ourselves. We must remember that without land there is no production.' So far the Federal government shows no sign of meetings these demands.

In the face of this refusal the organisation has begun building communities within communities. In cities like New York, Chicago, Detroit and Boston the Black Muslims have built temples and schools and started up restaurants, barber's shops, grocery stores and dry cleaners. The Black Muslims employ black workers and encourage all Negroes to buy from black-owned business.

The majority of Negroes are not prepared to join the Islam religion and live the very strict and pure life expected of a Black Muslim. They are, however, increasingly conscious of their blackness, their separate identity. In recent years more and more Negroes have accepted that to be black is to be beautiful. To emphasise this they adopt, for example, Afro haircuts and African clothes.

Like the Black Muslims Carmichael also rejects the present American society. He says America is organised for the benefit of middle-class white people.

'This class wants good government for *themselves*; it wants good schools *for its children*. At the same time many of its members sneak into the black community by day, exploit it, and take the money home to their middle class communities at night to support their operas and art galleries and comfortable homes.

'The middle class mouths its preference for a free, competitive society, while at the same time forcefully and even viciously denying to black people as a group the opportunity to compete.'

The laws and institutions in modern America and racist-designed to keep the whites superior to the blacks. Carmichael argues that the Civil Rights Acts do not really work, that neither political party represents the interests of the black man, that city planning commission, urban renewal commissions, boards of education and police departments all fail to meet his needs. Black people must form their own organisations and use the vote to choose their own leaders and make them responsible to the black community. Particularly in areas where the black people are in the majority they must exercise control. The sheriff must be black, the tax assessor and the tax collector must be black. The tax money must be spent on roads, schools and hospitals which black people need. Black power means the power of the black man to control his own environment and his own destiny. This means a revolution in American society. If necessary this revolution must be won by violence in the streets.

If you have read this section carefully you will realise that there are great differences between King's SCLC, the Black Muslims, and SNICK. Study the three carefully and try to summarise the difference in their origins, aims and methods.

A Race War?

The white backlash. The movement for civil rights continues to be resisted by extremist whites even today. In the South the Ku Klux Klan has been held responsible for many bomb attacks on Negro property and persons and for the murder of civil rights workers. It made an attempt to kill Martin Luther King after the Birmingham Demonstration in 1963. King was assassinated by a white man in Memphis in 1968. Both North and South continue to resist desegregation in education and housing: everywhere the Negroes remain in their ghettoes in poverty, despair and bitterness. The Negro violence in the towns and cities since 1964 has led to a countrywide retaliation by the whites, most of whom have little or no knowledge of the reasons for the Negro protest. In 1967 a *Times* survey stated that the Federal government had begun training courses for National Guardsmen, set up six secret arms dumps scattered across the nation with planes ready to deliver weapons to these men anywhere in the country, and devised secret plans for quelling riots in 150 cities. State and city police forces were reported to have obtained equipment like tanks, armoured cars, flame-throwers, and assault rifles capable of firing bullets through concrete walls. These police also possess tear gas, instant 'banana peel' foam—which makes the streets so slippery that people cannot stand up—and guns which fire tranquillising darts. Ordinary citizens are arming themselves. The report said that one American home in every two possessed a firearm.

All this is very frightening and very tragic. If the Negro persists in rioting and the whites insist on repression then the streets of cities all over the country will become very bloody battlegrounds. The two sides will understand each other even less. America will be torn apart by race war.

The future. The great American experiment is still not complete. A truly democratic nation has yet to emerge from the raw wilderness. While the racial problem remains unsolved America is not fully the land of freedom, the land of opportunity for all, despite what Conservative Republicans say. The solution to racial prejudice is not simply one of legislation. What is really needed is a change in the hearts and minds of white Americans and this is not simple. Yet it is necessary unless America is to become two societies, one Black one White—'separate and unequal'. In 1968 President Johnson received an interim report from the Advisory Commission on Civil Disorders which called for 'a commitment to national action—compassionate, massive, and sustained, backed by the resources of the most powerful and the richest nation on this earth. From every American it will require new attitudes, new understanding, and, above all, new will.'

For the moment Johnson's Great Society remains a dream of the future.

Further Reading

Baldwin, James, *Notes of a Native Son*, Corgi, 1965.
Commager, Henry Steel, *The Struggle for Racial Equality*, Harper Torchbooks, 1967 (contemporary documents).
King, Martin Luther, *Why We Can't Wait*, Signet, 1964.
Hansberry, L. A. *A Matter of Colour: Documentary of the Struggle for Racial Equality in the U.S.A.*, Penguin, 1965.

13 AMERICA AND THE WORLD

The Atlantic Ocean ensured the Americans were safe from invasion. For most of their history they had been concerned with taming the wilderness. They faced west; Europe was vital for trade but the United States avoided entanglement in European affairs except when her own interests were affected. This policy was known as 'isolation'. In 1783 the United States was only one of the powers in North America. Americans felt insecure and their 'manifest destiny' was to strengthen their position on the Continent. They regarded it as their own special sphere of influence and as early as 1823 in the Monroe Doctrine warned European powers not to interfere.

By 1900 they had occupied most of the modern United States and had begun to invest their industrial profits abroad on a large scale—particularly in Latin America and Canada. They used this 'dollar diplomacy' to influence and control their neighbours. Their overseas trade had led them to develop a larger navy and to acquire overseas bases, for example Pearl Harbour in 1887. Some spoke of 'Americanising the World'. By 1914 the United States was the most powerful nation in the world—in population, in industrial organisation and production, in technological and scientific skills—and it had, in spite of its beliefs in freedom, acquired an Empire. But it was still essentially isolationist, concerned with its own growth and not anxious to be involved in the quarrels of Europe.

Isolation or Involvement

Neutrality or war. In July 1914 the Great War broke out in Europe. America's first reaction was to treat the war as a merely European affair and observe strict neutrality. Even expansionists, with one or two exceptions, did not want involvement in a major war where the United States could have no practical interests.

But events made neutrality difficult. France and Britain controlled the sea and prevented Germany trading with the United States. They themselves greatly expanded their trade with her to get the supplies they needed for the war. In 1917 United States exports exceeded her imports by 3000 million dollars. France and Britain were able to pay for these purchases by selling to Americans the enormous investments they had built up in the New World during the nineteenth century. Germany had no such investments. Again by 1917 3000 million dollars' worth of these investments had been sold. To be strictly neutral the United States would have had to stop this highly profitable trade; but to do so would have been ruinous.

Allied resources were soon used up. The United States was faced with either the stopping of the Anglo-French trade—with disastrous effects on her own economy—or lending money to Allies. By 1917, before it officially joined in the war, America had already lent the Allies over 2250 million dollars—and only 45 million dollars to Germany. If Germany won, these loans would be lost. But businessmen could get profit from neutrality and these economic connections with the Allies did not make the United States take an active part in the war.

Restrictions on American shipping were resented. The Royal Navy acted according to international agreements; no American lives were lost and usually owners of confiscated cargo were compensated. So British interference did not cause serious enmity. But

Germany, lacking control of the sea, used submarines and attacked passenger and cargo ships as well as warships, neutrals as well as Allied powers, and often did not give non-combatants the chance to save themselves. The most famous incident of this kind was the sinking of the British liner *Lusitania* with the loss of 128 American lives. Germany took little notice of American protests and German newspaper comment was often arrogant. For instance the following appeared in a Berlin paper in 1915: 'We do not want any love among the Americans but we do want respect, and the case of the Lusitania will win it for us better than a hundred victories on land.'

This bullying contrasted with the friendly, conciliatory British approach and made Americans furious rather than respectful. It offended their sense of justice and civilised conduct and created a growing distrust and resentment of German policies. They began to be seen as a threat to liberty, justice and democratic government, the very ideals for which most Americans felt they stood. Could America afford to stand by and see such ideals ignored or defeated? American idealism began to counteract her usual isolationist attitude. In 1916 Wilson, in an attempt to find a basis for peace negotiations, asked both sides to declare their war aims. The Allies, although they had been losing and were there-fore at a disadvantage, did so; but Germany refused. The following year she went back on previous half-promises and started unrestricted submarine warfare, sinking eight Ameri-can ships in February and March. It was these German actions which converted Wilson reluctantly from a firm belief in neutrality to a war 'to make the world safe for democracy'.

America's contribution to the First World War. This can be summed up as follows:
1. The United States had already made a large contribution in advancing loans to the Allies.
2. As soon as America had declared war it helped the Royal Navy in convoy work* and in antisubmarine warfare. Until the convoy system was established Britain was losing one in every four of her merchant ships. You can work out for yourself why this was important.
3. By the end of the war there were one million American troops in Europe. They took part in the fighting of 1917 and 1918 including the last 'big push' which finally broke German resistance.
4. More important was the knowledge that the whole industrial strength of the United States and an unlimited number of fresh soldiers was now available. This knowledge helped to break German morale and revive that of the Allies.

But the most important contribution was to the making of peace. Early in 1918 President Wilson suggested Fourteen Points as a basis for settlement. His main ideas was for a League of Nations which would involve America in maintaining the future peace of the world. At Versailles the following year the European nations accepted the idea and it was written into the peace treaty. In a series of speeches to Congress in 1918 he outlined his ideas in greater detail.

He thought that aggressive nations could only be restrained by the threat of force and that permanent peace could only be ensured by treating all nations fairly. He wanted America to join Britain, France and other states in policing the world. This would involve his country in problems in Europe and elsewhere which before 1918 had been thought beyond its sphere of influence. This policy went directly against the traditional policy of isolation from world affairs.

Wilson's ideas were really an attempt to find a way of governing the world peacefully and justly so that further major wars could not occur. He felt that other nations would only accept this if they were given the same rights to a fair hearing, and the same freedom and

---

*Warships escorting large groups of merchant ships. This was the most effective way of minimising losses in submarine attacks.

independence provided they did not harm others, which Americans themselves expected and had embodied in their Declaration of Independence and Constitution. It was the spreading of these ideas that Americans meant when they spoke of carrying American civilisation to the world. They felt that the American way of life, for all its faults, was based on these democratic ideas and that they were essential to civilised life. It was America's first duty to defend and support them.

But many Americans could not accept the surrender of isolation and saw ways in which it would harm their interest to do so. Some Progressives had always opposed Wilson on the grounds that taxation could be better spent on reforms at home, midwestern farmers saw no reason why they should pay taxes to prevent war on the other side of the world. Republicans were anxious to defeat Wilson on any issue. There was widespread suspicion of government interference in everyday affairs which the war had made necessary and a strong desire to get back to 'normalcy', letting foreigners look after their own affairs. Congress refused to accept the Peace of Versailles or to join the League of Nations.

Between the wars. The First World War had shown that the United States was a world power, but from 1920 under Republican presidents Warren Harding, Calvin Coolidge and Herbert Hoover, Americans returned to a policy of isolation. You have already seen many of the reasons why this would happen. In the 1920s they enjoyed enormous prosperity and then suffered a deep economic depression in the 1930s. Both these distracted them from foreign affairs.

Although Britain paid off her debts by 1923 six other countries found it impossible and defaulted by 1932; others followed. This was not entirely their fault. A country could only pay its debts if it earned dollars from the United States. But the low cost of American mass production and the high tariffs on imported manufactured goods, made it very difficult for European industries to sell in America. But few Americans realised European difficulties and most were disgusted at their seeming ingratitude.

While the United States was preoccupied with her own problems Nazi and Fascist dictators seized power in Germany, Italy and Spain. Although these governments did carry out useful reforms they were completely antidemocratic. They based their power on armed force, suppressed all opposition and were prepared to use any means to increase their power. In the Far East Japan, another military dictatorship, invaded first Manchuria and then China. Most Americans felt that unpleasant though Fascism might be it did not affect them, that two great oceans were ample protection, and that Fascist ambitions were exaggerated. The League of Nations, which had been set up on Wilson's initiative, failed to preserve peace because it had no means of coercing individual nations; when Japan

convoy of American
ps approaching the
ench coast in 1918

invaded Manchuria she merely withdrew from the League. A major reason for this weakness was the failure of the world's most powerful nation, the United States, to join the League.

What sort of commitment? When open warfare broke out in Europe in 1939 there was no question of which side Americans supported, but Congress was determined not to become involved. It was sufficient to be the 'arsenal of democracy'. In 1940 France fell and Great Britain was forced to evacuate the Continent at Dunkirk. Germany now turned her full strength against Britain, Italy came into the war, and in September Japan joined them in forming what came to be called the Axis. These events shocked Americans. If the Axis powers could knock out Great Britain and Russia, they would turn the American continent into an island. Congress was sufficiently alarmed to begin military preparations for defence and Roosevelt sold Great Britain fifty over-age destroyers in return for Atlantic bases.

After the election of 1940 Roosevelt was able to push forward with his plan for aiding the Allies as much as possible short of actual war. But he still faced strong opposition. There was an influential minority which thought the Fascist danger was exaggerated, that Britain and France were bound to lose, and that the United States should save her resources. This opposition came to a head over Roosevelt's Lend-Lease scheme (what we might call hire purchase) to help the Allies buy munitions. They claimed that this would inevitably lead to war and asked whether the last war had benefited the States. Roosevelt appealed to the same ideals as Wilson had done—what he called the Four Freedoms. He claimed aid was essential to ensure freedom of speech, freedom of religion, freedom from want and freedom from fear. Here again we have the two threads which have run all the way through American foreign policy—on the one hand the belief in isolation as most in the

United States' interest, on the other hand the belief that the United States must be prepared to defend what it believes in wherever it is attacked.

By the end of 1941 it is difficult to speak of the United States as a neutral. Churchill and Roosevelt had already met to discuss the aims of a peace settlement and Congress had agreed to arming American merchant ships to enable them to reply to the attacks of German submarines. That the Americans could not expect to do this and not fight was finally made clear when the Japanese gained the mastery of the Pacific by their destruction of the American Pacific fleet at Pearl Harbour on 7 December 1941. America now had no choice but to declare war, which she did the following day.

But even had the Americans remained completely neutral from the first, they would eventually have had to face a world dominated by the Fascist powers, and face it alone. America would have been vulnerable constantly to attack. Once it had shown its sympathies were with the Allies, and once they began to lose decisively America really had no choice but war. America came into the Second World War because she wished to live according to her own beliefs, and believed that if she did not fight, her position in the world would be so weakened that she would not be able to defend them.

The Second World War. The United States played a far greater part in the Second World War than it did in the First. Indeed it is unlikely that Germany and Japan could have been defeated without American resources and men. The war forced it to cooperate fully with the other Allied powers. The Allies agreed that all their diplomatic, economic, industrial and military policies should be unified, and that the main strategy should be to hold up Japan's advance in the Pacific and concentrate on defeating Germany in Europe.

Since America had already started to organise for war in order to supply the Allies under the Lend-Lease scheme, and since there were already one and a half million men in training,

Liberty ships

Devastation of Eu▪
by bombing in Sec
World War

Map 28 The war ▪
the Pacific

it was able to help much more quickly. By 1943 its capacity for war production was at least equal to that of the Axis powers combined.

Find out the details of the campaigns for yourself. In Europe the Allies first cleared North Africa before invading Italy. Meanwhile the British and American forces severely damaged German industries by intensive bombing while Russia attacked Germany's eastern front. In 1944 the Allies crossed the Channel and invaded France in the greatest amphibious operation in history. The Seventh U.S. Army invaded the south of France and the Germans were trapped. On 7 May 1945, as the Allied forces converged, Germany surrendered.

In the Pacific the Americans, aided by British, Australian, New Zealand, Dutch, Indian and Chinese troops fought their way from island to island and up through the jungles of southeast Asia, towards Japan. (Look at Map 28 and you will see the routes.) By 1945 they

Mass production for
Second World War.

198

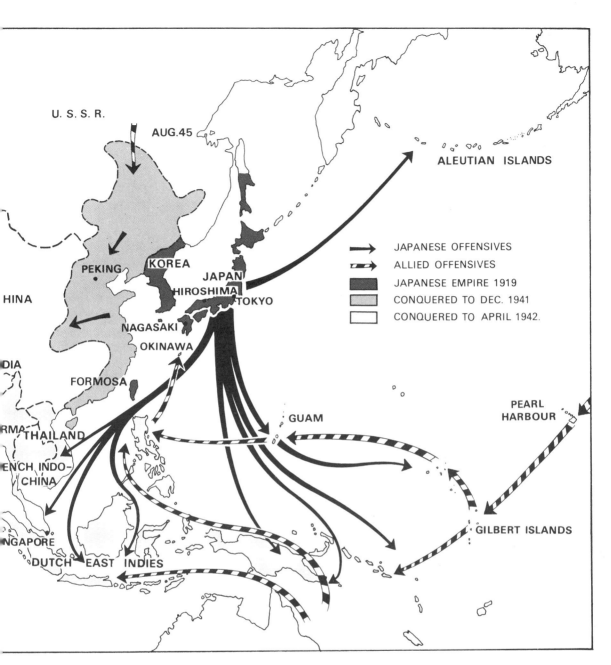

were ready to invade Japan itself. Since 1941 the Allies had been developing a new sort of weapon—the atomic bomb. This was ready by July 1945. Though it was small compared with modern nuclear bombs, it was immensely more destructive than conventional weapons. The new American President Harry Truman, who had been Roosevelt's vice-president, continued his policy of vigorous cooperation. He and Winston Churchill, the British Prime Minister, agreed to use the weapon against Japan to bring about a quick surrender and save the cost in lives of a conventional invasion. On August 6th and 9th two Japanese cities were wiped out—Hiroshima and Nagasaki. Japan surrendered on 14 August.

Reluctant Leadership

After the war. When the war ended most of Europe had been occupied by the Allied powers. Germany was divided between them. There was no final peace treaty because the Allies could not agree. Many of the problems of making peace are still unsolved; the reunification of Germany is one.

Relations between the powers developed in two opposite ways. First, the war had been so expensive and so damaging that all nations, even the United States, felt that the countries of the world should cooperate in preventing another world war. As early as 1943 the American Senate had voted in favour of 'an international authority with power to prevent aggression and preserve the peace of the world'. In 1945 a conference was held in San Francisco to settle the details of what was to be known as the United Nations. It followed closely the lines of the League of Nations which Woodrow Wilson had tried in vain to persuade the United States to accept after the First World War. Its headquarters was set up in New York. This shows the enormous change in American opinion which the experience of the war had made. The United Nations has done an enormous amount of valuable work by means of its agencies such as the World Health Organisation (W.H.O.) and the United Nations Educational, Scientific and Cultural Organisation (U.N.E.S.C.O.) but it has not always kept the peace. This is in part because of the rivalry of the United States and Russia.

Secondly, the United States had emerged as a superpower, far stronger in men, money and resources than any of the European powers. But despite this, it was no longer safe behind its two oceans. Pearl Harbour had shown that it could not rely on naval power to control them. The development of flight and nuclear weapons meant that its own homeland could be attacked. If America had to defend itself it would need allies.

Russia had emerged as a second superpower. Since the Bolshevik Revolution of 1917 she had been occupied in developing the political system called Communism and turning herself into a modern, industrialised state. This process had been largely completed by 1945 and under a new name, the Union of Soviet Socialist Republics, Russia had played a vital part in defeating Germany. It was not yet equal in power to the United States but showed every intention of becoming so.

Americans saw Communism as a threat to themselves. Communists believe that the state should own all industry, agriculture, housing and retail shops so that goods can be made and distributed for the good of the whole community, not for the benefit of rich individuals. The State employs everyone, pays everyone and sees that everyone is fairly treated. In the West individuals own property and compete to make themselves rich, often at the expense of others. Communists call this capitalism and claim it is unjust and harmful to most people and should be eliminated. Believing itself right, the Communist government has not allowed any opposition, and millions of those who opposed the Communist party have been killed. The Bolshevik Revolution of 1917 was carried out by quite a small group of devoted and fanatical revolutionaries who had channelled the very real and widespread discontent in Russia into support for Communism as the best means of overthrowing and replacing the old Russian government. Compare this with the American Revolution against England. As you can see, Communist ideas are the exact opposite of what most Americans believe in—free enterprise, competition, free speech, the right of each man to live as he wished, and hatred of government interference. These ideas are very important to an understanding of the world you live in. Discuss them in class.

Both the U.S.S.R. and the U.S.A. were convinced that their own forms of government and attitudes to life were best. Each feared the other would do its best to protect itself and undermine its rival. Each was suspicious and afraid of the other. Americans were afraid that Russia would encourage Communist Parties in other countries to take control of their governments and turn the rest of Europe and Asia Communist; and that they might suppress opposition by force as they had done in Russia. Russia feared that American money and perhaps troops would be used to corrupt other countries and crush Communist parties. Both were right, because if one side was successful the other would find itself isolated and in a minority in the world. To avoid getting isolated each country did exactly what the other feared. Each felt it must have allies, and that its own security depended on convincing the rest of the world that it was right, so that other countries would support it. This division of the world has dominated the whole period from 1945 to the present day and can be seen in many different ways, some of which we will now look at. You will notice, though, that this division forces the United States to take a full part in world affairs—no longer can she remain isolated. Notice, too, that the division is about rival ways of living; the American feels that their ideals, their way of life, the American 'dream' is in danger.

The failure of the peace: Hot War becomes Cold War. The countries who have usually supported the United States are often grouped together as the 'West' or 'Western powers', while those who support the U.S.S.R. are called the 'East' or 'Eastern powers'. It will be useful to start by showing how the seeds of this fear and suspicion between East and West affected even the making of peace.

Political problems. Map 29 shows the alignment of the countries of Europe just after the war. The Western powers wanted them to choose their own governments after the occupying troops had withdrawn. They could afford to be generous because they expected they would choose capitalist, democratic governments which would be friendly to the West. But if they did this, then they were not likely to be friendly to Communist Russia. Moreover Russia had suffered so heavily from German invasion that it was determined to use the East European states as a barrier, in case Germany started to expand again. Germany itself was to be very carefully controlled. To feel secure Russia therefore had to have the East European states, including her part of Germany, governed by Communists who would follow Russian policy. To the West this seemed merely an attempt to extend Russian power and territory. But from the Russian point of view it seemed most dangerous to allow a free choice of government to the occupied states, and the West's insistence on this seemed a deliberate threat to Russian power and to Communism. Neither side understood, or felt they should make allowances for, the fears of the other; and neither felt they could trust the other.

Economic problems. A second major problem was the economic recovery of Europe. Large areas had been devastated, industry destroyed and millions faced with more severe rationing than in wartime. European stocks of dollars were exhausted, so no country could buy the food and equipment it needed from the United States. Nor, of course, could the United States sell any of its products to Europe. The American Secretary of State, George Marshall, suggested a plan of cooperation by which America would loan Europe the money which it needed to finance its recovery. This would benefit the United States as well. Do you see how? In all, America loaned 12,500 million dollars; almost all of it to Western European powers. This was called the MARSHALL PLAN.

To the Russians this plan was suspect. American aid to rebuild capitalist industry would make it more difficult for Communism to spread, so the loans could be seen as a sort of economic attack on Communism. Some Americans did in fact intend it in just this way. The quickest way to European recovery was for the Eastern countries to concentrate on agriculture as they always had. But to compete with the Western powers on equal terms they needed to industrialise, just as Russia herself had done. So for these two reasons Russia refused to cooperate with the Marshall Plan and started a rival organisation of her own—the Cominform—to organise the recovery of the Eastern states. The Cominform also controlled the other European Communist parties, and under its directions they organised widespread strikes, causing economic chaos in France and Italy in 1947 and 1948. This seemed to justify Western suspicions which were strengthened when in 1948 the Communists overthrew the government of Czechoslovakia, the sole remaining non-Communist government in Eastern Europe.

The Berlin blockade. Open war almost occurred for the first time in 1948. At the end of the war Germany had been divided into French, British, American and Russian sectors. Berlin, the capital and in the Russian sector, was similarly split, and the Western powers allowed access by carefully controlled road, rail and air routes. The West wished to reunite Germany with a democratic government but this would be hostile to Communism and therefore to Russia, and Stalin, naturally enough, would not agree. As time passed and no agreement was reached the West went ahead with its own sectors, forming the present state of West Germany. West Germany recovered much more quickly from the war than East Germany. The contrast was an embarrassment to Russia and a threat to her control of the Eastern sector. The contrast was clearest in Berlin, right in the middle of East Germany. Russia therefore decided to drive the Western nations out of Berlin by shutting off all the ground approaches—officially for repairs. There were 2 million Berliners in the Western sectors and Great Britain and the United States decided to supply them with everything they needed by air.

This was a fantastic operation. Every available plane was pressed into service, two airfields in Berlin were extended and another built. Everything had to be carried—coal, oil, petrol, clothing, shoes, meat, flour, vegetables, potatoes, milk—for 2 million people. At one point planes were landing at ninety-second intervals and there were 14,000 landings in one day alone. This enormous effort was maintained for eleven months.

At last in May 1949, when it became obvious that Berlin was not going to starve, the Russians reopened the ground approaches. But the world had come very close to war, and the problem of Germany has not yet been solved.

It was now, by 1949, quite clear that Europe was divided into two armed camps, separated by what Churchill called an 'Iron Curtain' stretching from the North Sea to the frontier of Switzerland. See Map 29. What was meant by an 'Iron Curtain' do you think?

The United Nations Organisation (U.N.O.). You may have wondered why the United Nations did not prevent this happening. It had been founded to prevent war. In fact the fear and suspicion between Great Britain and the United States on one side and the U.S.S.R. on the other had made the United Nations ineffective from the start. From the point of view of peace-making the important parts of the United Nations are the General Assembly and the Security Council. All member nations are represented in the General Assembly but only a selected few, including the four former allies, Great Britain, the United States, France and the U.S.S.R., in the Security Council. The Security Council has the power to decide what action should be taken on a dispute but it has to have the consent of the Assembly. In its early years the Assembly showed a clear majority for the United States' policies, since in addition to Great Britain and France, America could rely on the support

ocks of supplies for
e Berlin airlift

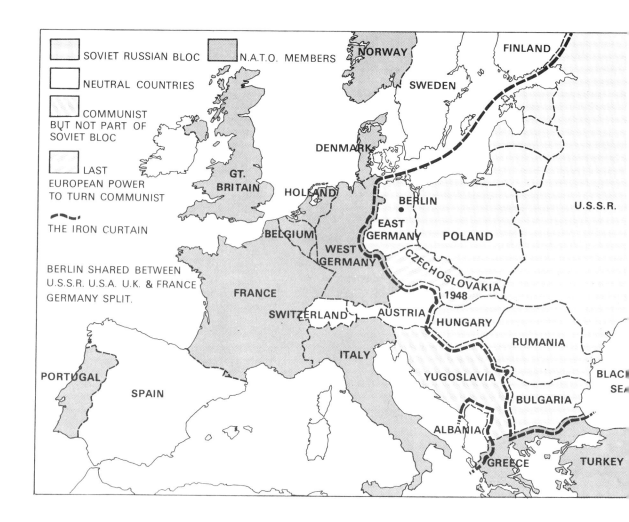

SOVIET RUSSIAN BLOC

NEUTRAL COUNTRIES

COMMUNIST
BUT NOT PART OF
SOVIET BLOC

LAST
EUROPEAN POWER
TO TURN COMMUNIST

THE IRON CURTAIN

BERLIN SHARED BETWEEN
U.S.S.R. U.S.A. U.K. & FRANCE
GERMANY SPLIT.

N.A.T.O. MEMBERS

NORWAY, FINLAND, SWEDEN, DENMARK, GT. BRITAIN, HOLLAND, BELGIUM, WEST GERMANY, EAST GERMANY, BERLIN, POLAND, CZECHOSLOVAKIA, 1948, FRANCE, SWITZERLAND, AUSTRIA, HUNGARY, RUMANIA, U.S.S.R., ITALY, YUGOSLAVIA, BULGARIA, BLACK SEA, PORTUGAL, SPAIN, ALBANIA, GREECE, TURKEY

of the South and Central American states who were dependent on her economically. Realising this would be so, Stalin had insisted that members of the Security Council should have a veto over any suggested policy. The result was that the United Nations could do nothing towards peace-keeping unless the United States and the U.S.S.R. were agreed.

In fact the situation was worse than that. To Russia it looked as if the United States intended to use the U.N.O. as a means of enforcing its own policies. Sure of its majority in the Assembly, it could in fact do this, and so from the Russian point of view it was hardly a fair way of deciding things. The Russians used their veto to block any action they felt was unfavourable to themselves; the Americans claimed the Russians were being obstructive and used the Assembly to show they had majority support for what they wished to do. No powerful nation would in fact allow an international body to interfere in any issue which it felt was vital to its own survival. Of course neither side would agree to setting up a United Nations army to settle disputes, in case it was used against themselves.

So, by 1949, it was clear that the peace had failed; no permanent settlement had been found; that the United Nations was powerless when it mattered most; and that the Americans were committed, despite themselves, to a worldwide rivalry.

The Cold War and containment. The Berlin Blockade was the first major clash in what is now known as the Cold War. It has been called this because the two principal opponents,

Map 30 'Containment' of communism Main treaty organisations, U.S. bases and trouble spots

204

Map 29 Europe after the second World War

Russia and America, have never fought against each other openly. Yet they have both been involved indirectly in practically every incident of importance since the war. One main reason for this restraint has been that for most of the time they have both had sufficient nuclear weapons to destroy their opponents. The weapons have acted as a 'deterrent' and made both sides cautious. But rivalry short of war has been all the fiercer. Each has built up enormous stockpiles of armaments, tried to consolidate its own strength by making treaties with its allies, developed spying to a highly refined art and tried to use all sorts of indirect methods to win over the poor countries which make up the largest part of the world.

America found this persuasion difficult. Many of the poorer countries had only just thrown off the rule of America's allies and did not wish to replace this by American domination. Some were impressed by Russia's rapid industrialisation and rise to world power. For these two reasons many poor nations found Communism attractive. For example, as early as 1949, the Chinese Communists under Mao Tse-tung had seized power from a corrupt and inefficient government supported by America. From the moment of the victory of the Communists in China it was clear that the Cold War could not be confined to Europe. To the United States the western Pacific was equally important. The struggle was to be worldwide. Within three years America and China were fighting each other in Korea.

America gradually devised a world policy to counteract what she saw as the menace of Communism. Look at Map 30 and you will understand why this policy is called 'contain-

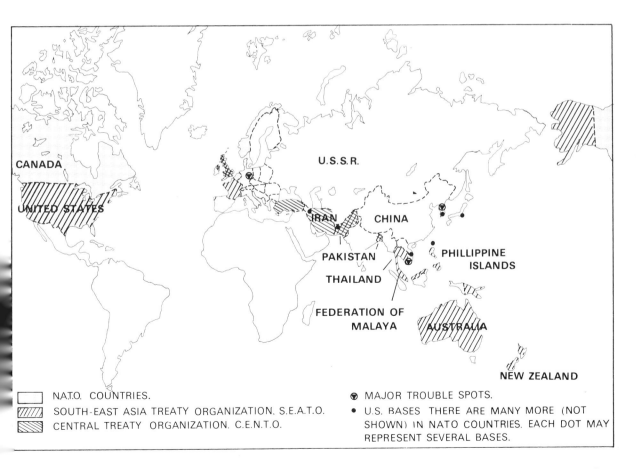

CANADA

UNITED STATES

U.S.S.R.

IRAN

CHINA

PAKISTAN

THAILAND

PHILLIPPINE ISLANDS

FEDERATION OF MALAYA

AUSTRALIA

NEW ZEALAND

☐ N.A.T.O. COUNTRIES.

▨ SOUTH-EAST ASIA TREATY ORGANIZATION. S.E.A.T.O.

▧ CENTRAL TREATY ORGANIZATION. C.E.N.T.O.

⊛ MAJOR TROUBLE SPOTS.

• U.S. BASES THERE ARE MANY MORE (NOT SHOWN) IN NATO COUNTRIES. EACH DOT MAY REPRESENT SEVERAL BASES.

ment'. In the map Russia is placed in the middle and Communism is seen as expanding outwards in all directions. The United States by means of treaties, financial aid, military bases and sometimes war, attempts to 'contain' this expansion. This policy was not developed all at once but only gradually emerged as the Western powers faced each new threat—or what seemed to them to be a threat.

In the early years after the war, Russia was much less powerful than the United States, and was afraid of war occurring before she was strong enough to defend herself. It was partly for this reason that she did not disband her forces in Europe. In addition to much greater industrial capacity the United States was the only nation with nuclear bombs. To Russia therefore containment did not look like defence, as the West thought of it, but much more like aggression. Just as the Americans had felt bound to join in the Second World War to avoid isolation in a fascist world, so Russia felt bound to break Western encirclement before it became a noose. So again fear and suspicion dominated both sides and each took the very steps which confirmed the other's fears, not merely because it wished to be aggressive but because it was, itself, afraid.

Alliances. Look carefully at Table 13. Notice that these alliances were formed only slowly as different dangers arose. Although these alliances were defensive you can see that Russia might well be alarmed. You will see this even more clearly after reading the next section.

The Arms Race. After the war Russia's superiority in soldiers was offset by America's possession of atomic bombs. But by 1953, through effective spying and the work of her own scientists, Russia possessed a full knowledge of nuclear weapons.

1945: U.S. perfected first atomic bomb.
1946: U.S.S.R. rejected plan for international control of atomic energy.
1949: U.S.S.R. exploded her first atomic bomb.
1952: U.S. perfected first hydrogen bomb.
1953: U.S.S.R. exploded her first hydrogen bomb.

Both sides then built up their stocks of bombs and concentrated on developing methods of delivering them. This was much easier for the Americans. They used their alliances to build a string of airforce bases around the Communist areas. They then equipped these bases with long-range bombers of the Strategic Air Command, *each* of which could carry nuclear bombs with a destructive power greater than that of *all* the bombs carried by *all* aircraft in *the whole of* the Second World War. These bombers were organised in such a way that there were always some in the air, loaded, and briefed on their targets, ready to fly to them the moment an alarm sounded. One can appreciate Russian fears. Russia had no bases close to America's borders, so it was much harder for it to attack.

Russia therefore concentrated on producing Inter-Continental Ballistic Missiles (I.C.B.M.s), rockets which could reach the United States in twenty minutes from Russia. They succeeded in 1957. Feeling themselves no longer secure the Americans immediately started building their own missiles, and both sides started working on missiles which would intercept and destroy those of their enemy.

Because these missile systems were designed to react very quickly and relied heavily on electronic devices it was possible that a mistake or breakdown might set the whole system of attacks and reprisals in motion. Since it has been calculated that each side had more than enough nuclear strength to eliminate all human life from the earth, such a mistake might well lead to the killing of most human beings. It would take only five hydrogen bombs, for instance, to destroy Great Britain. Map 30 shows the distribution of U.S. overseas bases. You can see how they encircle the Communist areas. In 1964 they had 115 bases manned by about 700,000 personnel.

Table 13.   Western Alliances

Date	Members	Comments
1949	U.S.A., Great Britain, France, Canada and other nations.	*North Atlantic Treaty Organisation* (N.A.T.O.) The West intended N.A.T.O. as a defensive alliance. Each member was to defend any other member who was attacked by an outside power.
		The U.S.S.R. saw it as 'aimed at the establishment of Anglo-American world domination'.
		In practice its military forces were weaker than those of Russia.
1954	U.S.A., Great Britain, France, Australia, New Zealand, Pakistan, Thailand and the Philippines.	*The South-East Asia Treaty Organisation* (S.E.A.T.O.) The result of increasing fears of Communist expansion in China, Korea, Vietnam, Laos and Malaya.
		The West saw S.E.A.T.O. as a defensive alliance.
		The U.S.S.R. and China saw it as an attempt at encirclement.
1955	Great Britain, Turkey, Iraq, Persia, Pakistan. The U.S.A. was closely associated with it.	*The Baghdad Pact* The result of fear of Communism in the Middle East. Again intended as a defensive pact.
1960		Renamed the *Central Treaty Organisation* (C.E.N.T.O.)

N.B. It is not surprising that Russia felt these alliances were a threat to her existence, because:

1. The countries involved received financial and military assistance from the U.S.A.
2. In return they provided bases for the U.S. strategic airforce (see next section).

Effectively the U.S.S.R. was surrounded by a ring of armed opponents.

The arms race was not confined to the air. In 1960 the United States had about 2.5 million men in her armed forces, Russia about 4 million. In 1958 Russia had 475 submarines, the United States had fewer but had a number of the much more powerful Polaris nuclear submarines armed with missiles which can be launched from underwater. More recently of course, this competition has led to the space race. But so far, despite prolonged efforts to bring about disarmament, little real progress has been made in overcoming the suspicions of each side.

The arms race has made both sides cautious but several times they have come close to a Third World War.

Korea. You can see the position of Korea on Map 31. Just as the Russian and American allies had met in Germany so they did on the east coast of Asia when Japan surrendered in 1945. Korea was divided between them at the 38th Parallel. The Koreans wished to reunite their country but America feared the Communists would try to dominate it. This would increase the threat to her power in the Far East. The situation became more dangerous in American eyes when the Communists gained control of China in 1949. For this reason America blocked the admission of China to the United Nations.

Both Russia and America had withdrawn their troops from Korea by the end of 1949 but the North Korean government was Communist and America had left military advisers in South Korea and granted 150 million dollars aid.

In June 1950 North Korea invaded the South. President Truman ordered American air and sea forces to give 'cover and support' to the South. In a speech justifying his action he voiced American fears that 'Communism has passed beyond the use of subversion* to conquer independent nations and will now use armed intervention and war'. Russian and Chinese Communists reacted promptly seeing American help to the South as clear evidence of aggression. Mao Tse-tung said it was good to see the 'true American face' and that the peoples of Asia 'will neither be bought by American imperialism nor duped by it.'

The majority in the United Nations at this time, as you have seen, supported America's policy. They proposed that the United Nations intervene to restore peace. It did so and seventeen nations supplied troops, but of course Russia and her supporters would not help. In fact, because of her great resources, America provided 95 per cent of the United Nations force which was commanded by an American, General MacArthur. After great initial success the North Koreans were driven back and most of North Korea occupied. At this point China intervened and drove the United Nations forces south again. A stalemate was finally reached at about the original dividing line—the 38th Parallel. Eventually peace was made in July 1954. Korea remains divided.

This dangerous episode confirmed the Communist belief that the United Nations was biased against them. It showed that already China was powerful enough to threaten American security in the Far East. It also revealed that Russia was still strategically weaker than America. America could reach Russian targets from her ring of air bases in Asia and Europe. Russia could not reach America easily. She was only just developing a solution to this problem—the I.C.B.M.s. Russian troops never fought in Korea because Russia could not risk a third world war with America at this time.

Cuba. The second incident arose because Russia tried to gain a nuclear base nearer the United States. In 1959 Fidel Castro became the Prime Minister of Cuba. Though not a Communist himself he wished to free Cuba from dependence on the United States and to provide it with a higher standard of living. He therefore invited Russian interest and support. His opponents, many of whom had fled from the island or been exiled, with the help of American intelligence, which distrusted Castro, invaded Cuba at the Bay of Pigs in 1961. Resenting this interference Castro allowed Russia to instal missile launching pads in Cuba. American spy planes spotted these and President Kennedy declared that all cargo ships bound for Cuba would be searched and turned back if found to be carrying weapons. Troops were concentrated in the southeastern states, Polaris submarines put to sea, nuclear bombers took off. Twenty-five Russian cargo ships approached Cuba. The American Navy waited for them. All but one at last turned away. The one was boarded and searched, but was found to be carrying no weapons, so it was allowed to continue. Shortly afterwards Russia agreed to remove the missiles and the United States agreed not to invade the Island. Look at Map 32 and say why America was so alarmed.

*The overthrow of a country's government by another not by open war but by, for example, propaganda and guerilla tactics.

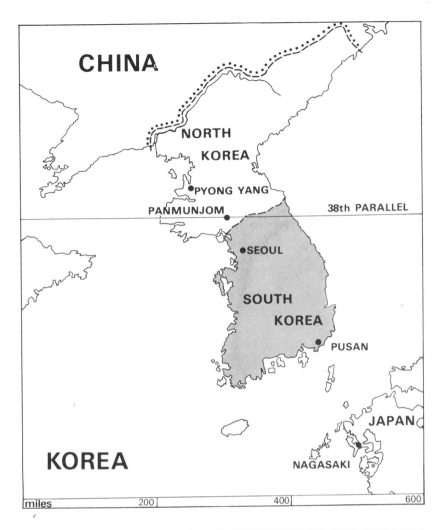

*our skybolt air to
rface ballistic
issiles being carried
) a B-52G bomber*

CHINA

NORTH
KOREA

●PYONG YANG
PANMUNJOM
●SEOUL

38th PARALLEL

SOUTH
KOREA

●PUSAN

JAPAN

NAGASAKI

KOREA

miles 200 400 600

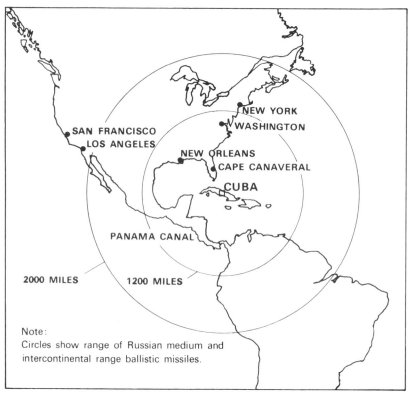

NEW YORK

WASHINGTON

SAN FRANCISCO
LOS ANGELES

NEW ORLEANS

CAPE CANAVERAL

CUBA

PANAMA CANAL

2000 MILES   1200 MILES

Note:
Circles show range of Russian medium and
intercontinental range ballistic missiles.

210

Vietnam. The third clash is not yet over. During the Second World War Ho Chi Minh freed his country from French rule. But in 1945 Vietnam was divided; the French regained the South and Ho Chi Minh was confined to the North. There is no doubt that Ho Chi Minh was then popular in the South and he soon led a second war of liberation against the French. In 1954 the French left Vietnam, and it was agreed that the division of the country should only last until free elections could be held to choose a government. Ho Chi Minh would undoubtedly have won, but America and the West would not accept him because he was a Communist. They therefore supported a rival government which refused to hold elections. On the other hand the North stuck to the 1954 agreements, for like the Western allies after the war in Europe, it could afford to do so since it expected a favourable verdict.

Like the Koreans the Vietnamese wanted to reunite their country. When the South Vietnam government refused to hold elections a National Liberation Front was formed by patriots and North Vietnamese Communists. This started a civil war against the government. At first America gave only munitions and advice but the South Vietnamese government failed to win the war. It is difficult in thick jungle to locate guerrilla fighters, and it is hard to distinguish them from ordinary peasants.

The United States became convinced that unless she intervened personally the whole of Vietnam might be lost to Communism. The Communists might then attack the rest of Indo-China. From 1964 the number of American troops in Vietnam was steadily increased and the bombing of North Vietnam started to stop supplies being sent to aid the rebels. By August 1968 there were over 540,000 American soldiers in the country and the United States had lost over 33,000 men. Between February 1965 and July 1968 the American air-

211

force dropped over two and a half million tons of bombs on North Vietnam and America has officially lost 2340 planes and 2103 helicopters. The cost of this war has drained even America's resources. For example, in 1966–67 alone, the bill was 19,419 million dollars.

The effects of napalm

Despite this enormous expense America has not won. In 1967 she claimed success in winning permanent control of many country districts in South Vietnam. The following year the opposing army, the Vietcong, launched one of their most widespread and successful offensives. The Americans lost most of what they had gained and it was several days before the Vietcong were driven out of the capital, Saigon. The places mentioned in this section can be seen on Map 33.

The cost of the war in money and lives, its effect on America's reforms at home, and the failure to win have made many Americans critical of their government. American methods of fighting, for example, the use of *napalm** bombs and *defoliants*†, have aroused strong opposition. Some observers came to believe that the war could not be won and that whatever the effect on America's position in Asia it would be better for her to get out of

*A highly inflammable jelly which is spread over a wide area when the bomb explodes. The jelly sticks to the skin and burns.
†Chemicals sprayed on large areas of jungle to kill the foliage.

212

Vietnam. President Johnson therefore made strenuous efforts to start peace negotiations. They finally began in May 1968 and in October America ceased bombing North Vietnam in return for a reduction in Communist military activity. Since then the talks in Paris have stagnated but President Nixon has now begun to talk of withdrawing American troops gradually as South Vietnamese can take their place.

The Vietnam War is important for two reasons. North Vietnam has the support of Russia, but much more vigorously of China. China has already developed nuclear bombs but not yet sufficient missiles to deliver them. She has been consistently more bellicose in her attitude towards spreading Communism than Russia. So strong is Chinese rivalry in the Far East that a few Americans have advised a war to defeat China decisively before she becomes too powerful. The second important aspect is that Vietnam shows a contradiction in American policy. In theory America supports free elections and independence for all states; in practice it tries to prevent people choosing to be Communists. America faces a conflict between her belief in freedom and her belief that if Communism is not checked it may spread to the rest of South East Asia and threaten American security.

To the uncommitted nations America's support of an unpopular South Vietnamese government makes a mockery of its claim to be the champion of freedom in the world.

Further Reading

Boyd, Andrew, *An Atlas of World Affairs*, Methuen (latest edition).
Heater, Derek, *The Cold War*, Oxford University Press, 1965.
O'Callaghan, D. B. *Roosevelt and the United States* Longman 'Then and There' Series.
Snellgrove, L. E., *The Modern World Since 1870*, Longmans 1968.
Stonier, Tom, *Nuclear Disaster*, Penguin, 1964

INDEX

Transport, in Civil War, 91–4
  in Western Movement, 58–60, 76–9,
    81, 106–9
  in twentieth century, 154–61
Treaties,
  of Guadalupe Hidalgo, 83
  of Paris 1763, 34–5
  of Paris 1783, 44, 54
Truman, Harry, 200, 208
Trusto, 127, 130–3, 135, 147, 150, 151,
  157

Unemployment, 164–6, 172, 174, 180
United Nations, 200–1, 203–4, 208

Vietnam, 211–13
Virginia, 19–20, 21, 28, 29

Wagon Trains, 76–9

Wall Street Crash, 164
Washington, George, 29, 31, 42–4, 48,
  49, 67
Wealth, 124–7, 128, 130, 133, 143, 154,
  163, 164, 172, 174–8, 179, 193,
  202, 212
Westward movement, 24–5, 36, 37, 39,
  49, 50, 54, 56–63, 87, Chapters
  5,7,8
  routes of, 58–9, 61, 70, 71–2, 77, 79,
    80–1, 106–9, 119
Wilderness, 1–3, 70–1, 79, 80, 106, 113–
  114, 128
Witney, Eli, 50
Wolfe, James, 32–4
Wilson, Woodrow, 147, 148–9, 150,
  167, 194, 195
Workman's compensation, 150
World War I, 193–4,
World War II, 196, 197–200